SCREENED OUT

MEDIA, COMMUNICATION, AND CULTURE IN AMERICA

Michael C. Keith and Donald Fishman, Series Editors

SCREENED OUT
How the Media Control Us and What We Can Do About It
Carla Brooks Johnston

WAVES OF RANCOR
Tuning in the Radical Right
Robert L. Hilliard and Michael C. Keith

SCREENED OUT

How the Media Control Us and What We Can Do About It

170201

CARLA BROOKS JOHNSTON

M.E.Sharpe
Armonk, New York
London, England

Library of Congress Cataloging-in-Publication Data

Johnston, Carla B.
   Screened out : how the media control us and what we can do about it / Carla Brooks
Johnston.
      p. cm. — (Media, communication, and culture in America)
   Includes bibliographical references and index.
   ISBN 0-7656-0488-4 (hardcover : alk. paper)
      1. Mass media—Influence. 2. Mass media and propaganda. 3. Mass media—
   Ownership.
      4. Media literacy. 5. Mass media—United States. I. Title. II. Series.

P94.J638 2000
302.23—dc21   99-056893

Printed in the United States of America

The paper used in this publication meets the minimum requirements of
American National Standard for Information Sciences
Permanence of Paper for Printed Library Materials,
ANSI Z 39.48-1984.

∞

BM (c)   10   9   8   7   6   5   4   3   2

Table of Contents

Foreword

The growing influence of mass communication as society's chief source of information has become a commonplace topic on the public agenda. The media's influence frequently is characterized as being two dimensional: ubiquitous and omnipresent, but difficult to discern and virtually impossible to oppose with alternate frames of thinking. Carla Brooks Johnston's approach to this problem of the media's influence is unique in three ways.

First, Johnston paints a vivid picture not only of what the media does to influence and entertain the public, but also what issues the media ignores or fails to pursue. Among the overlooked items are issues of economic diversity, a realistic portrayal of cultural diversity, meaningful discussions of healthcare, educational opportunity, the environment, and an intelligent analysis of economic questions. Instead, Johnston argues that the media more often than not presents discussions that pander to stereotypes and preexisting prejudices rather than probe emerging transformations in society. As a result, by ignoring meaningful discussions about children, the elderly, gender, racial and ethnic discriminatory practices, the media fail to grapple with changes of major importance as society evolves. Johnston intelligently asks whether it is in the industry's self-interest to "screen out" two-thirds of the population.

The second virtue of this book is that it provides an underlying and compelling explanation to account for the varied missteps of the media. Johnston analyzes many of the difficulties related to the "media influence thesis" in terms of Kurt Lewin's concept of gatekeeping, contending that the strategic role of the gatekeeper function is heavily influenced by ratings, advertisers, and self-interest by the ownership of media organizations. Collectively, these factors serve to undermine, or diminish, the "public interest" standard that the media should be pursuing.

Third, Johnston encourages action steps to change the current media malaise. Among her recommendations are steps to increase the public's lobbying of the FCC and Congress, expanded approaches to media literacy, and increasing the public's awareness of the rights and regulations that were designed so that the "public interest" standard could play a more powerful and encompassing role in guiding media decisions.

Screened Out: How the Media Control Us and What We Can Do About It is a book that challenges common assumptions, synthesizes a wide range of information, and provides alternatives to current frames of thinking. Johnston's book will inform, persuade, entertain, and even cajole the reader. In addition, this is a work that yields more that its fair quota of insights and observations about the influence of mass communication as the new century begins.

Donald Fishman
Boston College

Acknowledgments

Once people believed they shaped the world, that they—rather we—could change it. I am a product of this gestalt of the 1960s and 1970s. I know we changed the world in those years. We ended government sanctioned segregation. We ended the Vietnam war, and much more.

Screened Out is based on my belief that we need not follow the lemmings off the edge of a cliff driven by the self-interests of transnational media moguls and their handmaidens who care only about what we buy and what profits they make. *Screened Out* draws on the insights of many people who share my view that what we each do matters to the quality of life and the progress of civilization. The book spotlights the dangers and the opportunities before us at this millennial crossroad as we begin to emerge from the valley of self-indulgence and cynicism through which we have traveled in the 1980s and 1990s.

It draws on forthright commentary about the effect of our mass communications on the state of our nation from experienced and astute observers such as Jane Alexander, Ed Asner, Michael Dukakis, and John Randolph, all of whom continue to move society toward progressive change.

The trailblazers of recent decades, whose work validates the belief that societal change is possible, provide both inspiration and examples for this book. For example, Robert Hilliard pushed public broadcasting and government media toward increasing acceptance of the concept that all members of our society are entitled to access and the opportunity for free speech—even if they happen to be women or black or poor; and, Nicholas Johnson as Federal Communications Commissioner, unceasingly steered the Commission toward proconsumer policies for American media—a position that constantly disturbed the cozy symbiotic relationships among those in industry and government who placed profits before people.

Screened Out is shaped by friends and colleagues. Nat Segaloff, Susan Shaer, George Hover, Hubert Jessup, Paul Walker, Art d'Lugoff, Mark Potok, Bernard Mann, and Ramona Hernandez provided clear thinking, important insights, diverse views, and facile language that helped enormously as I sought to express a viewpoint tested against the broad backdrop of our democratic culture. To test my ideas and to provide examples that resonate within our culture, it is especially important to hear the voices of those who are not famous as well as those who are, for they determine where the common ground is in a democratic society. Their views strengthen the overall fabric of society. Here, numerous student researchers have offered valued insight, as has my family—Elise and John, Eric and Debbi. And every time I'm tempted to retreat from reality into more academic realms of analyzing problems rather than solving them, a look at my little grandson Jesse reminds me that retreat is not possible because his future is at stake.

Nonetheless, at the end of the day, without steadfast support from friends such as Michael Keith, executive editor Peter Coveney, the skillful production assistance of Esther Clark, and project editor Henrietta Toth, the manuscript for *Screened Out* would never have become a book.

Introduction

Only 12 percent of the public think the media influence them. If that is true, then why do corporate advertising moguls spend $270 million a day to put their products on television? Why would a company want to pay $2.4 million for one minute of advertising on the Super Bowl if it did not pay off in product sales?

"Corpocracy"—de facto government by megacorporations—is screening out our freedom to act independently. The megamoguls' objective is solely to make profits. To do so, they expose the American people to some 1,500 advertisements a day. They alter news and entertainment programming, thereby transforming real communication into propaganda for profiteering. Clearly those engaged in corpocracy have the profits to prove that they are influencing the hearts and minds of the public.

The tragedy is that most of us have no idea how much the media influence, often control, our feelings and behavior. The media moguls rival Hitler and Stalin in their successful use of propaganda.

True to the definition of propaganda, people today do not realize they are being programmed any more than did the people of Germany, Italy, Japan, and, later, the Soviet Union. In the 1930s, 1940s, and 1950s, the messages were delivered by Hitler, Mussolini, Hirohito, and Stalin—political leaders misusing the media. Today, corporate moguls peddling cosmetics, pharmaceuticals, and automobiles deliver the messages. Their success is based on a symbiotic relationship with a handful of media moguls like Disney, America-on-Line/Time-Warner, News Corp., and Viacom-CBS. Our government officials, left without the pressure of effective alternative lobbies acting for the public interest, capitulate to these moguls, guaranteeing their profits by bending the laws and regulations toward big money interests.

Just as in the fascist eras of the twentieth century, and as Aldous Huxley warned us in *Brave New World*, people today are allowing themselves to be regimented by media moguls into a regulated social structure. Citizens are reprogrammed into compliant consumers.

Today's propaganda influence generates mass buying frenzies for Beanie Babies and scores of other products that buyers neither want nor need, and that, in many cases, are not good for them.

This same big-money control is destroying democracy. It is responsible for the phenomenon of winning political candidates' being, with few exceptions, those who can spend the most money on television commercials. Those commercials are designed to buy people's vote through sound bites that sell would-be policy makers like cakes of soap with little or no discussion of issues or credentials.

Similarly, in the realm of entertainment media, this profit motif is taking the edge off a bright and creative culture. We are all "dumbed down." By centering on the lowest common denominator to get profits, the media have established silly sophomoric entertainment as the norm. This deprives younger generations of the knowledge and understanding of what truly exciting and stimulating entertainment can be.

Suitably hypnotized by today's propaganda, the public offers little objection to the non-news broadcast on news programs. Even if we objected, the management is so monopoly controlled now that only carefully crafted government regulation could change things. Such an effort would require public-interest backing that is weighty enough to match the corporate lobbyists. Only then could we restore a balance between the public and those licensed to transmit information we need on the airwaves that we, the public, own.

It is a truism that those who do not learn from history are destined to repeat it.

After World War II and the Cold War, the world's leading democracies worked hard to ensure that the media spoke with multiple voices. Multiple ownership provided the only institutional safeguard for free speech and the expression of diverse views in both news and entertainment.

Americans and our government still honor these principles when discussing abstract philosophical concepts and when dealing with foreign policy. For example, in the beginning of the 1990s, when the Soviet Union was dissolving into the Commonwealth of Independent States, advocates for democracy were at the forefront of urging the dismantling of state-owned media, disposing of censorship, and the creation of diverse media companies.

A double standard exists, however. At home, Americans and those we elect to govern have allowed increased monopoly control of media. Free speech may be guaranteed in the Constitution, but access to the microphone is increasingly denied to those without money and influence. The public is screened out.

In addition, most of us are ignorant about how screened out we are. American educational institutions from kindergarten through graduate school—

even graduate schools in mass communication—teach what they have always taught with little or no attention to the advancement of technology that necessitates teaching *media* literacy. Media literacy is understanding what you see, what you do not see, and whose bias is reflected in the messages portrayed in entertainment and in news. Media literacy is learning how to make your voice heard and how to be proactive in creating and sustaining diverse media outlets. Media literacy is the critical link between the media and society in this era of new communication technologies. Without a media-literate public, the quality of life for our society in the decades ahead has as little potential for success as did a society in the past when all decisions were made by print illiterates. We are staking our futures on the images portrayed by the shadows on the walls of Plato's cave.

In the United States, and increasingly across the globe, the public and its governments are blinded by media mogul money. Consequently, nothing is being done to prevent creation of a corpocracy controlled by the transnational monsters we are creating. Such a corpocracy threatens to become the twenty-first century version of the twentieth century's state-controlled media—the media that imprisoned people behind an iron curtain of censorship.

World War II happened because the people of Germany, Italy, and Japan were not aware of the propaganda they were buying. The Cold War followed when the ideals of equality and opportunity turned into communist propaganda, and people, believing they would be liberated, were instead imprisoned. So today we are compliant. We eagerly take the same perilous path, unaware of the propaganda's influence over us, unaware of what is happening to us. This time we trade free speech and individuality for the chance to buy, buy, and buy more—for the chance to make the moneyed moguls even richer.

If we do not wake up and take corrective action, a new era of corporate fascism may sweep the globe—this time using psychological, economic, and physical weapons much more destructive than the military weapons used a half century ago.

This book examines how we are being duped by our media, who is doing it, and what can be done to ensure that we and our culture are not screened out.

SCREENED OUT

Chapter 1

Stealing Our Futures

I have noticed a definite decline in the coverage of alternative thinking. It is as if the wind went out of the sails somewhere back in the '70s and no one trusts alternative thinking anymore.

Jane Alexander, actress and former chair,
National Endowment for the Arts [1]

You are probably illiterate!

As you read this, you are most likely able not only to understand what you read, but also to evaluate and criticize it. Most Americans spend twelve years being formally educated in our schools to be print literate. You are print literate.

But when it comes to the medium that dominates most of our lives, you are probably illiterate. Only a small percentage of us have had any education in visual literacy.

If you are the average person, you are watching 29.5 hours of television a week. If you live in the average family, the set is on for 60 hours a week. You are spending more time watching television than you spend doing anything other than working and sleeping. Yet, you are probably among the overwhelming majority of Americans who are visually illiterate, unarmed against the media gatekeepers who are screening out from your mind entire segments of reality, while reinforcing consumer-oriented messages.

Does an omission or distortion of material affect your future well-being?

The media, more than any other institution, shape the agenda of the country. People believe what they see.

For example, if the media say a horrible storm is coming or a collapse of society at the turn of the millennium, Y2K, people prepare. (How, other than via the media, would they have heard about it?) If the media say a movie is fantastic, long lines appear outside theaters where the movie is playing. If the media say crime is everywhere, people believe it even if crime data indicate otherwise. If the media say no free coverage for candidates at

3

election time, the public—unquestioning—just watches its government sold
like bars of soap.

The moguls who control the media control our lives, the future of our
culture, our governments, and our democratic lifestyle. And most people do
not even know it because they're media illiterate.

Media gatekeeping—the censoring of information, ideas, and groups
of people—happens in the shadows. It is hard to see, sometimes even when
it is obvious, especially by more than two-thirds of Americans who are
screened out.

The public has little understanding of the power of money linked with
media. Even the president of the United States is powerless to change policies that hurt people if those who control money and media object. The money
and the media buy elections and tenure in office. As Nicholas Johnson, former
FCC commissioner and maritime commissioner, said, "You can't get [cam-
paign finance reform] through Congress because Congress is controlled by
the very same big money that you're trying to get them to forgo and they are
not particularly enthusiastic about that."[2]

The deals about what is to be voted upon by the FCC or Congress as
national policy are cut before the meeting agendas are even printed. The
arguments are held behind closed doors. The votes are counted before the
meetings calling for discussion and vote are even convened.

The people, if they even know, roll their eyes. They ask, "Who cares?
Government is just waste and scandal anyway. . . . That is what the media
tells us." But in this twilight zone, things happen that affect the lives of
typical people. Campaign finance reform never comes to a vote. So Congress and the president remain beholden to the big-money contributors needed
to stay in office.

Why do they need so much money? To pay the media, of course. Candidates can't get elected without presenting themselves to the voters, and that
requires the media. The only airtime reliably available is that paid for in the
high-priced commercials. Because the candidates need these media images,
the media have a vise-grip on our government.

How do the media moguls capture the politicians? Nicholas Johnson describes the method, "There's more to corporate control of government than
just money." It is so subtle; the access to officials; what is often personal
influence. A lot of Jack Valenti's power in Washington comes from that little
private theater he's got and the dinners he hosts. You go over there for
dinner and you meet the Hollywood stars, and you see their movies. The
dinners cost him something, but it is nothing like the millions of dollars
other lobbyists have to shell out in campaign contributions to set that
kind of access.

"Face it," Johnson continues, "If Bill Gates plays golf my guess is it would not take him long to put together an influential foursome at the Congressional Country Club. Senators return phone calls from Fortune 500 CEOs. The truly wealthy, powerful people of this world are going to continue to have access, and to exert personal influence over officials even if they never give them a dime. Where is the average citizen in all this? You got it: outside."[3]

Not only does the public not really realize what is happening, but most people do not have any idea how to deal with it. Solving the problem is hindered by the fact that these shadow dealings are completely screened out of the mainline media.

A legitimate fourth estate would cover this shadow government. An informed public would care because the media moguls allow our taxes to increase while theirs decrease. The moneyed power brokers keep us from having health insurance and quality health care. They block affordable higher education, secure Social Security, and more. Programs do not deal with toxins that give the public cancer, and they would prefer not to deal with product and workplace safety. And, if government would just make certain that corporate practices are not regulated at all, that would be just dandy.

These issues are not remote from our lives. They affect the public every day. But the media moguls have figured out how not to have anyone get too interested. Just "let the good times roll!" The public need not pay attention to the profiteering.

The government will not infringe on the media moguls; it is beholden to them. The public will not know how bad it is, and certainly will not mount any opposition if the media keeps it screened out.

Content value is not a topic of debate. The issue is simply that something, other than color bars, must fill the time between commercials. The criteria for selecting programs is to find ones that reach the people who may buy the products advertised in as cheap a way as possible.

Any honest television program executive will tell you that programming content has no value in itself. Its only value is the number of rating points it generates. Ratings are the estimate of the number of people watching any given program, based on a statistical sample from which the Nielsen Company derives its data. Such data determine the cost of advertising, the lifeblood of broadcasting.

Assume that advertising is crucial to the existence of American television (under televisions present structure, it is). Assume that some method is needed to count how many people see the commercials. Assume that both broadcaster and advertiser want to please the viewer—in order to make more money, if for no other reason. Why, then, are there so many complaints about television programs?

The complaints stem from media gatekeeping, the denial of access to the airwaves for many segments of the population and the failure to present the diversity of ideas that exist in a pluralistic society. While much is screened out of public view, that which is left is carefully calculated to keep and direct the attention of the public in order to bring needed revenue into the industry. Serving the public interest gets lost in the race for dollars—unless, of course, sufficient public displeasure results in revenue loss.

We get news without content.

We get entertainment without context.

We are anesthetized, and we just stay tuned!

Television programming, in today's world, is the most powerful tool for affecting people's minds or emotions. Yet, it is a by-product of an industry focused on financial survival, and may pay little attention to whether it is a fair and responsible representation of our culture in all its diversity and pluralism. Across the board, program decisions are based on their alleged financial repercussions. This preoccupation is at the core of the gatekeeping problem that limits opportunities for the public, for the creative person in media, for the advertisers, and for the media owners. It is an enormous irony, because by focusing on the profits instead of the product, it is entirely possible that lower profit is the result. But the industry's programming profits may not matter much if one's focus is on control of the nation and managing the nation's assets, 90 percent of which are owned by just 10 percent of the nation's households. But it is even worse. One-half of 1 percent of the nation's households own 42 percent of the nation's assets.[4] The other 9.5 percent of the top 10 percent own another 48 percent. Mediocre media may be a price worth paying by the media moguls; they benefit from an anesthetized audience—90 percent of whom have little share in the nation's wealth or its policies.

If the media owners really wanted to maximize audience, they would not tolerate, even encourage, the door being slammed in the face of Emmy Award–winning programs like "Picket Fences" and "TV Nation." These two, plus others in the 1990s, including "Nothing Sacred," got excellent reviews but were taken off the air because they failed to bring in enough rating points.

"Picket Fences" was a mid-1990s sitcom that dealt with controversial issues in society and characters who followed their consciences rather than conforming to community norms. Michael Moore's "TV Nation" was satirical reporting on the actions and attitudes of American icons in industry and politics. "Nothing Sacred" was the story of a parish church with a commitment to the poor in spirit, the meek, those who hunger and thirst. Roman Catholic Church authorities called for a boycott because the program did not respect customary church bureaucratic traditions. This caused the low ratings, despite the excellent reviews. Cancellation of programs like these reveals the contemptuous attitudes of those in power toward the American public, and their insensitive exploitation of people in order to achieve their personal and institutional goals.

Even the classic original "Star Trek" was dropped because it did not rank high enough in the ratings. It survived for three years only because it had a cult following and enthusiastic network executives who tried to preserve it. Even they didn't succeed. Later the series was revived as "Star Trek: The Next Generation," and it became very popular.

The judgment on these programs and others like them is made not on the basis of their quality. The judgment is not about whether there is entertainment value or educational value or valid information provided. It is not even on whether they are well written, well produced, or skillfully acted. It is not a judgment about strengthening the culture or stimulating good entertainment. It is not even about the self-interest of the advertisers and the owners to enlarge their viewing audience. It is about finding the lowest-common-denominator programs that can appeal to the most people who might buy products based on the statistical sample selected by the Nielsen ratings service. That's the simplistic formula in which everyone is trapped—the public, the broadcasters, and the advertisers. All must adhere to "paint by numbers programming"—to demonstrate their blind faith in a simple, quick profit formula.

To use the media in a more creative way means: (1) that the owners care about their industry more than their wallets—enough more to pay attention to it; and (2) that the owners believe an informed public is more important than an anesthetized audience.

This book is about how the media gatekeepers steal our future—and, ironically, their own. The focus is on television news and entertainment, and on the films that might be seen on television. By structuring the viewpoints presented in news and entertainment, the gatekeepers screen out the diversity of ideas that is essential to the fabric of a pluralistic and democratic culture. Subsequent chapters examine the gatekeeping forces in the media that are, effectively, killing our culture and scaring us to death. They examine how we allow them to control the information and ideas that affect society's culture, politics, and lifestyles. The book then examines why gatekeeping happens, who the gatekeepers are, and how they filter what is presented to the public. Finally, it examines what can be done to move beyond this media mogul stranglehold on our lives, our government, and our culture.

But first, how could this little electronic box in the house really steal our futures—without our realizing it? Could we really be illiterate?

Visual Illiteracy

Look now at the messages we do get. In chapter 5 more will be said about the messages we do not get, and about addressing this problem.

Understanding how the programs we receive influence us is not really so difficult. You see, the message sent to us helps determine how we move ever forward, even while we ourselves remain stationary in our seats. Jason Furlong, Emerson College media arts student, explains the power of television this way: "It is like when a human drives a car. The body is stationary, the *vehicle* propels it forward. Just as a car with invisible fumes can poison its operator, the vehicle of television has the potential to intoxicate its user, tainting their ability to operate with a clear head."[5]

Another way to look at what happens without our awareness is expressed by Professor Richard H. Fehlman. "I vividly remember sitting in a biology class a number of years ago learning about the respiratory system. It had a tremendous effect on me because to that point I had taken breathing for granted, an almost invisible act." He goes on to explain the critical but nearly invisible messages sent by the media. "Look at the representations of reality that you see—the semiotic: (1) the sound or lack of it—the type of music and what it means; (2) the visual imagery; (3) the voice-over narration; (4) the make-up, character gesture and placement; (5) the set design and props; (6) how the camera is placed and how shots are assembled and organized into a scene. What are the formulas, conventions, and icons for various TV and film genres?"[6]

There are many steps to becoming media literate—being able to evaluate what one sees, and being aware of what is screened out.

How does the audience "read" the show? Fehlman says, "Reading is seen as a transactional process, one in which the reader's personal background and knowledge (or schema) act as vital forces in making meaning. Reading is also a process in which the reader's personal pleasure and enjoyment are as significant as more intellectual kinds of response."[7] Engaging and connecting are, according to experts, two major strategies people use to get meaning from the texts. Fehlman notes that the audience "reads" a media text from three viewpoints: "dominant" or the view that is most socially correct; "oppositional" or the view that strongly questions the ideological correctness of the text material; or "negotiated," a middle ground allowing for personal differences in meaning. For a text to be popular, it must allow for this range of responses.

Fehlman says that American teachers have difficulty teaching criticism because of the overtones of social power and political control, so the pedagogy has been to look for universal truths within the texts. Criticism, on the other hand, suggests that what we think of as "right" may be tainted by those who are best served by this position. Fehlman writes, "All texts, especially if they are presented as entertaining, have meanings which readers assent to unwittingly, agreeing with implied ideas and values, not really questioning their validity and power in their own lives."[8] For example, look at "The Wonder Years" in the 1980s, "Father Knows Best" in the 1950s, "The Brady Bunch" in the 1970s, and "Roseanne" in the 1990s. They all embody beliefs about the correctness of how families handle personal and social conflicts, and about social settings.

What can the media steal from our future today? The power of the media influences our sense of what are appropriate expectations for family, partners, children, and parents. It creates ideals for love, for lifestyle, for community. It tempers our behavior concerning a sense of safety, a feeling of security, and a level of comfort in different situations. It expands or constrains our dreams for opportunity and self-actualization.

Life is a candy store. There is so much opportunity for each individual: different careers, different places to live, good investment opportunities, different trips to take, new people to meet, new technologies to try out. There are so many dreams, hopes, opportunities, adventures, and things to accomplish. If one is fortunate enough to be middle class and healthy, only two things can limit one's future:

1. We constrain ourselves and limit our future, believing that we are doing what is best for our physical well-being and our safety.
2. We focus on the day-to-day activities of our personal immediate agendas and, like lemmings, we head for the edge of the cliff, without even knowing that we can suffer dire consequences by choosing to avoid life's real problems. We do not exercise our options to keep the future open. We allow others to constrain our well-being.

If one is not middle class and healthy, life has more constraints. But the underlying premise of a democratic culture is that even the poor and the sick should not be constrained from opportunity.

An example of how the media encourage people to limit themselves is how the media portray kids who like school. If young people believe that it is not "cool" to like school and do well, they likely will not excel or pursue higher education. How many teen programs or cartoons idolize the character who is brainy as opposed to the one who is a social or athletic success? How often are bright young people called "geeks" or portrayed in ugly horn-rimmed glasses?

Another example: How often do you hear about the laws passed and programs launched by the tens of thousands of elected or appointed officials and civil servants who do a good job and make a difference in people's lives? Most portrayals of American politics instill cynicism—are clever and snide to attract ratings—and leave people with a sense of hopelessness about the system in which they live.

Another example: How many portrayals of personal relationships value (or even show) women who are not virtually anorexic or men who are not tall, young, and handsome? What do teens experiencing puberty learn from television and film about how they should view their own self-worth, or how they should relate to someone romantically? Teens are usually too embarrassed to discuss these topics at home. Their cultural norm is communicated by the media.

Television is the genre of mass communication that is most able to expose us to alternative views of the future. It can transport us into a world beyond our immediate experience. This ability can either expand or screen out our view of the options before us.

Processing the words and pictures on the screen requires giving them a meaning. Social judgment theory in mass communications deals with degrees of persuasion. The extent to which the message sender can persuade the message receiver depends on what is known as the anchor, or the personal stance, of the receiver. The closer the message sender is to the receiver's anchor, the more likely the receiver is to be persuaded.[9] Adolescents are looking for messages, models, and formulas to adapt to their lives. Their "anchor" is not yet grounded. Advertisers know this, which is why the youth demographic is targeted for ads. The ability to persuade is as strong within the programs as it is within the commercials.

All of us design or constrain our futures based on messages that are communicated to us through words and symbols in the programs and films we see and believe.

In order to understand the meaning of words and symbols, even light and sound, one needs to understand how the meaning is created. For example, a picture of a dog or the word "dog" symbolizes a real animal. This symbolism means more when placed in relationship to other elements in a message—a terrified person just bitten or a child tossing a stick for the dog to fetch. Even when one knows this much, there are more questions than answers. The communication is only partial. And it may be biased. The image presented projects an idea in the mind of the image receiver. The projection may be influenced by camera angles, colors, size, lighting, composition, and much more. The receiver of the communication then attaches meaning to the idea, gives it a connotation. He or she determines that the message communicated is about something sinister because the lighting is dark, or the baby shown must be a girl because it is dressed in pink, or the soft edges on the images must mean the characters are in romantic situations.

Many people contribute to the meaning of the messages in the media; media production professionals making judgments about how to portray something, the public relation firms putting their spin on what a message means; viewers providing cultural and personal context for interpreting the message sent by the media.

The meaning we give to the pictures and words happens at several levels, like seeing an iceberg. The 10 percent above water looks quite harmless, but, as in the story of the *Titanic*, the 90 percent below the surface is the important part. The meanings we derive from television and films are steeped in our understanding of archetypes, symbols, and images. Let us examine how these factors influence the way we view our future through television and films.

Archetypes

Archetypes are the prototypes or patterns for understanding certain concepts. They may also be based on what we understand to be the meaning of symbols or images presented to us. Carl Jung argues that because all humans have the same bodies in terms of organ structure, it is reasonable to assume that they share some common mental development regardless of culture. Ian Mitroff and Warren Bennis wrote in their book, *The Unreality Industry*, that "archetypes constitute the deepest and most symbolic aspect of the mind that human beings use to give *order* to their world. Most often observed in dreams in the form of mythological characters, they are even more readily seen through an analysis of comparative world mythology, legends, fairy tales, religion, and so on. The more that one examines the great diversity of world cultures, the more one finds that at a symbolic level there is an astonishing amount of agreement between various archetypal images. Their agreement is too strong to be produced by chance alone. It is therefore attributed to the similarity of the human psyche at the deepest levels of the unconscious."[10]

Psychologist George Hover explains:

> An analogy, perhaps most apt for fishermen, can help one understand this idea. An electronic fish finder will give an image on a screen of the contour of the bottom of a river or a lake. This structure cannot be seen with the naked eye and only an electronic image is produced on a screen, which even occasionally shows fish as well as bottom structure. The archetypes, themselves unconscious, create images. Both archetypes and images are natural phenomena in individual humans and in our cultures. They influence perceptions and behavior in profound ways, from the most personal individual experiences to the most horrendous social phenomena, such as National Socialism under Hitler. On the other

hand, they can also produce the most altruistic behavior from the most unexpected quarters. We see these images most clearly in dreams, fantasies, ancient and modern myths, fairy tales, art, literature, movies, news coverage, advertising, and propaganda. Images can be manipulated and distorted to influence people and whole societies.[11]

Psychologists talk about projection or seeing a relevant image in a secondary situation. This helps to explain how the media influences our behavior, our choices about the future. Hover notes, "Projection refers to our well proven, but unconscious habit of behaving like movie projectors. We see an image in another person or group, but the image originates from our own internal film repertoire, heavily colored by archetypes."[12] We see messages sent to us. We give them meaning in accord with our own internal beliefs, and then project them again in our behavior, thereby influencing our own futures.

Following are some sample archetypes, how they are reinforced by television, and how they can limit our futures:

The Hero Archetype

The hero archetype is explained by George Hover:

> This archetype appears at all times in all nations, religions and cultures. To name but a few: Moses, Jesus, Mohammed, Arjuna, Gautama the Buddha, Odysseus, Orpheus, heroes in fairy tales and modern novels, movies, and TV productions. Heroism is also projected on political, sports, and entertainment figures, both male and female. The hero or heroine represents every person in his/her confrontation with the world. Paraphrased from Max Luthi, an authority on fairy tales, the hero is sometimes a rollicking daredevil, or sometimes a silent sufferer, often sly and wily, but just as often open and honest, sometimes a brave fighter, sometimes compassionate, sometimes merciless.
>
> But all heroes provide age-old symbols for values of nobility, purity, danger, and mystery. They reflect a human capacity for change from a problematic or superficial life situation to one that is healthy, fulfilling, and authentic. The archetype of hero is frequently embodied in such actions as conquering the dragon, marrying the princess, or becoming king. In each case, good triumphs over evil. More contemporary manifestations of this archetype include marrying the lover, achieving status or selfhood—recurrent themes in television, the movies, novels and in advertising. Heroes are also seen within the character of wanderers, prisoners of conscience, refugees, even the slain seeming to return for victory over their enemies. There is always a maturing, uplifting, and deepening outcome when a true hero succeeds in a great struggle." Hover notes that "heroism in the movies *A Bug's Life* and *Teen Wolf* are whimsical but generally authentic examples of the hero archetype.[13]

Playing on the real, or the distorted, hero archetype brought Hollywood an approximate gross profit of $6,860,000,000 in 1998.[14] The three top films of 1998 are not yet on television as this is written, but they will be. *Titanic*, *Armageddon*, and *Saving Private Ryan* grossed more than a third of the total box office receipts for the year. *Titanic* and one other film, *Armageddon*, grossed over $200,000,000 in 1998. Actually, *Titanic's* gross that year, including international sales, equaled $470,000,000.[15] *Titanic* also gleaned eleven Academy Award nominations. It is a movie where everyone already knows the ending. The boat sank, and still the profits rolled in. *Titanic*, according to writer-director James Cameron quoted in *Entertainment Weekly* Online, "messes you up emotionally—and audiences like to get their emotions messed up at the movies. It is the only business in the world where people thank you for making them cry."[16]

The heroes in these three movies differed greatly, but all were heroes. Emerson College film student Andrea Milford observed:

> By making the hero ordinary and reliable the audience will stand up and cheer. This is in evidence even in real life by the likes of Princess Diana and Prince Charles. She was reliable and seemed human, while Charles appeared to be rather lifeless. The public adored Diana and frequently deplored Charles because of his lack of humanity.[17] The image of Diana, rather like the hero in *Titanic*, punctuated our understanding of the true hero archetype—one whose heroism reflects a growth beyond one's own identity.
>
> In *Titanic*, Jack, the lower–class artist, falls in love with the upper–class Rose. Jack sweeps Rose off her feet by showing her how freeing life in steerage can be. The two fall in love, and as fate would have it, the ship hits an iceberg following their steamy love scene. As the ship sinks, all hell breaks loose. Rose gives up a seat on a life boat to take her chances foraging for survival with Jack. When the ship finally does sink, Jack gives up his space on a floating headboard for Rose, ultimately saving her life. As Jack sinks into the water, Rose tearfully states, "I'll never let go, Jack." She keeps his memory alive by adventuring out on her own and creating a new identity.

Who among us does not laugh, cry, and fantasize about Hollywood's characters and heroes? This is nothing new. What is new is that the media that create these fictitious heroes leave us with no "real world" heroes. Few people in the real world ever get airtime for their heroic deeds. The subtle message is "do not pay attention to your community or your government or your nation. Keep your mind off reality and tune in to fantasy."

George Hover says, "Distortions of the hero archetype are also widely distributed in our culture. They have to do with a pseudo-hero figure appearing to vanquish evil forces, usually by violence, then followed by a sexual conquest or love affair, or by assuming a position of power. In these distortions, there is no convincing change toward inner maturity, no conquest in the struggle with the hero's individual ego, no uplifting or deepening movement toward integrity or authenticity. The distorted archetype is likely destructive of both individuals and of the larger culture. The senseless violence, or sappy sentimentality decried in the media and electronic games exemplify this distortion." The distortion serves as a form of propaganda that clouds the individual's view of his or her future.

Is the distortion of the hero archetype applicable when looking at the hero in *Armageddon* and *Saving Private Ryan*? Perhaps those two films are good illustrations of weaving the essence of the hero archetype together with the distortion to further confuse the viewer.

The Spirit Archetype

Another Jungian archetype, the spirit archetype, is also believed to be part of all human subconsciousness. George Hover explains: "This has a meaning more akin to rebirth—and is thought of as a 'guiding spirit.' The spirit archetype refers not so much to the spirit in a religious or theological sense or in the sense of an 'immortal human spirit.' The spirit archetype appears often in dreams in which the wise old person—sometimes only a voice or feeling—gives advice, help, or suggestions that may or may not seem immediately relevant." This wise old person "can also appear in visualization, meditation, and may take the role of teacher, guru, therapist, doctor, priest, grandparent, or God. Occasionally the archetype of the spirit produces animal images." *The Lion King* is an example. Hover says:

> The spirit appears at times where courage, organization, tenacity, and understanding are needed but lacking. The spirit aids, fills the gap, offers clarity, even gives information that can be very specific. The advice or influence can however, appear to be completely wrong or even evil, and experience teaches us that the "help" may appear harmful. It becomes helpful only after a serpentine development of unforseen events. A wise old man also frequently appears in fairy tales when the hero is in a desperate or hopeless situation that requires the most profound or lucky experience. The spirit prompts reflection, promises success, and aids in growth toward maturity. A traditional "psychological" explanation may suggest that this is the voice of the personal unconscious. This is probably an oversimplification. In the media we see this image in the mentor, the psychic, the person with special intuitive insight, regardless of sex or age. One can also wonder whether the talking heads of the news commentator are given a "wise old person" projection that gives them status beyond their role as news reader.[18]

Examples of the guiding wise person are throughout the media. Indeed, look at the persona bestowed upon the people who simply read what is called "the news." Books that some of these personalities have assembled become best-sellers even though the contents may not reflect either excellence in news gathering or significant insight into world affairs. The old days of the rugged journalist out in the trenches gathering the news are, in most cases, a piece of history. They have been replaced by modern technology wherein the materials are gathered locally by releases from newsmakers, from public relations agents, and—in some instances—by local reporters, and are edited into a program read by a "personality" or "anchor." The networks work hard to turn their anchors into the icons that fit the archetype of the wise voice of guidance and authority—unless it is the partner anchor who is supposed to attract viewers through sex appeal.

The wisdom of our era seems to come mostly from fantasy film and artificial gurus created by the media. But how would the public know if there are real-world gurus worth hearing? The media cover events, not ideas. The clips are so short that one can seldom get enough information on any one person or on their ideas. It is quite amazing that Mother Teresa got even the small amount of coverage that she did for her service to the poor and infirmed.

Distortions of the spirit archetype appear when ideological rigidity is made synonymous with the archetype. Expressions intent on rigid control of thinking cannot replace the wonder found in experiencing various expressions of creativity and being exposed to the range of manifestations of wisdom.

Some examples of the media stretching our fascination with the spirit archetype include the 1990s' popular so-called Christian family dramas on TV: WB's "7th Heaven," CBS's "Touched by an Angel" and "Promised Land." These television sit-coms have succeeded despite continued network skepticism that they would draw an audience.

"7th Heaven," on the WB network, portrays the ups and downs of the Christian Camden family. The father is a minister. The mother stays home. Viewer support has been strong. Special episodes have frequently bumped both NBC and Fox from their number-one spot in this time slot. At the end of the 1998 season "7th Heaven" was voted "The Best Show You're Not Watching" in the First Annual TV Guide Awards.[19]

"Touched by an Angel" surprised the industry as the second most-watched show in America.[20] The show depicts three earthbound angels who appear in different situations helping people. By early 1999 the show had 6.5 million viewers in the eighteen to forty-nine year old demographic. The in-house production initially cost CBS very little. Viewer response made it a hit.

One reason these shows are so popular, despite network dismissal, may be because of the demographic shift toward an aging population in the United States.[21] The largest segment of the population was born when the GIs returned from World War II. These baby-boomers are growing old, and constitute the large numbers of middle-aged viewers. The theory based on observations of church goers is that older people are more "spiritual." Concurrently, their values have become the values of the American mainstream.

Another reason for the popularity of these shows may be the increase in interest in conservative religion that has arisen to cope with a cultural environment that appears to offer little hope for one's personal future and engenders cynicism.

The media provide little insight into the countless accomplishments and acts of decency that occur in real life. They tell us to be cynical about everything. If we believe that nothing of value can be found in the real world, retreating to the fantasy world of angels is a logical mental health move.

It is interesting to note, however, that despite the good ratings, "Touched by an Angel" cannot command a high price for its ads. Advertisers, obsessed with the youth market, will pay approximately $278,500 for a thirty-second spot on "The X-Files" while, for the same length on the more popular "Touched by an Angel," they will pay approximately $90,000.[22] The Nielsen ratings show that "Touched by an Angel" draws an older audience. While the highest per capita spending is by those between age forty-five and age fifty-four, followed by those fifty-five to sixty-four, advertisers still pursue the youth market because young consumers are believed to be more open to testing new products and new brand names.

There may be another theory to explain the popularity of these shows. This era is so consumed with violence on cop shows and blood on hospital shows that the public, whatever the age group, may be looking for ways to identify with the hopefulness of the spirit archetype. The angel-type family shows offer viewers a chance to end the day on a more upbeat note than if they watched "Walker Texas Ranger" or even the popular "ER." "7th Heaven" and "Touched by an Angel" may be a bit heavy-handed on stereotypical religious ideology, but they grasp at something beyond violence and blood— the wise voice of guidance and authority.

Apocalypse

A third archetype that recurs throughout our history is that of apocalypse, or a monstrous end of the present world. The end of the world brought on by flood or fire appears throughout cultural and mythological history. In the Indian tradition, human liberation comes only from annihilation of Karma— the law of universal causality, the justifying of the human condition, the symbol of human slavery. The myth of universal world ending conflagration as we know it in the West originates in Iranian culture.[23] In Hebrew tradition, it is expressed as an extreme decadence wherein evil and darkness triumph until the moment when the renewal of the cosmos dawns. The concept of a final judgment of history appears throughout world cultures. The evil are punished and the good rewarded. Find it in Christian tradition. Find it in the death and rebirth celebration of the winter solstice. Evil is an omnipresent, easy to magnify Jungian thought according to George Hover. Creativity seems to be balanced in nature with destruction, and this nature includes the human race." Hover continues, "One can study the history of religions and discover that the gods usually have radical mood swings, like Jehovah in the Old Testament. For example, in the book of Jeremiah, the father (God) is creating but also destroying everything that does not please him. Such a mood swing is also reflected in the Indian Hindu goddess Kali who wears a necklace of flowers that can turn into one of human skulls. She is both creator and destroyer challengeable only by Shiva, god of change. Jung's concept of an apocalypse archetype is often expressed as a shadow, a teeter-totter on which each of us rides."[24]

The shadow archetype comes from the Jungian idea of an inflated shadow. As humans existing in modern society, many of us have a persona or mask that we present as who we are. This persona is controlled by our ego. However, under this mask lies our subconscious, a force that we are not always able to control. Because we cannot control it, we fear this part of ourselves. We project this dark half onto monsters and villains.

The belief embodied in the archetype of apocalypse, or of the monster shadow, is manifest in the genre of disaster films and it takes on new forms in the modern era. Things we cannot control today go far beyond the shadows and monsters of past years. Today's monsters include the many forms of the technology god.

For example, *Godzilla*, clearly within the disaster film genre, was one of the top grossing films of 1998.[25] Here the archetype of the shadow, the monster, is intertwined with the all consuming power of nuclear energy. Nuclear weapons technology gives us the power to destroy much of the planet ourselves. *Godzilla*, a film about the destruction of New York City, might be interpreted as an allegory about the atomic bombs that destroyed Hiroshima and Nagasaki in 1945. Emerson film researcher Chahn Chung observes, "We can conclude that *Godzilla* is an archetype taken directly from the fear of nuclear weapons by a culture that understands that fear intimately."

Author James Iaccino notes that "our use of technology for war and mass destruction has brought the shadow to greater heights over the last century. We now have the capacity to destroy ourselves ten times over with weapons that we have created from our dark side. The horror realm has not been remiss in reminding us what we have produced by loosing this shadow on unsuspecting society. The giant monsters, from massive insects to huge dinosaurs and even incredibly sized aliens, are all reflections of the shadow blown up to outrageous proportion."[26] The media hype about Y2K devastation and the public reactions provide another example of our willingness to believe symbols portraying the archetype of disaster.

Those outraged at the messages in some media might wonder why the media do not put a preface at the start of every movie, science fiction program, adventure show, or news broadcast to explain how the human mind might deal with the program content—sort of a variation on a video content warning system. They might warn us that without proper understanding of what we are about to see, our confidence in the future may be altered. How absurd that would be, if only because it would be ineffectual. Imagine such a preface in the front of the hottest new paperback book. Publishers, authors, and the public assume that if one can read, one is literate enough to evaluate and critique a book's content. So why do we not teach our children and our adult population to "read" the visual and audio literature available—to be media literate in order to understand the influence of archetypes, symbols, and images?

Symbols

Symbols are those visual images, objects, sounds, or words that bring to mind something beyond the object or the image itself because of associations that can be made or relationships that exist. They are like abbreviations. They are everywhere on television. And symbols often are manipulated to cause the viewer to transfer an association from one concept to another.

The Eagle

One example of a symbol is the eagle, a symbol of freedom and reliability to Americans. Because the symbol has broad cultural understanding, many institutions appropriate it as their own. For example, banks often use eagles as a symbol for their institution. Those designing the institutional logos and preparing their advertising manipulate the symbol to encourage the consumer to unconsciously equate the national symbol with their commercial product. Michael Wachter, Emerson media arts specialist, explains how meanings are manipulated: "Let's say the symbol of U.S. freedom, the bald eagle, was taken by a terrorist group that manipulated the symbol to symbolize *their* freedom, and the end of ours."[27] Without countermessages strongly reinforcing the original meaning of the symbol, the public can become confused, maybe even switch loyalties. For example, militia groups may use the eagle as a symbol to further their end of freedom only for people who share their racial and religious agenda. Their use of the symbol is quite different from the historic American message symbolized by the eagle—a message of liberty and justice for all without regard to race or creed. Common use of the eagle symbol could, in this case, give militias unwarranted credibility.

Smoking

Another prominent symbol is smoking. Until the 1980s, smoking was common in movies and on television—used to symbolize sophistication. For example, George Burns, the American father figure and comedic icon, would step out of character for a moment during his television show and give you a bit of advice regarding selection of the best cigars. James Dean, Humphrey Bogart, and other idolized Hollywood stars smoked; imitating them linked the ordinary person with their symbol of a star.[28] Using tobacco as a symbol for being "cool" has changed only because television does not carry tobacco ads any more. It now carries ads from the American Lung Association and similar health organizations that portray smoking as a slow form of suicide. The news broadcasts report the lawsuits that are won against the tobacco companies for causing lung cancer and related diseases. The symbol is no longer cool, but is instead identified with irresponsibility and greed. Away from the electronic screen, smokers in the United States have declined from 54 percent of the population in 1954 to 27 percent in 1996.[29] Such is the power of the media in using symbols to stimulate action.

How is one to know what meaning to ascribe to symbols as one decides one's own future? Visual literacy requires looking past the symbol to the underlying substance of truth. This requires checking and critiquing numerous sources.

The Gun

Another important symbol is the gun, which has become equated with murder. In the late 1990s the debate about guns reached center stage, largely because of a rash of school shootings. As each incident occurred, the media promptly and appropriately reported on how the suspects obtain their death-delivering weapons. Usually they came from the drawer of a relative. The weapon is an easier symbol to deal with than the complexities of why someone uses it to kill. Killing is what it is built to do. Some people say that kids get their ideas for murder from violent films, talk shows, video games, and music. The media, fearing censorship, deny blame and point to inattentive parents. The point is that the gun has taken on symbolic meaning. Helping it to achieve this status is the fact that in the United States two-thirds of all homicides are the result of firearms, mostly handguns.

Three events, however, have begun to force the public to look beyond just the gun symbol and toward the motivations for owning and using guns. First, the Brady Bill was passed, suggesting that some gun owners could be irresponsible and should be denied ownership of guns. James Brady was shot and paralyzed in the assassination attempt on President Ronald Reagan's life in 1981. Brady became the symbol for victims of violence. Second, in the spring of 1999, the Littleton, Colorado, school shootings were so devastating to the American public that, again, attention shifted away from the weapons to the people who use them. In Littleton, two students planned and implemented a mass murder plot against their fellow students in the school cafeteria and school library. The event in Littleton had been preceded by gun violence in other schools. In Jonesboro, Arkansas, a child assassinated classmates on the playground. Third, in the summer of 1999, Benjamin Smith, setting out to kill nonwhites and non-Christians, undertook a shooting rampage through several Midwestern communities near Chicago. Other murders in recent years included the assassination of doctors who performed abortions, and the murder of the California U.S. Postal Service employee, killed in 1999 because he was nonwhite and worked for the government.

Why are *these* events powerful enough to shift people's thinking from a focus on the symbol—the gun—to what is behind using the gun? These events reached the anchor, or personal, stance of the people who are the dominant voice of U.S. culture—the white middle class. Data shows that in 1992 handguns killed 60 people in Japan, 128 in Canada, 33 in Great Britain, and 13,495 in the United States. Yet, in the United States, the kneejerk reaction was to blame the symbol, the gun. People did not examine why this behavior existed.[30] It is easy to objectify an act in a symbol and stand apart, shaking one's head, when the people involved are not "your own." Unfortunately, murders in poor and minority neighborhoods were given little attention by the majority of the American population. But the three events discussed above are beginning to change the dynamic. James Brady is a middle-class, white Republican, like a large number of people on Main Street, America. Littleton, Colorado, is a middle-class suburban school with "kids like ours." The hate crimes offend the basic sense of "fairness" that Alexis de Tocqueville cited as central to the American psyche. The symbol of the gun has begun to change its simplistic meaning for mainstream America. Let us see if either the media or the public really change the way this symbol fits into our culture. With a threat to the future of people and institutions the mainstream cares about, symbols can take on new meanings. The question is, what will they be?

John Glenn

An example of a manipulated symbol is John Glenn, American space hero, the symbol of American achievement.[31] The film about Glenn, *The Right Stuff*, won four Academy Awards for portraying the story of the Mercury astronauts' 1968 space flight and the dangers they faced.

In 1998, NASA took the seventy-seven-year-old Glenn, a U.S. senator, on a return flight to space. Much publicity was given to the event. Not only was it the thirtieth anniversary of the first suborbital flight in space, but it was an opportunity for NASA scientists to measure the effects of space travel on an elderly person. There are those who say that the U.S. space program needed a boost in public support to keep the necessary congressional support for its funding, and this public relations event par excellence was created precisely for that purpose. Indeed, after Glenn returned to space, 76 percent of Americans rated NASA as doing a good or excellent job. That's the highest poll results given on a basic NASA job evaluation since Gallup began asking the question in 1990.[32] The symbol manipulation of John Glenn, space hero, into John Glenn, public relations advocate for NASA, worked well.

Toy Characters

Symbols in the form of imaginative science fiction toy characters and icons from a favorite cartoon are used regularly to sell toys to kids. Just watch Saturday morning television. Toy company products feature prominently in the stories created for kids' entertainment. The expansion of this practice stems directly from the Reagan administration's repeal of the FCC ban on program-length commercials. The media moguls and their wealthy counterparts selling toys got the political support needed to increase their profits. Apparently they do not even care about their own children and grandchildren. Now kids regularly watch half-hour programs totally designed to sell one product. And parents buy.

Examples of the link between kids' cartoons and toys are countless. The classics include "Batman," "Spiderman," and "Superman." These programs link the archetype for heroism to the symbol for that heroism, the fantasy character that can bring young consumers into the stores to buy dolls, video games, trading cards, clothing, whatever a manufacturer can sell. Other examples include the dolls sold in conjunction with the kids' TV programs "Rugrats," "Barney," and "The Muppets." Public television's "Sesame Street" has been extraordinarily successful in promoting a range of ancillary products connected with the show's characters.

Over the years the quality of the animation has become much more sophisticated, further capturing the hearts and minds of young viewers with programs and products never before imagined. As computer technology advances, computer graphics play an increasing role in producing these animation programs that sell program icons or symbols to kids. An incentive for the industry is that animated programming is cheaper to produce.

The American Flag

The American flag has always been the symbol for American patriotism. But in *Armageddon*, one of the top revenue-producing films of 1998, you see this symbol maneuvered into one with new meaning. It is the saviors of the world who carry this flag. The movie's story line focuses on an asteroid about to collide with earth, threatening life on the planet. NASA sends a team to drill a hole on the asteroid, place a nuclear bomb in the hole, detonate it, and destroy the asteroid. The American flag is present throughout this cliffhanger. In fact, the flag is seen once every forty-four seconds—a record in the history of repetitive advertising.

The American flag symbolizes different things to different people. Chahn Chung, Emerson College media arts researcher, observes, "To many, across the world, it stands for freedom, democracy, the ability to make one's own selection of who will govern, the right to practice one's chosen religion. It stands for the right to choose life style, choose travel destination, choose where to call home. To others, the flag means consumerism and a cutthroat capitalism. The flag is given to widows when their spouse dies in the military service. It is flown at half mast on days of national mourning. People protesting the U.S. policies will burn or mutilate the flag. Everything this country represents is embodied in the symbol of the flag."[33] *Armageddon* uses the flag to symbolize family and things we hold dear, to symbolize why we fight to save the planet, and as an association with the heroes drilling to destroy the asteroid.

In this film, it is the planet that is being saved, but planet and United States of America seem to be used interchangeably. The attributes of courage and heroism are transferred to the flag and consequently to the United States. Remember the context for this movie. America's number two export globally is media. A very substantial piece of the film's revenue will come from the film's international distribution, not to mention the value of the persuasive message within the film. "In *Armageddon*," Chung notes, "the U.S. has little help from other countries in destroying the asteroid. The U.S. never asks others for help. The Russian cosmonaut is portrayed on a run-down space station that needs to be evacuated while our heroes are on board. Hollywood has made the cosmonauts look unshaven and disheveled in contrast to the perfectly groomed Americans. The film sends a powerful message to the rest of the world by utilizing symbols and images that already have strong meaning for the public."[34] These symbols are believable because they are close to the personal anchor of the viewers. Americans have seen themselves as saviors of the world since World War II. The United States has offered new opportunities to millions of immigrants from across the globe for over 200 years. But then, we have also owned slaves and virtually destroyed the culture of the Native American population. Nonetheless, if a symbol represents something sought after, there is one united message. If it is manipulated into something that forces people to abandon their own identities, then it becomes a weapon as powerful as gunpowder, perhaps more dangerous because of how seductive it is.

Chahn Chung writes: "Watching films or TV shows, we receive messages about many things from morality to what products we should buy. Often, screenwriters call on symbols that are already familiar. They already carry general social connotations—common ideas in the minds of the general populace. We walk away from the film or video with new ideas, although sometimes we are not aware of where these ideas came from due to the subtle nature of symbol manipulation."[35]

Images

A third aspect of visual literacy critical to understanding how we interpret what's on the screen is image. Image is the imitation or mental representation of something not present. It is illusory or an apparition. Today we have traditional images and virtual images. It is like seeing oneself in a mirror. Image provides a common focus and keeps conformity needed in a cohesive society, or in an audience. As the new technologies and personal mobility enable the public to split into niche groupings with common interests, symbols may not have the universal appeal they did a decade ago. Consequently, images are used in the media to create a common focus—to hold audiences and to sell products.

The Perfect Woman

For example, look at the image of the perfect woman. For decades the image of the perfect woman was objectified for little girls in Barbie dolls. It is said that the average little girl had eight Barbie dolls.[36] This image has served advertisers well as the air-brushed images that appear in magazines and on product ads. It has sold millions of dollars worth of fashions, cosmetics, and diet products. An anesthetized public again pads the wallets of big business. The media have no regulation that requires portrayals of people or of products to be honest. Profits would suffer. Never mind if millions of teenage girls, brainwashed by the perfect woman myth, suffer trying to please the boys who also believe the myth.

In recent years, however, there are a growing number of women who have spoken out in opposition to the propaganda perpetrated on their little children, their dieting teenage daughters, and themselves. With sales figures at risk, Mattel, the makers of the Barbie doll, responded by giving Barbie "situations." Barbie drives her sports car to work with her briefcase in hand. And the new Barbie is in more human proportions—the result of some plastic surgery of sorts. The image is reformed to encourage the current generation of parents to rush out to buy Barbie because it promotes the modern woman and offers the motivation to compete in a heavily male-dominated society. It should be noted that in all of Barbie's new clothes and accessories for her situations, none reflect any interest in the real-life social or political problems of the country or the world.

. Another example of the perfect woman is Supergirl in the "Superman" cartoon seen on WB. She has very long legs, a huge bust, and a tiny waist. Other cartoons have the same image of women, for example, Batgirl and Cat Woman on "Batman." The film *Who Framed Roger Rabbit?* portrays the wife, Jessica Rabbit, as a woman with hip-length blonde hair dipping seductively over one eye, huge breasts, big hips, and a nearly invisible waistline.

Psychologist George Hover comments on such images of perfection: "Other values sometimes masquerade as archetypes. For example, if 'perfection' were an archetype, we might understand better the proliferation of images of perfection that we see in our culture. One must have the right body shape, wear the right clothes, go to the right college, be in the right clique, drive the right car, live in the right house, have the right career and income, and have perfect children. Sometimes it is called 'being the best you can be.' It is a masquerade of real archetypes. Archetypes are images that are time tested and pro-social, arising as they do out of the collective unconscious of the human race."[37]

Images of female perfection, Barbie-style, may collide with the real message in female archetypes.

Hover refers to the feminine archetype is described in Clarissa Estes' book, *Women Who Run with Wolves*:

> In her magnificent story collection and commentary, she calls the feminine archetype the "Wild Woman archetype." Estes recounts two versions of a southwestern tale called "La Llorona." She refers to it as a "shiver story," a story that can cause listeners to experience a shiver of awareness that leads to thoughtfulness, contemplation, and action. This tale uses the metaphors of the beautiful woman and the clear river of life to describe a woman's creative process in its

normal state. But in the story, when she interacts with a destructive masculine impulse, both the woman and the river decline. Then a woman whose creative life is dwindling experiences, like La Llorona, a sensation of poisoning, deformation, and a desire to kill everything off. She is driven to seemingly endless searching through the wreckage of her former creative potential. In order for her psychic balance to be corrected, the river has to be made clear once again. It is not the quality of our creative products that we need to be concerned with, according to Estes, but the determination and care of our creative life. Always behind the actions of writing, painting, thinking, healing, doing, cooking, talking, smiling, making, is the river.[38]

Other better-known images related to the image of feminine redemption or emergence are "Snow White," "Cinderella," "Rapunzel," and the movies "My Fair Lady" and "Pretty Woman."

The other common view of a woman is also very different from the Barbie image. Hover describes the mother archetype. "This unconscious structure produces an almost infinite variety of images. For example, the personal mother, grandmother, spouse, goddess, virgin, mother of God, church, motherland, mother earth, sea, moon, lover, well, cooking vessel, flower. Jungian researchers have pointed out that the mother archetype projects both negative and positive characteristics as seen in the Hindu goddess Kali—both nurturer and destroyer. In western cultures, we attribute to Mary only positive attributes and leave the destructive attributes to witches, evil mothers, stepmothers, and hurricanes. Any production that portrays the mother in any of her images as all-creative, or all-destructive, in other words as an absolute that is dictated as the truth without room for surprise and creativity, is most likely a distortion of the true archetype." An example of the "absolute" model mother on today's television is Bill Cosby's wife Claire Huxstable on "The Cosby Show."

The Grown-Up Image

Another image, critical to young people who so often are the victims of violent crimes and tragic drug overdoses, is that of the grown-up. This image of independence is closely intertwined with the archetypes for rites of passage for adolescents. Here, the young person achieves full autonomy and liberation. Recent research has taken up this theme of initiation and suggested that a great deal of wisdom, accrued in traditional societies, has been lost in our culture. Some think this has severely hampered emotional and social development in our society.[39] Hover observes that "one could argue that along with attachment disorders, an important but almost never mentioned dimension of the problem of youth violence is the failure of our culture to provide meaningful initiatory experiences for adolescent boys and girls.[40]

Malidoma Some writes, "There is a wealth of material about traditional myths and rights of initiation. Young men, and sometimes young women, are forcibly separated or weaned away from their parents and through initiation become full members of the clan or tribe. The group becomes the second parent, in a death/re-birth drama where the young are symbolically sacrificed and then re-emerge into a new life. This is not done in a random fashion, but with exquisite sophistication by the elders of the tribe."[41] Some of the rites of passage are anything but fun, and some, such as female circumcision, are not only physically damaging to the woman but life-threatening. Nonetheless, there is a clear demarcation between childhood and adulthood which, by design, has much more depth of experience than the American group-achievement banquets, hazing, and graduation ceremonies.

In the United States the closest one might come to an actual initiation is the Native American vision quest. It is usually a solitary initiation.[42] The Jewish bar mitzvah or bat mitzvah and the Christian confirmation are religious ceremonies with the expectation that one will learn certain religious precepts, but they are not the profound and lengthy experiences found in other cultures.

Hover continues to comment on the image of "grown-up" as it is impressed upon those who experience actual initiation rites.

> Along with the loss of the fear of death, the young person will be deeply consolidated with the larger group, able to submit with humility to the responsibilities of adult life in a functioning social group. The profound movie *Pleasantville* examines working out of this archetype. The genius who created the *Pleasantville* story has black and white imagery to symbolize a frozen, unchanging, conservative, and parochial life approach. After a spreading initiatory experience, all the black and white citizens of *Pleasantville* learn to see themselves, and live their lives in technicolor. Even *City Slickers* can be seen as a whimsical version of the initiation archetype. Left without much cultural or parental framework for a meaningful passage from childhood to adulthood, some kids turn to the most persuasive models before them—television images of gangs, violence, and drugs."[43]

Television films provide a steady stream of images that attack the emotions more than does reality itself. Think how often one can be brought to tears by a movie; likely more often than in real life. The bottom-line message is that futures are molded by the force of these media messages—especially when the viewer is not media literate.

Look at how archetypes, symbols, and images are ways in which we limit our own futures. Look at when they become rationales for self-constraint in the name of safety. Look at where they become models for self-identity. It becomes clearer and clearer that one of the gatekeepers, screening out our options, is, in large part, ourselves—media illiterates and politically hoodwinked by the media moguls. This is all too often because we are illiterate with visual language and consequently have little if any knowledge of what is being done to us. Those who create the messages and selectively screen out parts of the picture are gatekeepers too. Archetypes are projected by those who write, produce, and direct a show, with meanings encoded into the basic story line. But it is the illiterate viewer who decodes these message, often sitting in a dimly lit room, with a screen in front of him or her. Reality is suspended. The viewer, in a dream-like state, can enter any fantasy, love any hero, battle any monster, and travel to other worlds—all from the couch.[44] The viewer reassembles the encoded messages to reflect the archetypal nuances of one's own contextual and historical viewpoint. Interpretation depends, to a great extent, on the viewer's visually literacy.

This literacy problem would not be an issue if we were dealing with written material. As media expert Dr. Robert Hilliard says, "We generally require every student, from entry into elementary school through high school and well into or through higher education, to try to become print literates: courses in reading, print composition, print literature analysis and evaluation, and the form and structure of creating, expressing, and distributing ideas and feelings in print. We rarely see a similar effort to help our students become knowledgeable about and functional in radio and television."[45]

We have dealt with the first way in which the media steals our future. The conclusion is that very often we are our own gatekeepers because we are visual illiterates. How quickly we would move out of the dark ages and out of the grips of blind consumerism if we could experience the enrichment of interpreting and critiquing the messages sent.

Tuning Out, Screening Out

The other way the media steals our future is that we focus on the day-to-day activities of our personal immediate agendas, and, as stated at the beginning of the chapter, like lemmings, we head for the edge of the cliff, without even knowing that we can suffer dire consequences by choosing to avoid life's real problems. We do not exercise our options to keep the future open. We allow others to really constrain our well-being.

For example, there is a commercial that plays on a Boston radio station, a public service announcement for the dental industry. The commercial has the dentist's office phoning a woman to schedule her annual check-up. The secretary suggests a time. The woman replies that she walks her dog at that time. Another time? She finds that too early. Another time? This one is too late. Another time? That's when she phones her mother-in-law. One more time? That's the time the woman said she plans to replace her shelf paper. No time for the dentist.

When it comes to dealing with the larger societal problems or opportunities, it is even easier to procrastinate, or to be unaware of what is happening. Most of us can barely get through a day of kids, cars, jobs, bosses, shopping, bills, and house maintenance.

But we need to pay attention. The news media, in recent years, rarely put in front of us the things we need to know. Our lessees, the media companies, rarely use as a criteria for news content what we, the owners of the airwaves, need to know. American culture is fortunate to have advocacy groups that pursue the advancement of one issue or another.

Advocacy is what created the Declaration of Independence, civil rights legislation, environmental protection, and consumer safety. But getting an issue on the air as an alternative viewpoint is very difficult. Susan Shaer is executive director of Women's Action for New Directions (WAND),[46] a nationwide advocacy organization created to empower women to act politically to reduce violence and militarism and redirect military resources toward human and environmental needs. Shaer says:

> There are so many crucial issues that are not getting any coverage now. When we try to interest reporters in our point of view on topics like curtailing bombing of Kosovo, they think what we talk about is old news. If we say, but you write editorials favoring foreign policy positions, etc., then how can it be old news to cover another view on the same issue? Only one side of the story is being told, only one approach to the problem, if that. The media wants to hear only from experts, so we have to make ourselves into experts. The experts on the left are mostly old hat. Who makes experts? Presidents and presidential elections do. The campaigns have changed so much and have made it impossible for third-party candidates. Twenty-five years ago you had John Anderson and Eugene McCarthy, strong independent candidates representing an alternative viewpoint. You do not get that kind of people anymore. Alternative ideas, in this land of free speech, are heard less and less."

The behavior that jeopardizes our future is that an honest exchange of the full spectrum of viewpoints on important issues has been nearly totally screened out in favor of running clips from the police scanner and labeling that news. Media focus is on the quickest route to the highest ratings; it is doubtful whether one even considers providing real information on the news. It should be no surprise that news programs are losing viewers; the public does not hear what it needs to know.

Domestic Terrorism

For example, one kind of advocacy on the extreme right has taken the form of domestic terrorism. This force is so active in our society now that we have, for the first time in over a half century, the potential for creating a new era of fascism. In May 1998, 238.5 hours of extreme hate radio were broadcast on short-wave radio. That's up from 152 hours per week in November 1997, up from 94 hours per week in July 1995, and up from 5 hours per week in 1990.[47] This is only short-wave radio. It does not count the hours of programs on AM, FM, internet radio, satellite radio, and micro-power radio. A wide array of hate groups broadcast on at least 366 AM stations, and 40 FM stations. Some 2,000 hate Web sites are on the internet. Their messages surpass the right or left views of the political system. They promote racism, bigotry, and violence. They link a religious apocalyptic millennialism and a white supremacy message with revolutionary rhetoric about overthrowing the U.S. government.[48] Evidence shows the connection between these groups and the Oklahoma City bombing; Francisco Duran, the man who opened fire in the U.S. Capitol; Benjamin Smith who, influenced by World Church of the Creator, went on a killing spree in the Midwest; the Littleton, Colorado, student killers, who committed their crime on Hitler's birthday and used Internet resources from Neo-Nazi sites.

Yet, for most of the 1990s, the mainstream media, especially television, told us virtually nothing about it. It is not likely this is intentional gatekeeping, for the media moguls themselves are at risk from the radical right. This is just total disinterest in their program base. And the stories they did carry were presented in such disconnected sound bites, and are so lacking in context, that it was not possible to see the big picture unless one did a lot of independent research. But if we do not counter this threat, we will find ourselves like lemmings at the edge of a cliff—robbed of a future.

Robert L. Hilliard and Michael C. Keith, in their book *Waves of Rancor*, focus on the hate groups that are part of the neo-fascist, Christian Identity, and Patriot movements and are skillful users of the media flying just below the radar. They note that "dictators, charlatans and even random opportunists know that whoever controls the media of a country controls its political processes. . . . It is not a coincidence that the militias and militia-related or supporting organizations are prolific users of radio, television, and the Internet to convey their messages of hate and violence and to influence and recruit people to implement their goals of terror and chaos and ultimate control of their immediate, then larger societies."[49]

Another example of domestic terrorism is the link between the far right militias and anti-abortion violence. Laura Flanders documents the evidence in her article for Fairness and Accuracy in Reporting, "Far Right Militias and Anti-Abortion Violence: When will Media See the Connection?" She says:

> Media investigations of where right wing militants get their violent ideas generally ignored the "Army of God" manual, which recommends sixty-five ways to destroy abortion clinics and includes an illustrated recipe for making a "fertilizer bomb" from ammonium nitrate and fuel oil. The manual turned up in 1993, buried in the backyard of an anti-abortionist indicted for arson and acid attacks on nine clinics. But headline-writers avoided describing it as a "Manual for Terrorists," as the *New York Times* identified a militia document on April 29, 1995. . . .
>
> In late 1993, *Nightline*'s Ted Koppel hosted an in studio discussion of doctor-killing. He had only two guests. One was Helen Alvare, a representative of the National Conference of Catholic Bishops, which issued a statement post-Pensacola [when Dr. David Gunn was gunned down outside his birth control clinic] comparing the violence of murder with the "violence of abortion." The other was Paul Hill, director of an anti-abortion group "Defensive Action," which advocates killing doctors on the grounds that abortion is violence . . . Although terrorism is one of Koppel's favorite subjects—Fairness and Accuracy in Reporting's study of *Nightline* counted fifty-two programs on the topic in forty months—the word "terrorism" was never used by him to describe anti-abortion violence. Instead, a sympathetic Koppel said that Hill's advocacy of murdering doctors raised a "very very difficult moral question. . . ."
>
> In December 1994, NBC refused to air a segment of the program *TV Nation* in which Roy McMillan of the Mississippi-based Christian Action Group said that assassinating Supreme Court justices would be justifiable homicide, and that the President was in "probable harm's way." *TV Nation* producer Michael Moore believes that the airing of the segment could have led to arrests that might have prevented the Brookline, Massachusetts, Planned Parenthood clinic killings. Flanders states that, "It is a federal offense to say that the President should be killed, Moore told *USA Today*. Eventually the interview aired on the BBC in Britain, but not in the U.S.[50]

Finally Flanders describes how, after it was decided that the Arabs were not the terrorists to blame for the Oklahoma City bombing, the president of Planned Parenthood, Fred Clarkson, was invited to speak on a major cable network on domestic terrorism—a topic he had learned about because of the clinic bombings. Just before the show, his appearance was canceled. Clarkson told FAIR that he was told that "they couldn't have someone from Planned Parenthood on about militias because they'd have angry pro-life viewers calling in and they didn't want to take the heat." Clarkson added that you cannot prove the "link" between the militias and the anti-abortion groups, but in very many cases, the people are the same."

One may or may not wish to advocate freedom of choice regarding abortion. But that is not the point. The point is that when a young woman with a severe spine injury goes to have an abortion because neither she nor the baby might survive the pregnancy, she is already distraught over the difficult choices life has presented her. She does not deserve to be bombed, or even to fear being bombed. Domestic terrorism should not be ignored by the media any more than it should be ignored by the police.

But why does not the media tell us about the activities of right-wing terrorism? It is because they are continuing the status quo, running on automatic pilot. Covering the extreme right advocacy crimes might indeed bring good ratings. But, more important, such coverage might tell people what they need to know to counter this violence. Paying no attention to covering real news steals the future from us all.

Potential Environmental Catastrophes

Another example of tuning out and screening out is potential environmental catastrophes.

In 1998, a liquified natural gas (LNG) truck overturned near Boston, forcing the evacuation of a suburban neighborhood near Boston. The media covered this precise issue. They gave no indication of the larger context, the real story. Physicist Amory Lovins said, "The energy content of a single LNG carrier of 125,000 cubic meters is equivalent to 55 Hiroshima bombs." Huge tankers of LNG regularly come from Algeria into the port of Boston, transferring their cargo to the Distrigas import terminal in Everett. This is one of the few ports so close to a major population center in the world. The public has no idea what would happen if those tanks leaked. Nor do they understand why the entire harbor is cleared and the U.S. Coast Guard escorts the Algerian ship bringing the replacement fuel. If a LNG gas leak occurred when the wind was strong, much of greater Boston could be engulfed in a fireball.

A spill of LNG is initially a white frozen vapor hugging the ground. That is not the problem. The problem begins as the gas quickly mixes with air, expands, warms, loses any color, and is caught by whatever wind is blowing. This gas has no odor and gives no warning. It is nearly inevitable that such a vapor cloud will encounter a lit cigarette, a pilot light from a stove, a spark from a worker's tool. Then, fire is instant and all consuming.

The local media has largely ignored the situation.

Certainly this industry, like the nuclear reactor industry, tries its best to avoid accidents. Fortunately, they have done quite a good job. But accidents have occurred. Should not the citizens of metropolitan Boston and their elected officials decide whether the benefit of hosting one of the globe's major LNG import terminals outweighs the risks? Should there not at least be some discussion of whether the terminal in Everett should be closed and relocated elsewhere?

Should not the media cover the whole issue, not just with occasional snippits that give no context?

Dr. Paul Walker, Legacy Program director of Global Green U.S.A., offers perspective on the importance of environmental hazards globally, far beyond the very hazardous LNG situation in Boston. The foundation, led by Mikhail Gorbachev, the last Premier of the Soviet Union, works on these important and life-threatening issues. It is work seldom covered in the media. Walker says, "One of the major challenges of the twenty-first century is environmental security—cleaning up thousands of badly polluted sites around the globe which threaten the public's safety and health. From fields in Kosovo and Kuwait ladened with unexploded bombs, to drinking water supplies contaminated with toxic petrochemicals, to regions infiltrated with radioactive waste, remediation of dangerous pollution has quickly become a most important goal. In support of our efforts, we need transparency of information and serious media attention and coverage in order to engage the larger public—all stakeholders in today's environmental cleanup."[51]

We live in an era when we must understand much more than we did in former times. We all pitch in to report the news of bad traffic jams. We operate crime watches, and kids' safety programs. We take precautions against disease with countless medical tests. But we are blissfully ignorant about the high-tech catastrophic hazards. We abandon all our good sense about taking preventive measures. We rely largely on the industry's policing itself. We pay little attention to any regulatory agency efforts. We assume accidents cannot happen, even while we know they do.

Return from the global environmental problem to one specific local problem. The media needs to cover each problem as if it were local. Then practical action, not just empathy, can happen. The public needs to know: (1) what LNG is; (2) the risks of transporting the LNG carriers from Algeria through Boston Harbor; (3) the views of Cabot LNG Corporation, the company that imports the gas from Algeria, and the extent to which it is prepared to compensate victims in the event of an LNG accident; (4) which government officials in the Massachusetts State House and in the Everett City Hall could take action to protect the public; (5) the preventive safety and security practices and who might monitor and continually strengthen such practices; (6) the realistic possibility of fighting a fire, should an accident occur; (7) what would be needed to close and relocate the import terminal away from a center of population; and (8) where we can learn about LNG so that we can compare the information disseminated by the New England Gas Association, the U.S. Bureau of Mines, and *Frozen Fire*, the book published by Friends of the Earth. The public deserves this same level of information about all of the other environmental threats to health and life.

Just do not expect to hear about this in the news media. Why? Perhaps because, as with LNG, the catastrophe has not happened yet. Perhaps because journalists do not have the slightest idea what is going on with LNG or with the other global threats. Perhaps the media does not want to upset the public. Yet, that level of discomfort would be nothing in comparison to that experienced in a real disaster—a cataclysmic disaster of LNG or nuclear or biological weapons—or a slow but lethal catastrophe of chemical or radioactive poisoning. Perhaps these stories are not in the news because the media executives are golfing buddies or neighbors of the Cabot Corporation executives or the officers of other corporations and governments responsible for creating these hazards. Whatever the reason, it is the public who is left like the lemmings enroute to the edge of a cliff, with their future stolen and without a voice in their options. Each person in the equation has become a gatekeeper to the extent that she or he has acted from self-interest and without regard to the public's interest—which, ultimately, and ironically, is their interest too.

Albert Einstein said, "Everything's changed except the way we think." Maybe it is time that the media rethink the extent of coverage that is in the public interest when the topic is high-tech hazardous materials. Maybe it is time the public rethinks its stance and insists that government officials take steps to minimize this enormous public safety hazard. Consider what is at stake if the best efforts of industry are not enough. Must we risk a Chernobyl-type disaster in metropolitan Boston?

Another way in which the story told does not give us what we need to know is when parts of the story are screened out due to personal bias.

Personal Bias within the Media

As reported in *Time* magazine, October 26, 1998, David Weston, chairman of ABC News, killed a story that was to have aired on ABC's news magazine program, "20/20." The story was critical of ABC's parent company, Walt Disney.

Another example of screened out information is the ABC News special program called "The Century." It aired early in 1999 and the segments chosen were looks at some of the most notable events of the last century. What we were not told is that the events were chosen by their prominent news personality Peter Jennings and came from a book he wrote. What he has done is perfectly fine—as long as the viewer understands the bias used in listing the purported key events of the century. His list included Charles Lindbergh's flight, landing on the moon, World War I, President Franklin

Delano Roosevelt's New Deal, Hitler's rise to power, the atom bomb, McCarthyism, Elvis, Martin Luther King, Jr., Vietnam, and the revolution in Iran. Had others had a voice in developing such a weighty list, they might have included things like Mother Teresa's work with the poor, the Holocaust, the invention of birth control contraceptives, the Peace Corps, the first heart transplants, the end to apartheid in South Africa, and democratic revolutions in many parts of the world. Individual choices made arbitrarily by media creators can limit the opportunities for the rest of the population to benefit from inclusion. The public should understand that the message sent is one man's view, not necessarily gospel truth.

War

Another example of the full story not being told is the coverage of war.

The Gulf War of 1991 offers a good example of free press not being as free as the Constitution suggests. As reported in *Winning the Global TV News Game*, "Many U.S. journalists were upset at the press censorship in the Gulf War. They were so upset that they filed a law suit against the U.S. government, claiming that it was unconstitutional for the military to overrule the press. Many believed they would win. When the war ended, the suit was declared moot and dropped."[52] *Winning the Global TV News Game* presents the comments of John Fialka, Defense Department correspondent for the *Wall Street Journal*, comments at an MIT forum.[53] "Although photographers produced some six thousand frames per day of the war, only twenty were released each day. Reporters were encouraged to cover the high-tech equipment for which the Defense Department sought continued congressional appropriations; they were given little opportunity to cover the conventional weapons and the troops that were actually responsible for most of the military action. Here, censorship took the form of interfering with news coverage in order to turn it into public relations for the U.S. Defense Department."[54]

A Greek student of mass communications from Boston University reflected on the war coverage of the May 1999 NATO intervention in Kosovo in the former Yugoslavia. Andreas Argyropoulos offered this comparison:

> When a refugee caravan was unintentionally bombed by NATO planes, killing an estimated eighty-six refugees, the reporting of this story was very nonchalant on CNN, merely referring to the convoy that was struck and that there might have been casualties. There were no reports, no camera feeds, no interviews. When I watched the same news on Greek TV, there a reporter was on site and the pictures were the most shocking I have ever seen. People's remains were all over the area. I cannot accept the excuse that these pictures were too shocking to show because, first, they

could have been edited. In addition the excuse isn't believable because we all know how eager television is to show shocking material. I believe that if the Americans were shown this and were told that their planes had killed all those poor civilians, many of whom were children, then there would have been a radical shift in public opinion about the war. There was so much coverage of the three American soldiers who were imprisoned by the Serbs and then released, yet the number of casualties among the Serbs is only a statistic for CNN. Why the double standard?"[55]

War coverage will always be a controversial topic because one does not want one's opposition to see too much on TV. In addition, each incident does not necessarily reflect the whole story, and there is room for interpretation. Nonetheless, citizens in a democracy should expect to have sufficient information to determine whether or not they wish to spend their tax dollars and sacrifice their sons and daughters to the cause of whatever the current war may be.

Water and Air Safety

A final example of critical news sometimes screened out of the public view: We all need to know that our water and air supplies are safe. The Union of Concerned Scientists, a national public interest group, tells people how to "Take Action: Protect Our Air" in their Winter 1998–1999 *Earthwise*. It tells who sets policy regarding emission standards, and how the typical citizen can contact those people. But you will likely never hear of either the problems or the solutions on prime time news. Every day, employees of the federal Environmental Protection Agency are dealing with legal and regulatory decisions affecting the air and water. Will the EPA be able to hold the automobile manufacturers to tight emissions controls or will the industry's lobbying result in Congress's weakening the laws? Will industry polluters continue to jeopardize drinking water supplies the way they did in Woburn, Massachusetts? Or will the EPA be able to enforce regulations to protect the water supply from carcinogens? In this case, a movie called *A Civil Action* actually told the story of how the local advocates won their battle with the polluters. That kind of coverage is rare, either in the entertainment media or the news. Covering stories like safe air and water are usually deemed less important than covering the fleeing convict found hiding in the limbs of a tree fourteen days after he escaped from prison. You'll never know, and not knowing might hurt you.

Occasionally, the entertainment media does tell us exactly what we need to know by raising critical issues to enough prominence for a reasonable debate to occur—the kind of debate that offers hope for a democratic culture.

Hollywood actor Ed Asner, former president of the Screen Actors Guild, identifies a couple of the rare moments when Hollywood raised the level of debate:

> Maybe *Dead Man Walking* will be one of the first steps toward fighting the death penalty effectively. . . . But to me the most meaningful event of that time, because I was so directly involved in the El Salvador situation, was when Oliver Stone came out with his picture of *Salvador*. Everything I had been calling people's attention to—the savagery and brutality of what we were inflicting on the people of El Salvador by supporting their military government—became clear in his movie. But his picture did not gain wide release and was not shown across the board. So most people didn't see it. But just perhaps, perhaps those who did see it may not have been aware of the process and may have been influenced by it."[56]

Asner is referring to two recent events that have cost huge sums of American tax dollars and have raised crucial questions about the civil society's concern for human rights. First, in recent decades, the death penalty has been restored in a number of states, and the question of whether or not to do so is very controversial in other states. Aside from the overall ethical issue of whether a modern state should engage in murder itself, numerous cases have been cited where persons on death row have been proven innocent or, in some cases, they are retarded and not fit to understand the act they committed. There have been cases in recent years where the pope and the secretary of state have each pleaded with governors not to carry out a scheduled execution. *Dead Man Walking* is a film about a nun's concern with a man on death row. The film takes the viewer past the stereotypes and into the extremely complex issues that must be faced if one wishes to act with some intelligence in passing judgment on the death penalty. The civil war in El Salvador was about the brutal dictatorship in that country using its power to control the indigenous population lest they show a preference for a socialist government. The problem was that many of the military forces were trained in terrorism by the U.S. military at our School of the Americas. The one event that brought the war to the attention of the American public was when several Roman Catholic sisters were raped and murdered and the government in power protected the attackers. Otherwise, most people knew little about the U.S. role in this activity. The movie *Salvador* did what films can do so well—put the issues in front of the public.

Indeed, much of the time, the media steals our future.

Partly it is because we have little understanding of what's not shown—the deals made by media moguls that control our government, our lives, and our culture.

And, in large part, the media steals our futures because top media moguls are too busy protecting their own bottom line. An anesthetized public is easier to deal with than an alert public.

Edward R. Murrow, one of the leading twentieth-century radio and television personalities, observed that "unless we recognize that television . . . is being used to distract, delude, amuse, and insulate us, then television and those who finance it, those who look at it and those who work at it, may see a totally different picture too late."[57]

Chapter 2

Killing Our Culture

> The quality of state and local news coverage has declined
> pathetically. But if you think it is bad in Boston, you have not
> lived until you see Los Angeles. . . . The networks are our
> franchises. These are public licenses.
>
> *Michael Dukakis, former governor of Massachusetts,*
> *Democratic nominee for president in 1988[1]*

"They think I'm weird, 'cause I really like weapons," said a twelve-year-old boy from an affluent Boston suburb. More and more youngsters sound like this one, youngsters very much like the two boys in the Denver, Colorado, suburb of Littleton, whose murderous rampage against their high school classmates in 1999 was influenced in no small degree by the media "entertainment" and "infotainment."

The above quote of former Massachusetts governor and Democratic presidential candidate Michael Dukakis opens the Pandora's box that the media try to keep closed. Instead of providing us with news that reveals the positive as well as negative aspects of our culture, the media concentrate on the sensational and the violent, giving the impression, especially to unsophisticated young people, that violence is our societal norm.

Why would a young teenager from a typical family be fascinated by weapons instead of outer space exploration or baseball or catching frogs? Why would he or she think this is the way to get attention rather than winning the science fair or hitting a home run or going hiking with the kids? If his parents and his neighbors have never owned weapons, could it be that the ideas come from the media?

So many cartoons and sitcoms are full of guns and violence. Even in well-written and well-produced programs that use weapons not gratuitously but as an essential part of the plot line—such as "Law and Order" and "NYPD Blue"—the weapon itself becomes glamorized. Perhaps that is because the "good guys" use weapons in what are portrayed as justifiable and worthy causes. Does this appear to the viewer as a reason to like, and not despise, tools that are designed to kill. The significant question is whether these influences have become a value base for American culture.

To determine whether media moguls are killing our culture, it is first necessary to understand what culture is. Most of us just live within it, the way the student "just breathed" until his course in biology introduced him to the respiratory system.

Culture is patterns of behavior and beliefs common to members of a society. It is the rules for understanding and generating customary behavior. It includes beliefs, norms, values, assumptions, expectations, and plans for action. It is a framework for seeing the world around oneself—for interpreting events and behavior and reacting to perceived reality.

Culture is learned, shared. Culture is how people adapt to the environment around them and it is dynamic, continuously changing over time.[2] Individuals and their culture are involved in a constant dialogue through which they define themselves. Everyone should have the right to develop her or his own culture.

Culture requires participation, community and place, language, cultural exchange, a way to redress grievances and conflict. Culture is acted upon through education, public communication, arts, public cultural policies, public services, and the media.

Tony award—winning actor John Randolph offers an example of how culture is portrayed in films from other countries. He finds the content to capture the rich dynamic of life for every character, young or old—capture a level of sensitivity not always evident in American film. He speaks from his experience screening foreign films for Academy Award nominations.[3] "I see the most magnificent pictures with children in other societies. If they make a mistake, the parents are there. The kids are honest. They cry. Then they are forgiven and they go out." Randolph is very excited about the vital change the inclusion of foreign films is bringing to the American Academy: "It's real people. Great artists in their own country and we've never heard about them. We moved a great step forward."

American culture has all these wholesome characteristics, too, we just hear little about them. They have been set aside by media moguls looking for quick profits. Because we rarely see the positive on TV, we come to believe the world is all negative.

Remember how the quote on the Statue of Liberty symbolized the heart of America? "Give me your tired, your poor . . ." How proudly Americans touted our culture, our land of opportunity? We still open doors to high-profile refugees from Kosovo. We can always add one more seat at the table. Come on in, we have much to offer. Despite its shortcomings, American culture has, to a greater degree than most countries, accommodated people with differing beliefs, backgrounds, and values.

Part of this ideal America summons up images of friends and neighbors sharing a barbecue after helping someone clean their basement. Homemade pie, ice cream, and everyone is family.

Once kids sold the newspapers on city street corners and no one worried if they would be kidnapped.

Once house doors were left unlocked and car windows were left open, and no one worried if a thief would come.

Once public schools were a place of pride, a level playing field for all kids regardless of background. No one worried they would shoot each other.

The 1999 movie *Pleasantville* captures some of these longing for the good old days. And then the movie story line, subtly but deliberately, moves people into a preferred technicolor today—a period with far more opportunity, for many people, than was the case in the "good old days." In real life, the longing for better times does not disappear so easily. People do, by and large, experience positive events in their lives, but they are so often overshadowed by the negative, especially when the dominant media message is to sow fear and anxiety. The longings for a viable culture are expressed daily in the decisions people make about their lives.

For example, gated communities are touted as safe and friendly places to live. They are sought out as a reaction to fear and a protectionist measure allegedly safeguarding one against those who are *different*. They are also sought out by people who feel isolated and want that community feeling of the old time barbecue or the church supper.

The "salon" movement, where people gather weekly at someone's home to converse, is an effort to escape the isolation of talking with one's computer—a sad, even tragic, commentary on many of today's people under forty. It is a longing to share life with fellow humans again. It is a way to find people who share this desire.

The charter school movement, publicly funded schools with a special focus—arts, science—apart from the normal public school system, represents attempts by people to find a safe and healthy place for kids, with a decent education.

It is born of a disenchantment with the public schools and a disappearance of the commitment to the equalizing intent of this honorable American tradition—free education for all.

The growth of the radical right's religious zealousness and fascist philosophy is an expression of people saying that they have "had it" with cultural disintegration.

All these decisions made today are symptomatic of three things: (1) A sense of desperation about our culture; (2) a longing to believe that the culture of the "American dream" is still alive—at least for "me and my friends"; (3) the fact that people have no clue how to create the culture they seek because neither role models nor teachers have a voice in today's media.

The median age in the United States today is thirty-six. That means that the historical American Dream is only in history books for them. Nonetheless, the longing remains for the place where the rash experiment in individualism, pluralistic culture, opportunity, and the pursuit of happiness exists.

The problem is that real-world solutions that attempt to find this "American Dream" today are largely exclusive, not inclusive—a total contradiction of our Constitution, our legal system, and the most admired moments in our history. This country is so huge and such a mix of people and ideas that exclusivity can never succeed.

For example, the radical right sees scapegoating and violence as a solution. It is not. It can only bring misery to everyone. The charter schools seek a new form of segregation. This can only return us to some of the difficult social problems we had in earlier decades of the twentieth century when separate and unequal schools were tolerated. The result can only widen the gap between those with enough education to get jobs and those who are unable to get jobs. The salon movement is a desperate attempt to formalize human understanding. Throughout history it has been evident that whenever people, on their own, care for each other, even fall in love, there is hope for humankind. If we live in a culture where basic human exchange must be structured, the joy in life is lost. Gated communities also bring a form of segregation of the upper-income, mostly white, population into ghettos. Whoever is enclosed in a ghetto—be they Jew, black, poor, elderly, or white suburbanite—loses freedom of movement and opportunity and increases the societal strain with those outside the real or imagined ghetto walls.

These behavior choices indeed reflect the outcry of a people losing their culture. The motto on the Statue of Liberty, the words in the U.S. Constitution lose their meaning.

Why are these responses to today's culture media-driven?

It is simple. The media are the largest, most pervasive instruments for persuasion and propaganda that shape the hearts and minds of people. Otherwise, why would advertisers spend so much money using the media to sell their products? Otherwise, why are the media the first targets for takeover in a military coup?

The media have promoted individualism at an extreme that has resulted in isolation. For example, inherent in media industry success is the selling of a "star." This is one person, an icon, for the public to follow. It is one person who solves everything, often in some superhuman way. The technologies of recent decades have only made it easier to promote and sell a star. The 1980s and much of the 1990s have been a growth period for rugged individualism. It is a recurrent theme in Republican politics. It is the mantra of the rich and famous who, enjoying a particularly good economic period, have forgotten all those who contributed to their good fortune. Rugged individualism is a logical outcome of a period when it has been fashionable to be cynical about the value of government and fashionable to be suspicious about the effectiveness of not-for-profit organizations.

Consequently, U.S. culture shifted from one of generosity and community to one of self-protection and isolation.

Why do we act like the figures in Plato's cave—believing that reality is in the shadows on the wall (or the electronic screen)? Why do those shadows become more important to us than the culture we create through our own personal involvement? Are the shadows (images) more important because they are larger than life or superhuman? Or are we transformed into passive receivers of electronic message, no longer proactive creators of our own community?

Shadows substitute for substance. The shadows initially were those on the silver screen, where people who are frustrated or alienated identify with the fictional characters or create a fiction by empathizing with their portrayers as a way to create a momentary different identity for themselves. When the real world does not get any better for them, they more and more lose themselves in the fictional world, using their new would-be identity figures as role models. This becomes more intense in television, in part because of the greater frequency of identification opportunities.

For example, on TV not only is the character a hero, but the actors and actresses themselves become larger than life. John Wayne is forever the rugged individualist tough guy. Candice Bergen is synonymous with "Murphy Brown," the sharp-tongued independent modern woman. Oprah Winfrey is another larger-than-life character, reaching the public through her very popular "Oprah" show. When she loses weight, much of America plans to lose weight. When she starts a book club, people across the country take up reading.

The media can shape our identity. It surely shapes our culture. Does the practice of including or screening out media messages constitute a form of gatekeeping that is killing American culture?

To answer this question, we will examine six cornerstones of American culture to see how they fare in the light of contemporary media: (1) free speech, (2) advocacy, (3) democracy, that is, self-rule, (4) economic opportunity, (5) human equality, and (6) priority care for our kids.

Free Speech

American culture is based on the notion that anyone is able to say anything they wish. In the marketplace of ideas, the best ideas will win. This cornerstone of the U.S. Constitution, the First Amendment, makes our culture different from that of many countries of the world where ideas are often considered dangerous, and where governments carefully control what is said—especially in the media. History has proven that when diverse ideas about society are not resolved in speech, they are ultimately resolved on battlefields. Few things could be more central to killing American culture than ending the right of free speech. Unfortunately, it is happening. While the media owners jealously protect their own First Amendment rights, as well they should, they do not extend the courtesy to the larger American public.

The issue is not free speech, per se. It is the "distribution of free speech," which is becoming virtually impossible without passing the gatekeeping of the powerful. This gatekeeping affects access to the media for the typical American and it even screens out many of those who have a foot in the door as media professionals.

Andrea Milford, Emerson College media arts researcher, looks at free speech in the context of the filmmakers. "Not only does an Academy Award nomination or win practically guarantee a film success, thereby increasing its chances of being heard, but the lack of a nomination for certain minorities has a tremendous effect on filmmaking. In 1999, not a single ethnic minority was represented in either the story of the film or in the portrayal of characters in any film."[4] Women as well had a low showing in 1999 films. The independent filmmakers, who usually are financially strapped, cannot exercise their free speech on a street corner with a brochure; their product is a film that needs distribution. In recent years, festivals like Robert Redford's Sundance Festival are beginning to open venues for the independent films to have an audience. But it is very slow.

Another example of restricting the distribution of free speech relates to coverage of controversial issues. PBS censored a documentary on nuclear weapons because it was negative. *Building Bombs*, made in 1990, shows what happened at the Savannah River Plant in South Carolina after forty years of making nuclear weapons. It talked of cancer and related health and environmental problems such as radioactive turtles and improperly buried nuclear waste.

The reason cannot be a fear of scaring people. The media has learned that its highest ratings and biggest economic success come when it scares people. Commercial stations understand this even better than do the public broadcasting stations. Of course, there is a fine line, albeit frequently blurry line, between fantasy-scared and real-world-scared—and *Building Bombs's* impact is definitely real-world-scared. The only other reason for not airing a well-researched, well-produced program like this is self-protection. That usually comes down to not angering those who send money—government and industry.

The documentary had been carefully reviewed for statistical accuracy. Erik Barnouw, the prominent film historian, says, "PBS didn't dare show [the film] for fear of offending the nuclear industry."[5] The film won an Academy Award nomination in 1990 for best feature documentary. It finally aired, after three years of lobbying, in a cut-down version.[6]

A third example of denying free speech is based on the self-interest of the media owner. *Variety*, the media industry trade magazine, demoted, then fired, a film critic who gave a negative review to a big-studio film. Joseph McBride made negative comments in his critique of Tom Clancy's *Patriot Games*. Paramount, which had produced the film for $40 million, pulled its advertising from *Variety*.[7]

Then there are those who genuinely believe that the practice of screening out free speech for all but the powerful is quite appropriate. For example, Michiru Onishi, an Emerson College film student from Japan, finds it hard to accept the American idea of free speech for all. He explains, "It is acceptable for only the powerful to have free speech because I see this control as the way to preserve accountability and to keep social order."[8] This attitude of assuming trust in a benevolent dictator is the stance often presented by those with the power. When one participates in the chaos and hears the offensive things sometimes said in a free speech environment, such benevolent dictatorship can seem appealing. Onishi further defends his argument by observing, "There are two types of power. One is social power such as celebrity, fame and authority, and the other is physical power such as bodies and weapons. Physical power prevails against free speech. The basic theme of free speech is that the pen is mightier than the sword. However, speech is no longer useful against violence."[9]

A former federal official recalls an informal conversation he had with several CIA officials at the time the Pentagon Papers were made known to the public by the *New York Times* and the *Washington Post*. The papers revealed to the public the false information and outright lies the military had disseminated to the American people during the Vietnam War in order to control and manipulate people's political attitudes toward the U.S. involvement in Southeast Asia. The official supported the right of the people to know the truth about their government's operations as long as it did not jeopardize lives. The CIA officers insisted that they alone had the expertise to judge what the American people should or should not know, and what was best for the country. Their point was that the public could not and should not be trusted to influence decisions that they believed should be made unilaterally by the country's leaders. They implied that there was something subversive about the official's belief that the people have a constitutional right to know in order to participate intelligently in the operation of their government. What effect does this attitude and behavior have on the functioning of a democratic culture?

America's founding fathers bristled at this way of thinking. They had seen violence. They knew that the only course to preventing violence, or ending it, is the exercise of free speech. Are we, in America, beginning to accept a de facto norm that only the powerful can have free speech? If so, the media can surely kill American culture as we have envisioned it. (Or rather, we the voting public are allowing the power of the dollar to speak louder than the voice of the people through the power of their vote.) The law, after all, is on the side of the public—so far.

Without free speech *for all*, American culture is dead. Free speech presumes content, not just amusing sound bites that divert people from reality. Without free speech, there is no room for intellect or ideas or progress.

Advocacy

Advocacy, or the existence of viable nongovernmental groups of ordinary citizens who want to advance or oppose something, is a cornerstone of American culture very much taken for granted. In some countries, people are arrested for suggesting that it is their right to organize in this way.

The Parents' Television Council (PTC) is a nationwide organization that promotes traditional family programming and attacks shows they do not like. They have been aggressive in their efforts for conservative values. Their Web site, *www.parentstv.org,* weekly posts the programs they dislike with the tagline "A message brought to you by—," fill in the names of those who advertise to sponsor that program. Howard Stern's raunchy subject matter usually placed him on their list, for example. Denise Gorman, Emerson College media arts researcher, says, "They are focused, persistent, and organized."[10] The PTC also produced a network "filth" scorecard with a green, yellow, or red light. It does not list which shows fit which column, it just ranks what they consider to be filth. For example, the new PAX network got no red lights. PAX programming tends to avoid senseless violence and explicit sex. The PTC also posts a "dirty dozen" each year, what they consider the least family-friendly programming, with a paragraph on why each show made their list. They post a "Diamond Dozen" list, which identifies the shows they support. The top three for the 1997–1998 season were "Touched by an

Angel," "7th Heaven," and "Promised Land." In 1999, the PTC ran a nation-wide newspaper ad campaign with full-page ads costing approximately $36,000 each. The ads used celebrities—Shirley Jones and Steve Allen are two of them—to draw attention to their activities on the Web. This is a classic example of how skillful advocacy works.

There are countless advocacy groups across the country. We generally hear little in the news media about their activity, until it reaches the point of an overwhelming public movement such as the Civil Rights movement of the 1960s or the anti-Vietnam War movement of the late 1960s, or the Nuclear Weapons Freeze campaign of the 1980s. Today, we hear some about the two sides of the advocacy movement concerning who decides whether or not one can have an abortion. But, in general, there is less news coverage of nongovernmental organizations (NGOs) on mainstream media in the early twenty-first century. The NGOs have headed toward the Internet, where it is possible to have a voice. That is great, except the dominant communication providing common news, information, and entertainment still is television.

The media's diminished coverage of NGOs seems to run parallel to the increasing reliance on public opinion polls. It takes less expenditure of news-gathering time and money to rely on a poll than to report on advocacy efforts. Polling has become an integral part of the whole cycle of communication. The polls give the policy makers information on what to say to best please the constituency whose support they need at the moment. The policy makers then release statements to the media, which report them to the public. The media then poll the public to see what their reaction is to the releases. These results are announced and become known to the policy makers, who add the results to their own polls and the cycle starts again.

Polling is not a substitute for advocacy. First, it is incredibly superficial. Issues such as public attitudes toward health care are far too complex to be dealt with in polls. Second, statistically selected samples may have only a small margin of inaccuracy, but they still have enormous limits. They are valid only for the moment the information is gathered and the time period *before* that, and they are only as good as the questions that are asked. For example, a political poll once asked the public who they preferred for "congress*man*" in a race with ten men and one woman. The wording alone might have excluded the one woman in the race from being selected. Enough misreadings of the word could alter the poll results. Covering NGOs allows a far more in-depth debate about the alternative ways of viewing a given issue. The presentation of alternative views that may differ from government views makes possible a forum in which the public can have a voice as well as a debate platform facilitating the public in thinking through all sides of an issue so they can decide their own position.

Turning from news to entertainment, one sees even less coverage of NGOs. The entertainment media rarely have a film that provides an example to the public of how advocacy works. This lack of a role model, and lack of coverage of substantive activity on behalf of something one finds important may well contribute to the isolation, lack of community, and sense that it is not possible, in today's culture, to join with people to change something.

Here are some views of advocacy leaders about their areas of interest and the media coverage thereof.

Susan Shaer, executive director of Women's Action for New Directions, thinks women are undervalued and underheard. When she realized that no one in power ever listened to the League of Woman Voters, she turned her attention to real politics, money, and lobbying. Shaer says:

> The media ignore advocacy groups. The media is interested in confrontation, uniqueness, and eccentricity. They're not interested in mainstream activities. Most lobbying and taking actions is fairly ordinary stuff. If a lobbyist pays hundreds of thousands of dollars to a politician to get a vote, that is a story. On the other hand, if hundreds of people are protesting to get a vote, it is not high visibility. Women have always been marginalized unless they do something unique, eccentric and bazaar.
>
> Similarly hundreds of letters written to lobby for or against something, letting a legislator know that to stay in office, they need to reflect voter interest, are discounted by the media. But we will certainly get media reports on poll results. Why? For one thing, the polling companies are in collusion with the media. When you see the poll results, it's a *Time/Newsweek* poll or that of another media outlet. They poll for many reasons. They do not just do a poll about politics. They do a poll that has multiple layers that show what mainstream people are interested in so they know what to put on the air.
>
> People are not in the streets showing their support or opposition for something the way they were twenty years ago. We do advocacy differently. We do it by e-mail or by faxes, and it is harder to be visible. Unless you jam the switchboards or the e-mail equipment on Capitol Hill, it's not much of a story. When you do, it is still not a story because you can't take a picture of it for the electronic media. You can't make it into a sound bite. The media wants sound bites, pictures, and glamour.
>
> We as an advocacy group always try to think of the "photo op." Most groups like ours can't afford a staff press person to "spin" the story and make the headline come out the way we want it to.
>
> To get media coverage, you must be relentless and tenacious. You will call them until you just wear them down. No one I know can do it part time. Twenty years ago Dr. Helen Caldicott made people crazy and she was tenacious in her outspoken opposition to the nuclear arms race. You could count on her to break through. You never knew what she'd do next. It is not that Helen Caldicott knew things that others didn't. The point was that in "media land" Helen Caldicott had become an image, an icon. So, rather than getting into detail,

click on the icon. And indeed, throughout the 1980s, this Australian was a household name in the United States.[11]

Susan Shaer notes other differences in advocacy since the 1980s:

> In the 80s we talked about the bomb. People had a very visceral reaction to that. Now we talk about the money. So and so votes this way because he gets so many dollars in Lockheed money. The votes influenced by money affect the policies of the nation, and they're not even a story in the media. . . .
>
> The land mines issue only became a media story because they took it out of the United States. E-mail about the land mines went international and they just hugged the U.S. from all sides. When weapons are made in the U.S., they are made in more than eighty congressional districts quite intentionally. The weapons contractors don't just own the congressperson in that district because the money brings jobs, they own the media in those districts. We can only succeed in having an alternative view heard if we try to get under the radar. That takes a lot of work—especially to sustain it.[12]

Another leading national advocacy organization is the Southern Poverty Law Center. Mark Potok, its director of public affairs and information, talks about the SPLC work as a nongovernmental organization specializing in watching the activities of the radical right:

> I think what we do is critically important. We are able to collect all this information and present it in a way that is compelling. In the case of this list I just drew up, the point is that in the years since the bombing at the Oklahoma City Federal Building, the radical right movement has not receded. In fact, the terrorist wing of the movement has greatly increased. Presently, there's probably the largest state of terrorism in this century, or certainly since the late 1960s. I remember as a reporter, you tripped across a story, and you know you have an idea. But the liability exposure is enormous. However, if you can call a commission or an organization, do you just quote them? That does not entirely cover the libel exposure, but it diminishes it hugely. That allows you to put things in the paper that you could never get in otherwise. Otherwise, everybody would have to be an investigative journalist and every story would take forever to do. You could simply say that the SPLC claims that so and so is an extremist. That's better than allowing someone to say, "I'm from the knights of the Ku Klux Klan and I'm not a racist." At least this way the reporter can quote both sources, the KKK and SPLC saying, "That is funny, because they've been arrested for burning down a biracial couple's house," or whatever.
>
> We do not need to be shrill and make pronouncements that racism is bad. Racism *is* bad. We have a great role to play in trying to be more of a think tank. I try to give the *Intelligence Report*, which I edit, the feel of authority. We've stopped quoting ourselves. We do not write stories. We quote academics or people who know their field. What's different for me is that in the past, when I worked as a reporter, I covered both sides of stories. This is odd now, because I really do not talk to the other side. That is ended for me.[13]

Free speech and the expectations of freedom in America are very m...
linked to advocacy—the right to work on what matters to you. As is evident
in some of Mark Potok's comments, citizen organizations can be enormously
helpful in getting a story told. But, much of the time, from many of the
sources, alternative viewpoints are not heard. TV news often screens out the
news generated by those who believe it is their right to speak out. Sometimes
this is intentional; do not rebut the media owners or advertisers. Sometimes
this is thoughtless; just stick to the formula of a few established voices pep-
pered with inconsequential tidbits and call it news. As TV screens out advocacy and alternative views, it spreads the poison that kills our culture. It kills
the spirit of hope.

Democratic Self-Rule

"I do not get involved in politics. I know better." One of the nation's leading
media experts, not a media owner, said that. There's much dissatisfaction
with government in today's American society. Why wouldn't there be? The
media tells us to hate government, never tells us that government is our only
recourse when seeking to protect the general public and a way of life from
the excesses of media mogul greed. Government alone can make and enforce laws, unless we want to return to Wild West vigilantes.

Art D'Lugoff, New York theatrical producer, who was the owner and
director of The Village Gate, where some of the finest new performers of the
1950s and 1960s were introduced, observed:

> "I think the media has cut up our efforts to understand, because it lacks deep
> analysis or any analysis. Television is all bites. The radio, outside of National
> Public Radio and Pacifica, does not give you any in-depth understanding even
> if it is wrong. There's nothing in-depth on television. There's only small bites—
> photowise and wordwise. There's just not a way for people to understand
> what happened, whether it is Kosovo, or Vietnam, or the Holocaust, or our
> national economy, or globalization, or whatever you want to look at. It is all
> very narrow.
>
> "With the Internet too, you cannot get things in depth. You cannot read a
> book on the Internet. A book is still going to last through the centuries. You can
> sit down with it at any time and think and focus and take it in. I think the other
> things are just engines to help you find information. But past that it is not a very
> substantive way of doing things."[14]

Who, besides the media, have the microphone to communicate information to millions and millions of citizens entitled to self-govern?

In recent years, most of the media, news, or entertainment criticizes government as unnecessary, inept, scandal-ridden. Remember that the job of
government is to provide some checks and balances on giant corporate inter-

ests so that there is a balance in how tax money is spent. For example, the job is to make sure that industry puts a special effort into food production so that the public is not poisoned, to make sure that toxics from industry are not entering the environment. Government's job is to be a watchdog of the very industries who finance the media to ensure that the rights of the public are protected. The job of government, additionally, is to safeguard public access to the media.

Is it any surprise that in these decades of corporate supremacy it is fashionable to attack anything and everything the government does? If the public turns off on democratic self-government, it becomes all the easier for those not concerned with the public to have their way. Indeed, government has its share of laziness, corruption, and scandal. Name an institution in society, including the church, that does not. "Cynical press coverage is helping to create a nation of cynics," said Paul Starobin, writing in *Columbia Journalism Review*.[13]

Cynicism is fueled by news media that rarely tell the public about anything that government workers do on behalf of key issues. The sitcom "West Wing" is the first equality attempt by the entertainment media to appraixse the public of "how things work."

Nonetheless, even those among us who complain have the expectation that part of American culture will guarantee them roads for travel, fire and police protection, libraries, schools, garbage collection, a safe and respected status when traveling internationally, and the ability to speak freely without interference from those who disagree. We have come to believe that self-government is our birthright.

Former Masachusetts governor and 1988 Democratic nominee for president Michael Dukakis, talked earlier this year about the health of America's democracy and the role of the media today, "All during my local career as a legislator and as governor, each of the major newspapers and television stations in Boston had a full-time State House reporter. Today, they're all gone. I always had a good relationship with the press. You're criticized. You expect that. I respected the press around me. They never were intrusive in a personal sense. They all knew that Sundays were family days at the Dukakis house and I can almost never remember when they were pounding on my door on Sunday. Nobody was ever staked out in the hedge. But they were aggressive and they were critical in the best sense and they did a good job—both TV and print. They were an important force in this state. There was coverage all the time. People were engaged. The press was engaged. That is no longer the case.

"I think that the media is no longer as large a force in Massachusetts politics as it used to be and that is sad. Because as a point of fact, they held us to account. We would worry about them—especially the TV. But the *Boston Globe* led the TV. The first thing the reporters did at the State House was to read the *Globe*.

"I don't think politicians are particularly concerned about the media today. It doesn't have any impact so they ignore them. There's not the kind of follow-up today in the media. In the past, they would not leave you alone until you responded. They're just paper tigers these days. They're pussycats. Nobody pays attention to them. There's no follow-through.

"The quality of state and local news coverage has declined pathetically. But if you think it's bad in Boston, you have not lived until you see Los Angeles.

"The Annenburg Center at USC did an analysis of local television news coverage of the recently completed statewide political campaign in California in the November 1998 election. This is the largest state in the country. It's the world's eighth largest economy. In November 1998, the public voted for a U.S. senator in a hotly contested race, and a new governor for the first time in eight years. They voted for state legislators, county supervisors, and other officials. Local television stations in California devoted one-third of 1 percent of their news broadcasts to the candidates running. About 60 percent of that coverage was horse race coverage (coverage of who's ahead). The conclusion for candidates was, do not do any events where you expect to draw the media. They won't bother to come. Just keep dialing for dollars. The only way you'll get on television and reach the voters yourself is to raise money and pay for it."[16]

How can the public even decide whether it is worth taking the time to vote if they do not understand how the decisions of the elected official matter in their lives? Who would possibly deliver this information on a large scale other than the media? There is no other voice so powerful. How can we maintain self-government if the public does not have the opportunity to meet the candidates and question them?

Maybe we should just forget about the election thing. Let self-government run on automatic pilot. Just leave it to whoever is impassioned enough to assume power. That might be Jesse Ventura, the former wrestler, or David Duke, the former Ku Klux Klan leader. It might be a military leader. It might be someone very rich like Steve Forbes, who uses his own money, or George W. Bush, who is backed by the nation's wealthiest power-brokers. Maybe it is media commentator Pat Buchanan, whose rhetoric reflects much of the hatred and bigotry of the extreme right. Can there be any danger is letting one of them assume leadership? No need for elections and checks and balances; those formalities just slow down the business of moving ahead, don't they?

What right does the media have to screen out all the information we need to know about a candidate's experience, views, and past actions? How presumptuous of the media to tell us "who's ahead"? The only real poll is on election day when the people vote. Focusing election coverage on horse race speculation means nothing except on the day the poll was taken and among the sample that was polled. It is simply hype for the ratings. It is either total recklessness about the culture in which one lives or it is ignorance on the part of the young journalists who have never been taught that covering elections is a wholly different activity from covering a ball game.

Arthur D'Lugoff points out that, fortunately, some people in the culture are able to understand the substance of the issues. They just do not understand the full story. "We have the information," he says. "There's a tremendous amount of information in magazines and books and so forth. It doesn't reach people. You have to be in a major city to get it. And even if you're in the major cities, you won't find out the truth unless you're directed to it, know where to look for it, and know what to look for. A large part of the United States might as well be rural America a hundred years ago. They get what they get on their local television stations."

Michael Dukakis comments on the national press corps and its role in election coverage.

> The national press corps! There's too many of them. They're running around. They're wallowing in crises. What to do after Lewinsky (the scandal about President Clinton's mistress)? For a while it was out to Denver for the poor Benet kid (JonBenet Ramsey, the child model who was killed). Then Kosovo hits (NATO bombing and ethnic cleansing in former Yugoslavia). Then Littleton Colorado hits (two high school students open fire on their classmates).
>
> "If I see one more analysis of where we went wrong at Littleton, I think I'm going to scream. They get psychologists on the TV. The Colorado state legislature was in the process of passing a bill giving you a statutory right to carry a concealed weapon. There were billboards with Charlton Heston with a rifle all over the state. What do you expect? There has to be some reason why the level of juvenile violence in Massachusetts is so much lower than it is in the West. It is not because our kids are inherently better. They're all watching the same TV. They're playing the same video games. It is because we're tough as hell on guns. That is a message you get from the get-go. The U.S. Attorney just put a guy away for twenty years for selling guns to minors. The messages kids get are where we go wrong. It is this wallowing in the sensational story of the moment.
>
> "When you're a candidate for president, the national press corps and the twenty-four-hour television channels are there. You deal with them. But lest we forget, in total, all of the nationals put together do not have more than a million

viewers. If you're a candidate for president, you want to be in on that local media market. If you can do twenty-four local interviews in one and one-half hours, as I did from Raleigh, N.C., it saves time. It is not a question of end-running the national press corps.

The national press corps itself these days is another matter. There are too many to make it workable logistically. They're competitive. Campaigns are long. They follow you for months and months and you can only say the same thing about fifty times differently and then they start getting bored with you. You get bored with yourself. After that, it is a game of 'gotcha' and it is all this silly stuff and so forth.

The folks I respect in journalism are even more unhappy than you and I. They think it's terrible, but nobody seems to be able to do much about it. I think a lot of it has to do with who owns the media these days. It may well be that the citizens of this great country, in their wisdom, aren't paying much attention to this. You look at the impeachment thing. It is clear that about 67–68 percent of the people in the country decided early on that what Clinton did was wrong. It was dumb, but it was not impeachable. Nothing seemed to persuade them otherwise despite all of the wallowing in it that the press was doing. So maybe there's a kind of a wisdom amongst the public, that's not affected by all this stuff.

"But one would think we'd at least be better informed citizens if we had a press corps and media that dealt with the issues. When I think back to the days in the sixties and seventies when you and I and other people were deeply into so many fundamental issues, which I like to think for the most part we success-fully resolved, there was coverage and information and analysis. The media played a major role in this stuff."

Dukakis turns to why he thinks the media has screened out the real issues of politics. "It's a competitive ratings game in which you somehow try to find a sufficiently large part of the market—although these segments are a small percentage of the total—to justify whatever it is you're supposed to justify to the remote boardroom that owns you."

What can be done to prevent this death of self-government?

Dukakis has several thoughts. First, in elections:

Can't we get less focused on the horse race? Please, stop paying pollsters to do polls a year and a half in advance, for that matter, six months in advance. Everybody knows those polls are absolutely worthless. Spend more time on whatever it is the election is being fought over. You'd hope the media would seriously look at what the candidates are stressing."

Dukakis adds:

"Paul Taylor, the *Washington Post* national reporter, was the one who asked [Gary] Hart the famous question in the 1988 campaign about whether he'd ever committed adultery. He was on a one-man crusade trying to get the national media to provide free time for the candidates. His proposal was to provide five minutes of prime time for each of the two major presidential candidates on alternate nights, five times a week. I think John Ellis actually came up with this discussion of nine Sundays. It came out of the Kennedy School at Harvard. They proposed that the two-hour slot from 7 to 9 p.m. on each of the nine Sundays from Labor Day to Election Day would be devoted exclusively to the campaign. There would be two debates between the presidential candidates and one debate between the vice presidential candidates. The other six Sunday evenings would be jointly produced by the networks. They would look at a one political issue—a policy area—and examine what the candidates' positions were. They would offer the candidates interview time, but nothing big. They selected the time of day assuming that people are usually home Sunday evenings. It is the "60 Minutes" slot. When you look at the audiences that the debates have attracted—ninety million to a hundred million viewers—it is pretty impressive.

The TV networks turned them down. The networks are our franchisees. These are public licensees. I think the FCC, using their existing regulatory jurisdiction, could require the five-minute proposal. Why don't they? This is a pretty good FCC. A president could do this.

Is the issue one of screening out the public interest in favor of network and incumbent public official self-interest? Members of the National Association of Broadcasters make campaign contributions to members of Congress. The Congress approves the budget for the FCC. Incumbents in Congress are likely to prefer the status quo. At present, it is difficult for challengers to get access to the microphone unless they buy it. Free air time for presidential candidates might trickle down to other races as well.

Making democracy viable means the gatekeepers in the media, in Congress, and in the FCC need to decide it is in their self-interest not to kill this cherished part of American culture.

Michael Dukakis summarizes:

> The only way to overcome this is to go right to the grass roots. A grassroots effort needs to be sustained for twelve months, a year—thousands of people knocking on local doors, using the local media, using free radio in the region. They'll put you on the agenda. There's good research that will tell you there's eight to ten points in that. Not too many elections are won by more than eight to ten percentage points. Why aren't we doing it? Too many people are buying into this consultant crap. You do the media piece because you have to, but you really communicate through the grass roots."
>
> You organize the hell out of the grass roots, something you did and I did, but candidates are doing less and less. I think it's a terrible mistake—especially for Democrats. We're not going to outspend the other side, we're going to out work them. We can outwork them. You do what you've got to do with the media, because it is a factor and you certainly do not want to be wiped out. You're looking at the guy that didn't do it, and here we are, right. Nobody's going to make that mistake again. But you put time, energy, and resources into the grass

roots and maximize your most effective way of communicating. And that's the way you win. You overcome this dead media environment.

I'd just like to see in a major media market, a channel or two that decides as a matter of sound business strategy that they are going to break with the current thinking and market themselves as such.

Economic Opportunity

Economic opportunity is another cornerstone of American culture. This is the country to which people come from all across the globe seeking economic opportunity. The promise has been that your background is irrelevant. Hard work and initiative can create for you the American dream. It is eye-opening to see the extent to which the media has not encouraged this cultural standard.

Before looking at how the media deal with economic opportunity, check out the stage set. Exactly who has economic opportunity? Who needs it? What are the trends?

U.S. Statistical Abstracts provides enough detailed information on this topic to put an insomniac to sleep. Just do not expect to find it summarized very often in the news media, or woven into entertainment scripts. The data show that the wealth/poverty gap is enormous and growing, thanks in part to changes in the IRS tax codes that date from the early 1980s Reagan era.

In 1976, the top 1 percent of the nation's wealthiest people owned 19 percent of the nation's wealth. By 1995, they owned 40 percent, and by 1996 they owned 49.8 percent.[18] To help put these numbers in perspective, the assets of the nation's wealthiest person, Bill Gates, constitute more than the total wealth of the bottom 100 million poorest Americans.[19] The entire U.S. population is less than 300 million.

The chasm between the very rich and the rest is finally defined in the statistic that shows that the wealthiest 10 percent (including the 1 percent very rich) in 1997 held 89.8 percent of the nation's wealth. This means that 90 percent of the U.S. population has just 10 percent of the nation's wealth. Within this context, fulfilling the American dream of economic opportunity becomes increasingly difficult for the majority of the population.

Occasionally one finds rich people who think the change in wealth distribution since twenty or thirty years ago is a problem. They find it culturally destabilizing. Many others—including many media professionals—just do not bother to think about the extent of their privilege or the well-being of the larger society. Consequently, it is not surprising that the media often does not deal with the nonwealthy side of the economic-opportunity equation.

For example, this is a nation of immigrants. Today, 9.65 percent of the American population is foreign born, less than the 11.6 percent in 1930 or the 14.7 percent in 1910. We all have family stories of our ancestors, many not so long ago, who came here in search of a better life. Let us look at what immigrants are doing today to work toward economic opportunity, and look also at how the effects are reflected in the media.

Jose Jorge Dias came to the United States from Puerto Rico in 1991. He has a university degree in mass communications. Most of his class- mates got into film, TV, the recording industry, or journalism. He told Emerson College researcher Lauren Grossman that he "attended Catholic schools in Puerto Rico and was seen as wealthy and elite. However, as soon as he came to the U.S. and started college here he became a 'low- life.' He didn't really feel accepted, and was upset with the apathy and with the angry rich white kids rebelling against their parents. He said, racism was in your face. Students of color felt—and were—left out. In order to be proactive, he took an internship, later a job at Neighbor to Neighbor, a nonprofit advocacy organization for poor people. He helps people gain power for themselves and to get health services without the horrors experienced in some of the clinics where those without insurance experience long waits, rude staff, no translators. He's working with Healthy Cities 2000, a neighborhood-based program, to help people write legisla- tion and elect leaders interested in better health care. He started a political theater group to present the issues of the community in an engaging way. Jorge's view of mainstream media is that 'once an issue is no longer hot, it is dropped. But the problem hasn't been solved. And, whenever they cover the Latino community, it is negative.' 'The media doesn't understand the issues and doesn't let people speak for themselves.' "[20]

Oscar Chacon, administrator of El Centro Presente in eastern Massachu- setts, a Latino advocacy organization interested in helping people get basic skills and develop leadership capacity, came to the United States from El Sal- vador in 1980 as part of the wave of immigrants seeking to escape persecution for political activity. Many of those who were outspoken and sought demo- cratic reforms for their country either "disappeared" or were executed. Chacon told Lauren Grossman, "Most people have mixed feelings about being in the U.S. They are grateful, but they don't want too much attention focused on them as they fear it will be negative. Their lack of access to the media and to public policy makers has caused people to fear the media and to struggle to defend themselves against the negative image that the media offers. By and large the immigrant voice is mute. The immigrant is the perfect scapegoat. You can kick it left and right without consequences. Things aren't likely to change. Immigrants have no money and no power to get the attention of the media."[21]

Roosevelt Simil, a founder of a regional Haitian Coalition in Boston, told

Emerson College researcher Kheven Lee LaGrone, "The Haitian immigrant community had numerous individual discrimination problems in the early 1990s. Four Haitian high school students were harassed by teachers. One teacher sprayed the room whenever the Haitian student left the room. White kids would provoke fights with the Haitian kids and the Haitian kids would be expelled. White kids spat on the Haitian kids. The schools were lenient on the white kids but harsh on the Haitian kids. A Haitian couple was attacked by a white youth at a flea market. When the man went to use one of the portable toilets, the youth pushed it over. The man had excrement all over him. In response, the Haitian Coalition was started in 1991. It runs citizenship classes to get more citizens who then will be active so local politicians will listen. It teaches people how to buy houses, teaches the mainstream about Haitian culture, helps people get skills training and education, and helps to find jobs for people. The media doesn't cover any of this—neither the discrimination nor the self-help efforts."[22]

Jean Marc Jean-Baptiste, statewide assistant coordinator for the Center for Immigrant and Refugee Community Leadership and Empowerment (CIRCLE), a major program operating in conjunction with the University of Massachusetts, seeks to empower immigrants and bring them into the mainstream, spoke with Jeremy Thompson, Emerson College researcher, about the immigrant community, economic opportunity, and the media. Thompson reported: "Jean-Baptiste deals mostly with Cambodians, Asians, Latinos, Haitians, Irish, Russians, and Somalians. He works with the media to educate them about immigrant issues. He works with the immigrants to teach them how to articulate their positions in interviews and in public meetings. He believes that media literacy is connected to power, and media illiteracy is connected to powerlessness. This is a well-funded statewide organization reaching thousands, providing educational and employment opportunity. It is not likely that anyone even knows that it is happening. The media coverage of immigrants is usually only crime related."[23]

Michael Parenti, author of *Make Believe Media*, comments about how prime time TV misrepresents and under represents working people. "Blue collar and service workers compose 67% of the U.S. work force, but only 10% of television characters, usually waiters, bartenders, and store clerks."[24] Parenti observes that working-class people are not usually seen as reasonable and intelligent. Rather, they are portrayed as emotional, visceral, simple-hearted, and simple-minded. They do not take leadership. Those who strike are portrayed as selfish; and they are shown as harming the public. In the media, unions demand, but management offers.

Check the bias reflected in the choice of words that label rather than report; words that offer value judgments rather than neutral information.

Perhaps the portrayal of economic opportunity, or lack thereof, is understandable when one examines the media industry's own understanding of economic opportunity. What is seen on the air is what is seen through the eyes of media owners.

The news covers the owners' interests—the Dow Jones. It rarely covers the interests of the average American workers—contracts, layoffs, pension cuts, or strikes. It covers items that appeal to the self-interest of the 10 percent of the population who own 90 percent of the nation's wealth. There is little coverage targeting the 67 percent of the workforce who are blue-collar and service workers, or the scores of others who are old or poor or adolescent.

Not only are the interests of this segment of the population minimized, when reference is made to them it is often negative. Even on the entertainment programs on television, the "criminals" often turn out to be working people. Unions are often equated with the Mafia with the implication that they—representing working people—disrupt society. Somehow the white, middle class, reacting more from emotion than fact, minimize their own stake in protecting the majority of the population from the few whose greed can undercut democracy.

You seldom see shows about the workplace where people prevail in organizational debates, perhaps through union action; yet there is no indication that viewers would reject such real-life issues. *Roseanne* led a wildcat strike when her boss told her to speed up the assembly line, and no viewers complained. *Roots* was widely acclaimed and you cannot say this was a show for people who wanted to escape reality. The industry says that fear of a negative public opinion is the surface reason to keep it from dealing with more socially relevant issues. But could it be that presentation of a cross-section of views might reveal practices by the economically powerful that are harmful to the majority of the viewers?

Actor Ed Asner, former president of the Screen Actors' Guild, observes, "We have reams and reams and reams of business news. The *LA Times* used to have a couple people writing up the labor news, but to my knowledge, unless a strike is going on or negotiations, nothing is said about labor. *Norma Rae* is probably the main Hollywood production about labor. What else? Not much. In the media industry itself, the labor practices have gotten worse. Runaway production has decimated the labor market here and impoverished a lot of technicians. Certainly there's no gain for the main actors."[25]

Yegi Hong, Emerson College researcher, notes that "studies show that there are about 110 times as many servants on television as in real life. The 'oil operas' of the 1980s such as "Dallas" and "Dynasty" are classic examples of programs that did show true self-serving greed, while the public was invited to participate."[26] The programs showed the art of what author Michael Parenti calls "reducing sex, family, land, career, and other things to property acquisitions."[27]

Similarly, soap operas lack any portrayal of economic class issues. In "All My Children," for example, everyone is professional and rich.

Even in sitcoms, people are affluent. For example, "Friends" is a sitcom about six friends living in New York City. Their apartment is unrealistically large and elegant for the jobs they supposedly have. One is a chef. One works in a department store. One is a folk singer and massage therapist, one an office worker, one an actor, and one is a paleontologist. The focus is to laugh or cry about personal issues—never about economic realities.

Occasionally one sees films or TV programs that try to address the economic issues, but in squeezing classism into the script, they glamorize the situation. *Good Will Hunting*, even though it is an excellent movie, is an example of this approach. In *Good Will Hunting*, a local kid who is a janitor at MIT, turns out to be the genius who solves the math equations that the academic cannot solve.

Classism lives in the media. People in blue-collar and service jobs are usually depicted in what some nastily refer to as "white trash shows." "Married with Children," a popular sitcom, depicted a housewife and a shoe salesman and their family. The story lines do give some sense of their economic struggle, but part of the humor is how their neighbors make fun of the low salary of a shoe salesman. "The Simpsons" has attempted to deal with a working family. But again, one theme for the humor is to make fun of people who are not rich.

For example, one scene from "The Simpsons" exemplified this unspoken reinforcement of classism expressed through humor.[28] "The Simpsons" frequently do a better job of confronting the stereotypes than do other programs. The scene depicted a clown actor coming home from work. He works for a Spanish TV station, does not speak much English, but lives a comfortable life. He drives a nice car and has a nice, good-sized house, which he proceeds to destroy to maintain his "clown" character—or to show his neighbors that his possessions are disposable too, lest they think that money is important to him. The character Nelson laughs sarcastically at a man who is crammed into a car. The very tall man gets out, and tells Nelson that this was the largest car that he could afford. Then he asks if he should be made fun of because of that fact.

Humor is a tricky issue, however, because often it is created by poking fun at the expense of someone else. One certainly would not want to eliminate humor, the breath of fresh air in our daily lives. We are learning to preserve humor without racism and sexism; can we preserve it without classism?

Humor or comedy makes a point. We laugh because our brain perceives an anomaly, something unexpected. Satire is a form of comedy, a direct commentary on the foibles of a segment of society. The variety show, which featured both comedy and satire—programs like "Your Show of Shows" with Sid Casear and "The Steve Allen Show"—are long gone from the air. Remnants of such programs remain on late-night shows such as the "Tonight Show" with Jay Leno and the "David Letterman Show." Satire is too provocative for advertisers. Consequently, excellent political and social satire programs like Michael Moore's "TV Nation" do not last long. Tame versions of such a program, which are careful not to puncture any sacred cows but stick to easy targets, are sometimes seen in programs such as "Politically Incorrect." Good comedy and satire, however, are largely missing from drama on television. Situation comedies, with rare and few exceptions, rely on visual and verbal slapstick, principally sophomoric (and why not, since that seems to reflect the mentality of most of their viewers as counted by Nielsen audience households) sexual-innuendo jokes. Humor is rarely a means by which television will do more than titillate its audience—rather than educate and stimulate its viewers. The targets all too often are the "safe" ones—those without the economic ability to cause trouble when offended.

Both news and entertainment media provide little coverage on the real issues facing the public or the role models for improving one's economic opportunity.

If the media fail to hold out much opportunity for the working families of America, what does it do for the poor?

Poverty is common among those who have a hard time getting jobs—the elderly, the handicapped, the single parent without anyone to care for the kids, the chronically ill, the mentally ill, and the immigrants who may not know either the language or how to make the system work. TV may act as a baby-sitter sometimes, but there's little on the air in sitcoms or cartoons or in the news to offer role models for those seeking a route out of poverty. Newly arrived immigrants may learn some English by watching television, but they are not likely to learn much about improving their economic opportunity.

Over 20 percent of all children in America grow up in families whose income is below the government threshold that defines poverty. That is one in every five kids. Those kids are at risk of becoming adults with poor health because of poor nutrition. They are less skilled for entry into the job market because of lack of educational opportunity. Perhaps the most serious problem for these kids is that they are trapped in their environments, and, unless the media opens a window for them, they often cannot imagine a life outside of the one in which they now live. Why would they? They have never seen the options and certainly know little about any bridges they can cross to get from here to there.

Overall about 13 percent of America's population is below the poverty threshold; 75 percent of America's poor are women. Some are parents of small children, and either do not have day care or cannot get jobs because they have insufficient education or they are working in minimum-wage jobs (where the salary before taxes is about $12,000 per year). Others are older women. Many of these women were housewives and never had a career. They did what the culture told them to do—stay home and take care of the kids. Now they are widows and divorcees and, as a result of having stayed home, their social security is minimal, and there is little opportunity to improve their economic well-being. Nonetheless, their costs increase as does their life expectancy. So, the longer they live, the poorer they will be.

If the poor are visible at all on the media, they are likely to be portrayed as incompetent, mentally or physically ill, drug addicts, lazy, law-breaking scroungers. They are, effectively, blamed for their own poverty, as if they had much ability to alter their situations. Even on sensitively written programs like "NYPD Blue," "Law and Order," and "ER," these stereotypes prevail.

Travis Searle, Emerson College media arts researcher, observes that "the welfare reform policy struggle makes headlines. Welfare abuses make headlines. Civic groups helping the poor do not make many headlines. No one talks about what the Red Cross, Habitat for Humanity, Project Bread, or the churches do.

"While the issues surrounding our policies on welfare are debated almost daily, and covered in the news, it seems to be a taboo issue in the entertainment media. In the last five years, not one of the top twenty movies dealt with the issue of poverty or welfare."[29] Characters in movies and on TV may be portrayed as poor or homeless, yet they are almost never the focus of the story—except perhaps during the holiday season.[30] One could say the media does not touch issues, only actions. But, as Searle points out, they certainly do deal with issues like drugs. "First the news media reports on drug busts, drug dealers who are caught, crimes resulting from drug trafficking. Then, entertainment television focuses on the problem on various cop shows like "Law and Order" and "Homicide." Movies take on drugs in *Pulp Fiction*, and *Go*, which feature the life of a part-time drug dealer." Why do the media deal with some issues and not others? Why deal with some troublesome problems and avoid others?

If one wants to hear from the poor, speaking for themselves, one cannot hear it on the media. There is seldom a distinction made between those who could work and those too sick or too old to work. There is no coverage of advocacy for poor people's rights even though there are a number of articulate spokespersons on this topic, including former welfare mother Diane Dujon, now a college graduate and author of *For Crying Out Loud*.[31] Many organizations advocate for alleviation of poverty. Each year delegations of people develop "The Poor People's Budget," raising alternative ideas for appropriations that would help reduce poverty. Others wage "Up to Poverty" campaigns, pleading that welfare benefits at least provide people the amount determined to be the poverty threshold—the minimal level needed to feed, cloth and house a family. Others advocate for a "Head Start" for little kids so the next generation will be better equipped educationally. Others run campaigns for lower wage workers urging "Health Care for All." What all these groups get, usually, is a rebuff from a Congress that would rather cut the taxes of the wealthy than give this nation's poor the education and opportunity needed to rise out of degradation and poverty. The Welfare Law Center in New York can provide numerous spokespersons as well as stories that would make great plots for entertainment programs.[32] And to understand how the concept of economic opportunity as one of the cornerstones of American culture is being undercut, one needs only to contact a group like United for a Fair Economy in order to get the layperson's translation of how the rich get richer and the poor get poorer. Economic opportunity is not just about the rugged individualism usually shown in the media. The media seldom show the real story of those born into poverty or living with handicaps.

In a country whose culture puts forth the idea of economic opportunity, why is it so seldom dealt with in the media? Why does it avoid programs and topics covering the 67 percent of the workforce who are in blue-collar and service jobs? Why does it ignore the 13 percent of the population who are poor?

Effectively, media programming has little "real world" relevance to 80 percent of Americans seeking economic opportunity, except that it creates for them a fantasy world.

The media certainly offer little reinforcement in either news or entertainment for the American cultural cornerstone of economic opportunity. Rather, they offer an unspoken reinforcement of classism. This undercuts the U.S. middle class and underutilizes the potential contributions of the poor.

A group of university students whose career goals are to take up professions in the media were asked about their standards for quality programming after a discussion about portrayals of stereotyping and classism. Again and again the response was, "I don't have standards. I just want to laugh."

Maybe it is true. There are no messages, no content, nothing to remember or to do. America just wants to laugh. It is as Neil Postman said in his book aptly titled *Amusing Ourselves to Death*. But if that is the case, why do the advertisers spend so much money placing their product ads in front of the viewing audience?

The advertisers understand how to separate the rich from the rest in placing their ads. For example, "Frasier," a sitcom popular in the 1990s, is written so the advertiser can reach upper-income, college-educated consumers. In October 1998 the Nielson rating service found that "Frasier"'s audience had more college educated heads of households and more high income households than other sitcoms.[33] In other words, Nielsen has provided the advertisers with the tools they need to target their product to their chosen audience. If one wants to advertise products that the well-to-do will purchase, advertise on *Frasier*. The broadcasters can set their advertising prices to profit from the sale of ad space that will reach a well-to-do audience.

While the rich who own the media need money from the rich (advertisers) to keep the industry profitable, they also need the nonrich to buy their products. The really poor cannot even buy products. So what is the point of thinking about how they are portrayed in television programming? Leslie Gelb, a former editor and senior columnist at the *New York Times*, summarizes the manipulation of news to serve only a selected audience: "The principal business of journalism consists of recording what people with power say . . . the power of the media resides in its power to choose which ideas to present."[34]

Little thought is given to whether screening out these ideas is killing our culture, killing our sense of opportunity.

Human Equality

Human equality is another of the principal cornerstones of American culture prominently stated in the Declaration of Independence. History has shown that practice has often fallen short of the promise, but have the media—who are, after all, licensed to use *our* airwaves—supported this part of the American dream?

A block to human equality has always been discrimination against or stereotyping of groups of people. Those who defend stereotyping say it is helpful to a script writer trying to establish character, or as a base for humor. At whose expense? It is hard to dismiss the stereotypes as harmless entertainment when, in reality, behavior on TV is sometimes taken as a standard for the public. We all know this is true when it comes to fashions and products. Why would it not be true with behavior?

The media, much of the time, stereotypes or discriminates against the

American majority. The majority? Of the total population, 12.1 percent are black, 11 percent are Latino, 3.6 percent are Asian. Nearly 1 percent are Native American and approximately 37 percent are white female. There is no figure available for the number of white males who are disabled or poor.[35]

This total 65.4 percent of the American population are called "minorities."

There is much debate and less action about how the American media deal with the group classed "minorities and women." Think of what this means to the concerns of two-thirds of our population, not to have their voices heard. It not only kills our culture, but it greatly shortchanges our potential as a leader among the nations of the world when only one-third of the people are afforded the opportunities that come with human equality. What a waste!

Surely it is in the self-interest of the one-third of our population of 273 million people who are white male to look seriously at what they are missing in terms of national growth potential.

This is not to say the task is easy. Making room for other people—adjusting to power shifts—may be more difficult for these men than it is for the rest of the population seeking to find their places on the horizon. The traditional roles that our cultural past has ascribed to men are all shifting. Men alone no longer control procreation. The pill was invented. Men have to share these decisions now with women. Affluent white men no longer control the workplace. There are women and people of color wanting to share the jobs. Affluent white men no longer control the Ivy League academic institutions. There are equally bright people of all backgrounds knocking on the door asking for equal opportunity. In fact, even some of the neighborhoods to which the affluent white male drove at the end of the day now have some "affordable housing," some people of color who are also affluent, and some homes owned by women who are economically comfortable. This represents a sea change in identity for the affluent white males. They are beginning to understand what is happening, and while many are supportive of equality intellectually, it is tough emotionally when things in one's personal life change.

The media, by and large, perpetuate the "Leave it to Beaver" and "Superman" image for white males. And they still cover mostly male news and sports. This only perpetuates a fantasy that is no longer fact when the guy turns off the TV set.

The media coverage of the reality shift, if any, covers little beyond the attempts to halt this shift toward human equality. For example, the media covered the group called the Promisekeepers, who portray themselves as caring husbands—if, of course, their wives are subservient rather than equal partners. There is less coverage of the two-salaried families where both families struggle to keep a home and raise kids, giving them opportunities for the future. The media deliberately self-censor the misogynic character of the male Promisekeepers. The media cover some of the efforts across the nation to eliminate affirmative action. Often there is little coverage of those whose success stories are because of affirmative action—people like Supreme Court Justice Clarence Thomas. Thomas, ironically, turned against affirmative action once he had had the advantage of it. Eliminating affirmative action may be a nice goal, but not until the race and gender divide on economic opportunity is history. At present, in 1999, women still earn 72 cents for every $1.00 a man earns. Median family incomes for whites in 1997 were $47,023, compared with $26,522 for blacks and $26,179 for Latino/as. There is little media coverage of the wage divide, except to stereotype women as "pushy" when they complain that their household bills are the same as the household bills sent to a man. And the nonwhite/white wage divide is either totally screened out or dismissed as the differential for people who are "still on their way up." The excuse does not work when comparing two people with the same education, same intelligence, and same number of years of experience. At the turn of the millennium for the first time several TV shows, produced by David E. Kelley or Steven Bochco, portray a mix of race and gender in nonstereotypical professional roles. These include program series such as "Chicago Hope," "City of Angels," and "The Practice."

Most important, our culture and its media need to find ways to make human equality real while also creating new and healthy roles for affluent white men. A society that ignores this need jeopardizes itself just as much as when it ignores any other segment of the population. Solving this problem will not be easy. The media's neglect of the economic shifts now occurring in our society makes it more difficult to reach an equality that does not stereotype and does not discriminate.

Occasionally, you see a man doing the dishes in a commercial, but this is a tiny step forward. The substance of the problem for society goes way beyond such superficialities. Creative people could use film, cartoons, and news programs to put forth both role models and ideas for how to design a twenty-first-century culture with a significant role for everyone regardless of gender, skin color, or economic class.

The revolution of the last several decades has focused on making room for people of color and women.

Ed Asner comments on this "revolution":

> While president of the Screen Actors Guild and as a board member, I became aware that there was the constant cliché utterance of presenting the American scene as it really is, in terms of sex and age and color and belief. It was always a losing battle. It would have some advances in some areas and it would drop behind in others. I would say that, significantly over the years, black stars have

certainly risen in prominence in the last ten or fifteen years. I notice that every commercial has its token black out of every four. I do not think the elderly have been brought forward. They probably feel guilt because they made it to old age, so they do not necessarily fight for representation. Latinos have been very squeaky lately about their ungreased wheel. I see now that there's a token homosexual on every sitcom.

But at the same time, let's face it, when the Greeks wrote their tragedies, they wrote about kings and queens and they weren't a high proportion of the population. So I guess, in a macho culture, we're going to focus as much as we can on men—viable, handsome, pretty, *young* men. It is hard, first of all, to get derailed from what society has given us for a hundred years in terms of advertising—that look of the blonde, or perhaps the sexy vargas brunette, or the strawberry blonde, or the New Deal nymph. The male, that would be the Marlboro man, I suppose.

None of that is real life, yet it has every American aspiring to do it, or to achieve it, or to capture it—the man in terms of a woman and the woman in terms of the man. It's only the wise, sage individuals I come across who know enough to realize that prettiness or handsomeness carries too much baggage with it."[36]

There has been enormous progress in the portrayal of blacks in TV since the days of "Amos 'n' Andy" in the 1950s. It started in the 1970s when Norman Lear put "The Jeffersons," "Sanford and Son," "Chico and the Man," "All in the Family," "Maude," and "Good Times" on TV. At last, we had moved past black-face characters played by white actors, and the demeaning character portrayals for nonwhites and women that marked earlier media portrayals. While controversy still swirls around how the media handles the representation of minority populations, at least black roles on television did grow for a while. In the 1974–1975 season, ten top-rated shows either had black stars or dealt with the issues of race.[37]

Some of the controversy swirled around how blacks were portrayed. For example, "The Cosby Show," a show that did extremely well in the Nielsen ratings and was very popular for two decades, was criticized for not accurately portraying the typical black family. In "The Cosby Show," the parents were both college-educated. One was a doctor, the other a lawyer. They lived in a fashionable townhouse in Manhattan, and were almost always around to spend time with their children. Money was never an issue and the children were fed, clothed, and happy. The critics argued that the show should be moved to Harlem and portray the real struggle of black people, that is, living in a poor neighborhood without the economic resources to improve the quality of life, dealing with prejudice, and fighting hard to make ends meet.

Cosby, instead, chose to give middle-class white audiences the idea that blacks can also be middle class. And he chose to give poor black audiences the idea that blacks need not always be downtrodden.

Dr. Alvin Poissaint, professor of psychiatry at Harvard Medical School, was a consultant on "The Cosby Show" script. He said, "Some of the networks shied away from it because they didn't think it would appeal to the white audience. When it became the most popular series of the decade, the same network executives were stunned, and confounded." Poissaint thinks the executives are behind the times.[38]

Ed Asner comments, "Very rarely have I seen something that truly challenged the status quo as we recognize it—or at least popularly recognize it. I suppose you can say that the slow introduction of blacks over the years into leading roles, and into romantic arenas, has been a progressive approach to things."

While black acting roles at times came close to mirroring their 12.2 percent of the U.S. population (some 33 million) by 1999, blacks accounted for only 1 percent of news directors.[39] Black scriptwriters, producers, and directors of entertainment films in the mainstream media are rare, too.

However, as noted earlier, the turn of the century in some respects marked a step backward. In the 1998–1999 season only two of the top ten shows featured blacks or minorities in key roles. These were "ER" and "Touched by an Angel." And the programming lineup for twenty-six new shows in the 1999–2000 television season had no blacks in lead roles, no Asian-Americans, and only one Latina actress in a minor role. This prompted outrage on many fronts. Kweisi Mfume, president of the 500,000–member NAACP, called it a virtual "whitewashing in programming" and threatened legal action and boycotts of both programs and advertisers.[40] By early 2000, the representation improved.

Black television programming is more common on the smaller, new networks, WB with its teen oriented programming and UPN.

Black Entertainment Television, the black cable channel, is very busy producing a series of ten movies for the 1999–2000 season. Robert L. Johnson, chair of BET's parent company, BET Holdings, expects this will enhance BET's standing with cable carriers drawing more advertisers. "We felt one way to do that was to produce movies that spoke to the black middle-class experience and dealt with themes that are not usually on television. So there's romance, suspense, mysteries involving attractive black men and women."[41] Diane Wynter, the writer and director of one of the movies, *Intimate Betrayal*, explains: "The characters and stories aren't filtered through the prism of black-white conflict, as is often the case when Hollywood pays attention to blacks. . . . What is so sad is that quite often black women are portrayed very negatively or not at all. That is heart-breaking, especially when there's a growing middle class, and we watch television and spend money like everyone else. . . . How can you have a dream if you do not see an image of that dream?"[42]

It is doubtful, however, that a return to the "separate but maybe equal" philosophy can be a step forward for our culture.

Tony award winning actor John Randolph, who is active in the Screen Actors Guild, Actors Equity Association, and AFTRA (American Federation of Television and Radio Actors), notes that opportunities have begun just recently to appear for Latino/as. "There's a whole change in the Latino/a situation in Hollywood. In the beginning they were pushed around and they weren't treated well by the unions. The unions began to get the message, do not fool with us. We're interested. We know film. We're skilled. It is changed in just ten years."[43]

Latino/a researchers are, however, busy documenting that it hasn't changed enough. The media coverage does not represent their community either in quality or in quantity.

There are thirty million Latino/as in the United States, making it the fifth largest Spanish-speaking country in the world. Latino/as in the United States are 65 percent Mexican, 15 percent Central American, 10 percent Puerto Rican, 5 percent Cuban, and 5 percent others. The Spanish heritage people in the United States live mostly in Texas, California, Florida, New Jersey, and the cities of Chicago and New York.[44]

Charles A. Erickson, founder and editor of Hispanic Link Inc., said the problem with mainstream media is that, for the most part, they still will not allow Hispanics to be authorities on issues that concern them. The media view of the Latino/a community is a stereotype. They do not provide the information that people in this community need to know. For example, they tell you nothing about organizations that are critical to one's welfare or progress in the society. And the media does not hire representative numbers of Latino/as.

In 1999, Latino/as represented 11 percent of the United States's population. These 30 million people have a purchasing power of over $190 billion. Yet, in the mid-1990s, they represented only 1 percent of all the speaking characters on prime-time TV.[45] Complaining that this is institutional racism, forty-five national Latino organizations comprising the National Hispanic Media Coalition organized a collaborative action promising boycotts and demonstrations. The networks, meanwhile, pointed to progress, citing Jimmy Smits on "NYPD Blue," Hector Elizondo on "Chicago Hope," Robert Beltran on "Star Trek," and Daphne Zuniga on "Melrose Place."

Professora Ramona Hernandez of the College of Public and Community Service at the University of Massachusetts embarked in 1999 on a project to examine Latino/a media coverage in prominent newspapers. For over two months in the spring of 1999, the *Christian Science Monitor* had only sixteen articles about Latina women, not too many more about other women. The number is very small compared with the number of articles covering men. More importantly, the articles that covered or involved women often did not quote the women giving their direct views and opinions.[46] For example, one article, "Hands Across the Border" by Howard LaFranchi,[47] is about Mexicans and Native Americans protesting a proposed toxic waste dump site. Most of the protesters are women, but most of the quotes are from men. Women, while the primary activists, are not allowed to speak in their own voices.

The 1998 census update shows that Texas is 29.4 percent Latino/a. Yet, the *Houston Chronicle*, studied in the spring of 1999, lacked coverage of women in general and Latinas in particular. They were not columnists, writers, or subjects of articles. University of Massachusetts researcher Amanda Escamilla said, "The coverage on the Latino/a community was generally negative and mostly about criminal activity. There were a few exceptions on a positive note, however, even the positive coverage had nothing to do with the intellect or success of Latina women. When women are covered, the paper covers weddings, beauty and fashion, not intellect and success."[48]

The *New York Times* was also examined. In a two-month period in 1999, thirty-three articles appeared about women, five of which were about Latina women. Jenepher Gooding, another researcher on the University of Massachusetts Latina project, observed, "There are more women than men in the U.S., and the majority of the immigrants form Latin America are women. Even in the local news section covering this city with a large Latina/o population, women are far less covered than men."[49]

The *San Francisco Chronicle* was studied for the project by Juan Reynoso, a University of Massachusetts researcher, in early 1999 because of the large Latino population in California. Reynoso found, "Out of ninety days, only sixty-four articles were written about women. Only eight of those concerned Latinas and two were about black women. The rest were written about white women. The newspaper focused mostly on the negative aspects of Latinas in this country as opposed to depicting their lives as any other decent human being. Women's political, economic and career interests rank so far below men's that they are not reported on at all."[50]

Another growing segment of the U.S. population is Asian. There are less data here than on other population groups. In many U.S. census reports, the data do not even track Asians despite the fact that, in 1999, there were about 10.8 million Asians in the United States or 4 percent of the total population. The reporting will, no doubt, improve, because Asians represent the second largest group of new immigrants to the United States.

In addition, the United States, the one remaining global superpower, operates in a global economy where one in five inhabitants of the world is Chinese. If one included those who are ethnically Asian and from other countries such as Japan, Korea, Indonesia, Cambodia, Laos, Vietnam, Mongolia, Singapore, Taiwan, the Philippines, and Malaysia, the number would be still higher. Many of Hollywood's media products are made for global export. Indeed, a number of Hollywood studios are owned by Asian companies. One would think the media would be less parochial about the portrayals of Asians. It is time to leave the World War II stereotypes behind.

Hironobu Maeda, Emerson College media arts researcher, notes that "when we see Chinese people on television, they are usually either kung fu masters or gangsters. All Chinese don't fit these images, but that's how producers and directors portray them. Japanese are usually seen as businessmen or in a group of tourists carrying cameras. This is not an accurate reflection of all Japanese either. Most Americans never see entertainment or news media about Koreans or Filipinos or Indonesians, or Malaysians, or Cambodians or Thais, or the many other population groups within this huge and important part of the globe."[51]

Remember "Superman" played by Christopher Reeve? One of the most memorable events in Hollywood news was the tragic accident that paralyzed Reeve from the neck down in 1995. It has taken that tragic event to give media attention to the 43 million Americans who are disabled—even though the Americans with Disabilities Act was passed in 1990. Those who are blind, in wheelchairs, or otherwise impaired continue to struggle to live with the quality of life experienced by the majority population. In the last two decades, public buildings have built ramps and curbs have been cut across the nation to accommodate wheelchairs. Buses now "kneel" by lowering their front steps to accommodate people who cannot climb. Many theaters provide hearing equipment to amplify the sound for those who are deaf. Universities arrange special services for disabled students who cannot attend a regular class without someone who signs or without a tape recording that can assist the student who is blind. What has Hollywood done? A little bit. Occasionally a film or sitcom has an actor who is disabled. But still, disabled Americans are visible in only 1.5 percent of prime-time programming.[52]

One of the most compelling groups hoping that human equality will remain a cornerstone of American culture is the elderly. After all, one day we all will be elderly.

The aging population is growing as a percentage of all Americans. In the mid-1990s, 12.2 percent of Americans were over 65. By 2050, 29 percent of our population will be over 65. In 1995, 1.4 percent of our population was over age 80. By 2050, 4.6 percent of the population will be octogenarians. The cohort of centenarians, while small, is increasing rapidly.

The elderly watch a lot of TV, according to studies. Older men are more likely to get roles than older women, even though society has more older women. When one sees older men, usually white men, on news and talk shows, they are portrayed as experienced, wise, and trustworthy. In other situations, older men are often seen as eccentric or incompetent or laughable. Nonwhite elderly men are seldom seen in the media, unless they are heads of foreign governments like Nelson Mandela and United Nations Secretary General Kofi Anan. Elderly women of any race are often stereotyped as meddlesome, eccentric, and not to be taken seriously.[53] Older women are frequently seen as being overly talkative, but not people who are listened to. One rarely sees portrayals of the elderly in the media as intelligent, experienced leaders and experts in their fields.

It will be interesting to watch how long the stereotypes are allowed to last. Those becoming seniors now are all better educated than the generation preceding them. Today's seniors include more and more women who have had independent professional careers outside of the home. The old stereotypes are not only harmful, they could contribute to a loss of business for the media and its advertisers. This affluent segment of society may not switch brands as often as the young folks, but they are an empowered group of people who learned the ways of the world by crusading for the Civil Rights movement, stopping the war in Vietnam, inaugurating the movement for women's equality and initiating the environmental protection movement.

One wonders if there can really be a bright future for films like *Harvey*. It is a story about an elderly, seemingly intelligent and capable man whose best friend is a six-foot-tall white rabbit. The point of the story is that those tuned into the practicality of life do not have nearly as pleasant a time as he does with his imaginative life. The humor is at the elderly man's expense.

Another example, the film *Cocoon*, poked fun at the idea that the elderly might be interested in sex, and in diving into a swimming pool. The film is really for the young to reinforce all the stereotypes about the elderly.

Perhaps the most positive view the media takes of older women is the feisty older-women stereotypes in films such as *Family Matters* and *Driving Miss Daisy*.

The elderly also are used as symbols of death and decay, a topic that often frightens people. Another stereotype commonly used to portray the elderly is the doddering old senile fool. "The Simpsons" uses this for comic relief (humor at other people's expense). Grandpa Simpson is the basis for much of the humor in the show. He is helpless and he cannot remember a thing.[54]

Some years ago the House Select Committee on Aging, under the leadership of Representative Claude Pepper, asked the television industry to examine the purchasing power of elders and use that to reprioritize shows for elders. Shows like "Golden Girls" and "Murder She Wrote" were examples of shows targeted for older people.

TV advertisers' argument for not paying top price to place ads on programs watched by seniors is that, despite the size of the group's purchasing power, they do not warrant investment because they are fixed in their ways and are not experimenting with different brands. They are not perceived to be active consumers. Yet they spend significant amounts on new housing and furnishings, new cars, equipment to make living easier, travel, pharmaceuticals and other products or services.

Another suggestion from the House Select Committee on Aging was directed at the media industry. It urged stations/networks to maintain a mix of ages on their staffs and to discourage retirement at age sixty-five. While there has been some change in the presence of older actors on screen, more now than a decade ago, the situation regarding the industry's age discrimination policies are shocking.

In 1999, "60 Minutes" did a segment on age discrimination in Hollywood. It focused first on Reilly Weston, a supposed nineteen-year-old who hit Hollywood with widespread success as a writer and an actress. She was featured widely in magazines and was the talk of the town. She was a fresh new face and carried the hope that a young person writing for young audiences might be a big financial winner. It is the young audience that the advertisers want the Nielsens to identify. Then it was discovered that she was really Kimberly Kramer, a thirty-two-year-old. The phone stopped ringing. She told "60 Minutes" that if age is "dirty," then so ought to be implants and all the other Hollywood lies.

The advertisers are really screening out the market and shrinking their own profits if they support the idea that thirty-two-year-old actresses are "aged" and that aged equals rejected.

"60 Minutes" went on to describe how Hollywood program producers have executives in their thirties and media buyers in their twenties. The Writers Guild did a recent study showing that most writers in their twenties have jobs, most in their forties do not. The theory is that the young audiences are more likely to watch programs written by young writers. Chris Kaiser, executive producer of "Party of Five," a program about a family of orphans, told "60 Minutes" that it is hard not to discriminate against older folks. One screenwriter in her fifties described for "60 Minutes" her experience going to an appointment with a network to pitch a new show. The young woman who met with her rode an exercise bike while they talked. Then her interviewer asked her if they accepted her pitch, would she "have the energy to stay with it?"

Bert Purletsky, a screenwriter of considerable reputation whose credits include eight episodes of "Mash," said that once he turned fifty, he got no more jobs.[55]

Even when presumably trying to be aware of the contributions of the elderly, the media instead condescend. Carmella Adario, a latter-day Grandma Moses, began painting when she turned 80. At one of her many exhibitions in the Boston area, she was interviewed by the media.

"How long ago did you take up painting?" she was asked.

"About ten years ago," she replied.

"How old were you?"

"Eighty. I'm ninety now."

"Isn't that wonderful," the journalist commented.

"For whom?" Carmella said.

Unfortunately the media's perception of the elderly as achievers or contributors to society is based on a youth-oriented stereotype that is both insensitive, uninformed, and frequently insulting.

The elderly have a wealth of stories, both entertaining and informative, to share with the society. What do we gain by screening this out and making them just a bit less than eligible for human equality?

One of the issues for Native Americans is representational ethics—who has the right to represent others and under what circumstances. The Native American population has been stereotyped in the media for a hundred plus years. In the early years of establishing this country, the white population developed representations, then stereotypes for the Native Americans. America's stereotypes for its indigenous people have usually depicted them as warriors, medicine men, and naked savages. The indigenous woman is often seen as a bare-breasted sex fantasy.[56]

Now we see a Native American advertising the Mazda four-wheel drive vehicle, the "Navajo," with the tag line, "No one knows the land like a Navajo." Kodak used a Washington Redskin fan, complete with brightly colored headdress, and the tag line: "Show your true colors."

On television programming and in film, the classic 1940s Western seems to be a thing of the past. Films like *Dancing with Wolves* are a major step forward. However, there is little in media entertainment or in media news where contemporary indigenous peoples are the writers, the actors, the owners, or the spokespersons for their own issues.

The media in some countries have had to deal with a far more demanding indigenous population, and have been more attentive to incorporating them into the culture as equal partners. For example, the *New Zealand Herald*, on July 1, 1999, reported that the New Zealand government was about to grant sovereignty over a part of the entire radiomagnetic spectrum to its indigenous people, the Maori, giving them independent access to broadcasting stations.

The battle for women seeking human equality has been waged now for decades. And slowly, progress has occurred.

Actor John Randolph comments. "I think the view of women is getting stronger. It used to be that after age thirty-five or thirty-eight, the women disappeared from the screen. And, all along, they weren't well paid. Now you see women on screen who are sixty, seventy, eighty. It is my feeling that the women who are older are now being honored. It is not uncommon to say, my—she was a star!"[57] (It should be noted that Randolph, at the age of 84 in 1999, was working steadily in films television and radio.)

The media have, however, often portrayed women as emotional, dependent, less ambitious and less intelligent than men, and dominated by them. In the 1970s, for the first time, there were shows depicting women as other than just wives. For example, "Mary Tyler Moore" was a newspaper woman, and "Charlie's Angels" were detectives. Later came "Cagney and Lacey," policewomen.[58] While we are beginning to see women as leading characters, they still nearly always have a man to "help" or "take charge" if the woman cannot handle something. For example, in *Twister* the man is there to inject logic into situations where the woman is apparently lost. In *Volcano* a respected woman scientist works to save a city from disaster—something she might have done with another woman, but no. And even when a woman is given the lead role, it is invariably a romantic role. Frequently it is in a demeaning romantic role as a "bitch." For example, *True Lies* is a film about a bitch who gets paid a lot to help terrorists smuggle nuclear warheads into the United States. At one point, the terrorist she works with slaps her face and calls her an "undisciplined bitch" for flirting with the good guy. She had every right to point out that the whole strategy is hers and without her their plan would fail. Instead she takes the slap as an occupational hazard.[59]

The sexy businesswoman persona is most visible now on television. For example, "Melrose Place" has a character who is a cold-hearted aggressive business woman who uses sex as a business tool. On the other hand, "The Practice," a 1999 David E. Kelley creation, weaves its story about a law firm around a broad mix of characters who are, first, characters in their own right, and, second, people with gender and racial identifications. Another twist on the businesswoman motif is the marketing potential. Note Fox TV's "Ally McBeal"'s lead character, a defense attorney in the Boston courts. Ally's very short skirts were featured in a fashion line of business suits promoted by Fox—blurring the line between fantasy and reality. "The message being sent," says Beth Sekul, Emerson College researcher, "is that women might as well give in to the erotic fantasies of men and try to live up to a sex kitten standard at the workplace."

Sekul notes that things are changing a bit in Hollywood, in that not all the executive decisions are being made in the men's room. One finds more women in decision-making seats in big studios. Penny Marshall directed *A League of Their Own*. Amy Heckerling directed *Clueless*. Gillian Armstrong directed *Little Women*. The executive producer of *The Firm* and *Sabrina* was Lindsay Doran.

The bottom line, however, is that we are still a long way from solid ground for women. Their roles still, all too often, are as physical ornaments—stereotypical sex symbols. And too many programs still give a negative mental health portrayal, too. For example, in *Fatal Attraction* the female lead is obsessed with a man—going out of her mind over a man.[60] That depiction does not offer much hope for those seeking human equality.

The stereotyping and screening out of subsets of the American population is killing our culture, now more than in the past because of the fast pace of communication technologies. Minimizing opportunity for human equality kills the culture's sense of community.

A Healthy Environment for Kids

A healthy environment for children has always been a cornerstone of American culture. According to the Annenberg Public Policy Center of the University of Pennsylvania, kids spend an average of 3.25 hours per day watching TV or videos. That becomes 4.35 hours if video games and computers are added. Half of all kids have TVs in their bedrooms.[61]

The same 1999 study found that the percentage of low-quality kids' shows dropped from 36 percent to 26 percent and the proportion of shows containing no enriching content dropped from 46 percent to 25 percent. Nonetheless, 28 percent of kids' shows still feature four or more acts of violence and three-quarters of the high violence programs are not marked with the FV (fantasy violence) rating they are supposed to have. Less than one in five parents in the center's national survey reported having a positive opinion of children's television. Only one in four kids say they like what they see on TV. It is speculated that one reason for the improvement may be the "three-hour rule" imposed by the FCC, requiring broadcasters have at least three hours per week of educational programming to get their licenses renewed.

A deterrent to cable companies' picking up extra children's networks is, according to Emerson College media arts researcher Anthony Miller, that "most cable networks cost cable companies ten cents per subscriber, but license fees for a quality children's program channel can run twenty cents per subscriber."[62]

The price is higher because kids' shows cost more to produce. In 1994,

Children's Television Workshop (CTW), the flagship of children's television, spent $20 million to produce 130 episodes of "Sesame Street." [63] CTW produces "Sesame Street," "The Electric Company," and "3–2–1 Contact." It is working on its own cable network called "New Kid City." An animated half hour costs from $300,000 to $500,000 to produce. Yet licensing fees have dropped from $250,000 per episode to $150,000 per episode, so it is hard to see the profitability.[64]

With government dollars eroding, more merchandising deals are developed to help finance children's television. Some of the biggest campaigns belong to "Barney and Friends" and "Sesame Street." CTW has granted licenses to some 350 firms in more than thirty countries to produce "Sesame Street" products. Tyco makes toys. Sony Wonder produces audio and video tapes as well as books. The home video market is soaring: 27 percent of parents with kids ages two to five buy at least one video a month. Touring shows also bring in money. In 1996, in less than four months, Barney, everyone's favorite purple dinosaur, sang and danced on stage for 5,000 screaming kids, and the show brought in $7 million.[65]

How children develop mentally and what the media offer them is important to a wholesome environment. Kids between ages three and nine can be very influenced by television. This is because until age six or so, they are interested in copying adults. Between six and eleven they are looking for role models.[66]

Many kids who watch violent programming use aggression to resolve conflict; they copy the violence. Ann Norton, Emerson College media arts researcher, notes that on Saturday mornings alone, kids see twenty to twenty-five violent acts per hour. Kids see about 20,000 commercials per year, and, while being programmed as the next generation of consumers, they are not old enough to realize that the purpose of commercials is to sell.[67]

Kids who watch lots of TV have short attention spans. Also, TV can give kids a warped sense of roles racially and socially.[68] For example, African Americans, Asian Americans, Hispanics, Native Americans, women, the elderly, and people with disabilities have stereotyped images that children see and believe because they may have had no other opportunity to see differently. Similarly, kids have a difficult time distinguishing reality from fantasy when they watch fake violence.

On the other hand, some television is very good for kids in that it introduces them to new worlds. And some of the programs focused directly on young people serve to develop self-esteem. Authors Barrie Gunter and Jill McAleer explain that a program like "Mr. Rogers' Neighborhood" is unique in that respect.[69] Mr. Rogers deals with fears of the dark, divorce, death, going to the doctor, etc. "Reading Rainbow" is another positive show, and introduces kids to good books and to libraries. "Sesame Street" emphasizes learning numbers and letters and assumes cultural diversity. It also teaches that it is okay to be grouchy, or sad, or happy. The industry still likes to point out that high-quality programs appear to draw smaller audiences than the low-quality ones, according to Nielsen.[70] But getting accurate records of the preferences of two-to-eleven-year-olds, the desired demographic, is really open to question.

The 1990 Children's Television Act mandated that, beginning in the 1997–1998 season, stations earmark a minimum of three hours per week of children's programming that serves their educational and informative needs. The requirement is vague and ill-defined.[71] Author Lynette Rice notes, "NBC has the laziest approach to educational shows on the major networks, and I think it is sad. If they think they can put on five teenage sitcoms and one NBA program and it will educate kids, they should have their heads examined."[72] Nonetheless, Peggy Charren, founder of Action for Children's Television and one of the industry's harshest critics, gave the industry a better grade in the 1997–1998 season than in the past. "I think there's some good stuff this year. The real question is will parents and teachers get involved enough to guarantee that next season there's going to be more good stuff and more of the stuff that is still missing: news shows and local programming (for kids)."[73]

Charren warns that aside from getting the programs on the air, parents and kids need to know how to find them. "Newspapers and other media need to do a better job of covering children's television and their advocacy groups. Policy makers must work to inform parents about broadcasters' public interest obligations. Such outreach might raise parents' awareness about the existence of educational programming and might initiate a dialogue between parents and broadcasters about the programming efforts."[74]

In summary, the media has been aware of some of the cornerstones of American culture and has made both efforts and progress toward supporting them.

As Ed Asner said, "There was the constant cliché utterance of presenting the American scene as it really is—in terms of sex and age and color and belief. It was always a losing battle. It would have some advances in some areas and it would drop behind in others. What are the trends? First of all, you do not have a studio system anymore, which of course used to enforce the stereotyping very strongly. Right now we seem to have denigrated into the pocket of the youngest prettiest boy to come along. I'm sure a studio system could change things. I thought they were changing a few years ago when *Shine* won an Academy Award, and when the independent producer Billie Bob Thornton's movie took prizes. It was a year for independent production. Then we reverted right back to the huge spectacular. So it does not seem to last. Or if the small Merchant Ivory type people succeed in what they're doing, then when they're bought by the majors it seems they go on according to the big money winners. *It is money, money, money.*"[75]

Is it greed, or thoughtlessness, or apathy that is killing the culture? Is it the fault of the station owners, the advertisers, the government, or the citizenry? Wherever the fault lies, the price of screening out so much of the population from access to the media may not be worth it, either to the culture or to the industry and the advertisers.

Chapter 3

Scaring Us to Death

> The truth we get now featuring every known murder and
> mayhem possible on the evening news just turns us all into
> frightened mice.
>
> *Ed Asner, actor, former president, Screen Actors Guild.[1]*

Most Americans will tell you:

You have to be careful everywhere. Someone might break into the house. You might be mugged, or raped, or murdered!

This has become such a violent nation.

Has it? It is true that our violent crimes far exceed those in most parts of the industrialized word. However, from 1993 through 1996, homicide rates dropped by 20 percent.[2] In fact, among children, despite the high-profile school shootings, crime is also down. According to Dr. Duane Alexander, director of the National Institute of Child Health and Human Development, "In 1997, there were 31 serious violent juvenile crimes committed for every 1,000 children ages 12 to 17. That's down from 52 per 1,000 in 1993, and it's the lowest rate since 1986, according to Justice Department figures. . . . There are also fewer teenage victims of crime. There were 27 victims for every 1,000 people age 12 to 17 in 1997, down from 44 in 1,000 in 1993."[3]

The interesting part is that the media coverage of violent crime, according to the Center for Media and Public Affairs, has increased by 721 percent. You read that correctly. Based on media coverage, a viewer might believe that instead of dropping—as it has—crime increased by over 700 percent!

Why would the media want to give people the false impression that crime, including murders, has increased? Because scaring us increases our level of anxiety and our viewership. We watch more, just to keep on top of the problem. Coincidentally, this has the effect of increasing ratings and, of course, revenues to broadcasters paid by advertisers.

Alternative coverage could include a shift from emphasis on murders and bizarre crimes that are more rare to the more common unreported violence—

the violence of child abuse, spousal abuse, and the violence of elder abuse, for example. If, in an ironic way, the media focus has contributed to lowering the murder rate, maybe it could contribute to reducing other types of violence. These types of domestic violence are also scary, or should be.

Let us look at another "scare" exploited by the media to increase ratings and revenues. Many Americans will inform you that you have to watch out for those welfare mothers. Why do they not just go out and get a job like the rest of us? We just keep paying and paying taxes and it all goes to subsidize these women who do not know enough not to have more kids. There must be some inherent evil in poor mothers.

Is that where most of our tax money goes—to pay for welfare families? The federal budget pie has many slices. Less than 1 percent of the federal budget goes to welfare families. Welfare is the Temporary Aid to Needy Families program, formerly Aid to Families with Dependent Children. The budget figures can be confusing because the federal budget has so many different categories. About $112 billion of the Fiscal Year 2000 U.S. budget of $1.8 trillion, or 6 percent, is for means-tested programs (i.e., programs for distributing money based on family incomes that are below certain thresholds). Within this 6 percent of the U.S. budget are many programs, one of which is welfare. Some of the other programs, ones that spend more money than welfare, include Food Stamps, Food Aid to Puerto Rico, Supplemental Security Income (for old and or disabled people collecting social security who are very poor), child nutrition, Earned Income Tax Credits (tax refunds for working poor), and veteran's pensions.

Why is there tax money available to help the poor? After the depression, in 1935, the Social Security Act was passed with the intent of ensuring that children whose mothers were widows would have some of the same opportunities that children in other families had, and that elderly and disabled people who could no longer earn a living would not lack food and shelter.

Today's situation was created initially by the 1929 stock market crash and subsequent depression when there were few jobs. Then, the nation at war in World War II experienced economic recovery and afterward a postwar boom. During the 1950s many poor families from rural areas migrated to big cities in search of jobs and opportunity. This migration coincided with increased automation and a shift in the economy away from unskilled industrial jobs. Concurrently, the black GIs had returned from fighting for their country to find themselves, once again, second-class citizens. Many saw the irony of being so mistreated while their white counterparts were given hero welcomes. The old ways no longer seemed acceptable. Impatience grew. In the early 1960s, Michael Harrington wrote *The Other America*. The book caught President Kennedy's attention. The early 1960s saw the peak of Martin Luther

King's leadership of the Civil Rights movement. Kennedy and his administration listened to King and others seeking to close the gap in American
culture. After Kennedy's assassination, President Lyndon Johnson committed the nation to a War on Poverty. Laws were passed making discrimination
illegal. Schools were desegregated, as were beaches and other public facilities. Poll taxes that prevented low-income people from voting were discarded.

Before this War on Poverty was abandoned by subsequent Republican
administrations, first in the early 1970s and then in the 1980s, the nation's
poverty rate did fall from 19 percent in 1964 to 11 percent by 1973. In the
late 1990s, despite a strong economy, in fact a boom economy, about 13
percent of the U.S. population fell below the poverty threshold established
by the U.S. government. The thresholds stipulate the dollar amount below
which a family of a given size is eligible for financial assistance, half of
which usually comes from the state and the rest from the federal budget. A
family unit of four would be below the 1999 poverty threshold if they earned
less than $16,700 gross per year.

The idea of providing tax dollars for the poor is not just a humanitarian
one; it is compelling for the self-interest of the mainstream population. Uneducated adults and unhealthy people are a burden not just to their families
but to all of society.

Why would the media want to give people the false opinion that money
for welfare mothers, 1 percent of the federal budget, threatens the entire U.S.
economy? It is simple. The frightened mainstream keeps watching to see the
latest report on how we are allegedly being scammed. The poor are an easy
target for scapegoating because they are not major contributors to political
campaigns, and because their complex and troubled lives keep them from
spending time organizing voters or boycotts. And, in other segments of society, scapegoating the poor increases viewership, ratings, and revenues. For
TV and film producers, scapegoating the poor is like watching the school
bullies pick on the littlest kid; it becomes a form of theater. In addition, the
average reporter has little reason to know how to find the real U.S. budget
documentation and never bothers to learn about the exaggeration of expen-
ditures. Most report on anecdotes, not facts.[4]

Alternative coverage could focus on the other 99 percent of the U.S. Budget. What is it spent on? Are there special favors, scams, corporate welfare,
or waste that should concern the taxpayers?

Another "scare" exploited by the media is a fear of cities. Many subur-
banites tell friends in the city, "Thanks for the invitation to visit you. I don't
think I should come. Cities are dangerous places, you know. There are drug
addicts, and all those people who look a little different."

Some people from small towns and rural areas, even well-educated young

.ently say, "I've never been to a big city. It's scary. If you get lost,
.now what evil thing might happen to you." The general belief,
engendered by the media, is that most crime occurs in the cities of the north-
eastern United States. In fact, the crime rates are higher in the West and
southwestern United States.

In actual fact, some of the most wonderful cultural assets of this country
are in cities. The nation's major museums, concert halls, and theaters are in
cities. Most of the headquarters for major corporations are in cities. The
experts from academia, government, and science are usually based in cities.
Magnificent architecture can be found in cities. Some of the best magazines are about all those fascinating people from the far corners of the
globe—many of whom speak different languages and have different skin
color—just like the people in America's cities. Some of them have even won
Nobel Prizes.

Why would the media want to scare people into thinking they should just
stay put? Lock the doors. Do not go anyplace you have not been before. And
do not get too near anybody who looks different—has a different color skin,
speaks another language, or who might be poor or old or disabled.

Picking up the age-old habit of scapegoating other people, the ones least
able to retaliate—coupled with the fear of the unknown—works well to
keep the viewers attention. The media not only prey on prejudices and
fears, but reinforce them. It increases viewership and ratings and revenues
for the media moguls.

Alternative coverage of cities could focus on things that actually do happen in cities. For example, land use wars constantly engage residents fighting developers. Sometimes the battles are about actual removal of housing to
make way for commercial development. Sometimes the battles are less visible and are about raising residents' taxes in order to give concessions to
major sports teams building new stadiums. Transportation conflicts rage continuously. Sometimes the issues are about whether the government will build
more roads or put more money into mass transit. Sometimes they concern
flight patterns of noisy planes over residential communities. In this new high-
tech era, transportation battles are often over whether phone companies or
cable companies will transport Internet data in the cheapest and highest-
quality manner. In all these battles, money is usually at stake, sometimes
neighborhoods, and a way of life. In addition, the media might cover the
many human struggles that rage in the city—struggles for affordable housing, for decent schools, for health care, for job training and livable wages.

Sometimes the media scare people to pursue their desire for ratings and
revenue, but, ironically, scaring people sometimes serves the public interest.
For example, consider those who proclaim, "If crime doesn't get me, disease

probably will." Medical care is very scary because you hear all th
about medical malpractice. It is outrageously expensive. Do you
it cost my neighbor for an ambulance? And he has good health ir. _____.

In actual fact, the costs of health care in this country are exorbitant, and some forty-five million Americans have no health insurance—nearly one in seven Americans. Most of these people are working people from age twenty-one to age sixty-five. They are above the poverty level. They either have no access to health insurance through their employer or cannot afford a private policy. Some are elderly who do not have sufficient income to pay the doctor bills and prescription bills that are not paid by Medicare. This is a national crisis. It needs to be solved. In fact, many thoughtful people have given a lot of time to examining ways to solve it.

In the early 1990s, First Lady Hillary Clinton met over many months with a task force of the nation's experts to find solutions to this complex economic and human service issue.

The media coverage of the reform efforts tended initially to dwell more on the novel idea that the First Lady, a lawyer with a degree from Yale, might oversee a major activity aside from hosting state dinners. The public attention was not directed to the substantive alternatives for health care, nor was it directed to the crisis that required action.

The motivation for the White House attention was the impact that rapidly increasing costs of medical services and pharmaceuticals were having on both public and private organization budgets. The high costs brought three results. First, employers began bailing out of benefit packages, choosing to outsource jobs. By reducing the size of their workforce and hiring temporary workers instead, companies can save money. Second, the downsizing and outsourcing has contributed to the rapidly increasing numbers of people without health insurance. Third, the accountants tightened their grip on health care plans resulting in decreased quality of health care.

The public understood little about the real issues here. The media news coverage, when it focused on the issue, met the usual deadlines and format constraints by providing sexy anecdotes, sound bites, and little context. The health care industry, not wanting to see its profits capped, produced the clever "Harry and Louise" commercial. In fact, what most people remember about the health care reform effort is that "Harry and Louise" raised doubts. And the entire health care reform effort never came to a vote in Congress. It was all a political game. Congressional Republicans could not let the Democrats solve this problem, especially not when the health reform task force was led by a woman. It was the mentality of the early 1990s.

Why did the media choose not to cover the details of health care reform planning? Why would they help to stop health reform legislation by screening out coverage of all sides of the story? Probably because the news system was running on automatic pilot. No time was factored in for thinking about the full picture, the need for the fourth estate to tell the public about the stakes.

The media role in health care is complex. On the one hand, the public should be scared about the cost and quality of health care. The media has helped that in some respects. On the other hand, the public has not been told what it needs and deserves to know about how to influence health policy decisions. This is a democracy, and policy made only by politicians and accountants is unacceptable. It is easier for the media to avoid thinking about the reality of health issues and to deal instead with the entertainment value thereof.

In TV news, as in TV entertainment, increasing viewer fear by showing the dreadful things that can happen in accidents makes the programming easier to produce and more profitable. One does not have to spend the time and money on real investigative reporting to give the solid news if the news can just be selected from the police scanner. Entertainment programs about hospitals and disaster offer a good substitute for gun violence in programming. You cannot accuse the TV of being excessively violent if the show portrays what, in fact, happens in a place where most people have been at one time or another—a hospital. The scripts rarely address the controversies and the catastrophes surrounding how one pays for health care or who dies for lack of it.

Alternative coverage could still program dramas that get high ratings and more revenue for the station. Scripts could mirror the real-world debate. Many media professionals may have never thought about including the "real" debate, or may well have little knowledge of the issues at hand and the stories to tell. Veteran journalists sometimes lament the fact that younger journalists often lack the broad-based liberal arts education needed to understand in-depth newsgathering.

Advertising is another way in which the media scares people. The "Harry and Louise" ad, mentioned above, was a very clever commercial produced by the health industry companies to undercut support for health care reform in the early 1990s. The ad showed a typical family discussing the "what ifs" of health care reform. The objective was to frighten the public into lobbying their legislators in Congress to abandon health care reform. It worked. The ad campaign's strategy was impressive. By getting news coverage of the ad, they multiplied their impact. The incentive for the pharmaceuticals and health insurance companies to block health care reform was and is enormous. Simply put, the more the system is unregulated, the higher the prices can go, and the greater their profits.

Now, several years after killing health care reform, the news carries stories of more HMOs restricting health coverage and increasing prices because they cannot stay ahead of the mounting industry costs. The same group that produced "Harry and Louise" is jumping into television advertising to influence the reforms in Medicare, the health insurance for all seniors. If they succeed and if seniors leave Medicare and buy private insurance, the insurance companies would reap a 66 percent increase in profits in just seven years.[5]

Scaring us to death is good business for advertisers as well as for stations—good for the media moguls.

It is not that a meeting was held and people in power made a conscious decision to perpetuate this practice; rather it is a low-key, default position. Over time, scaring people has proved to be a tactic that works. So, why not continue what works? It makes money. And it keeps people from asking too many questions. Few in the industry emerge as spokespersons for operating a legitimate "fourth estate" as envisioned in the U.S. Constitution. Challenging the status quo is never easy.

The advertiser differs from the programmer only in the respect that there is some understanding that what she or he is doing is persuasion. Few understand the persuasive influence of news and entertainment programming. Persuasion is the route to making profits for the advertiser. It is the hook that keeps people tuned in to increase the ratings for the programmer. The mode of persuasion that has been most prevalent in recent years is the kind that is designed to increase fear and anxiety.

Today's persuasive argument has strayed from its origin in ancient Greece. Today's persuasion tactics as used by the media more resemble propaganda— a one-sided brain washing that convinces the public that something is right without much thought about alternatives.

In ancient Greece, the argument never ended with a one-sided presentation. Sophists trained citizens to argue, to present their case in the most convincing way possible. It was expected that one would be presented with a counter argument. Rebuttal defending one's position was part of the game. Those who listened to these rigorous intellectual arguments were not bored. They found themselves cheering, booing, laughing, and crying throughout the process. At the end, it may be that neither the thesis nor the antithesis prevailed in their pure form. Rather, a new position, a synthesis, might arise.

Today's media provides little exposure to such debate. The television program "Cross Fire" ostensibly is for this purpose. Unfortunately the participants do not represent the real cross-section of views in society—only the two dominant views within the government. And the program format is designed to create more heat than light, probably with the intent of boosting ratings.

Today, media programming rarely has time for persuasion in the classic sense. Propaganda is easier since the objective is not the health of society, but the wealth of the media owners and advertisers. It is all about money. The media may, or more likely may not, recognize the need to place the diverse viewpoints next to each other so that the public has the benefit of thinking through the arguments.

Anthony Pratkanis and Elliott Aronson, psychology professors at the University of California, Santa Cruz, write: "A fear appeal is most effective when:

- It scares the hell out of people.
- It offers a specific recommendation for overcoming the fear-arousing threat.
- The recommended action is perceived as effective for reducing the threat.
- The message recipient believes that he or she *can* perform the recommended action."[6]

The authors go on to say that people who have a low opinion of themselves may have difficulty coping with threats to themselves. A high-fear communication overwhelms them and makes them feel like crawling into bed and pulling the covers up over their heads.[7] Using fear is a common propaganda technique.

The media, by presenting only the frightening aspects of an issue and omitting the steps one can choose for countering the fear, are turning us into frightened, manipulated consumers and we do not seem to know what is happening to us. We are too media-illiterate to see how we are being used.

In the past, within news presentations, the scary items were carefully placed by the editors. Ed Asner observes, "When we were doing "The Lou Grant Show," we would cover aspects of the news. The story of the black welfare mother who got murdered for her welfare check was buried on page twenty-two. The white Pasadena widow who beat off the burglar with a golf club makes page one.

"On the other hand, you can see that there is a benevolence in that— which you no longer see on nightly TV, of course. It shows that the little guy can win. So there's a positive piece to be gained from that. The other horror of a poor mother murdered for her check is buried so as not to depress the public. None of these cases are truths, but the truth we get now featuring every known murder and mayhem possible on the evening news just turns us all into frightened mice."[8]

Let us look in more detail at how the media is scaring us to death. We will examine media coverage of violence, drugs, HIV/AIDS, and of urban and rural places. Then we will look at some of the techniques the media use to hype suspense and heighten fear.

Are we being mugged by the media?

Violence

A 1994 report from the Times Mirror Center for People and the Press on viewer opinions of American movies and TV programs showed that people across the globe believe American television has too much violence.[9] This view was held by 45 percent of Canadians, 49 percent of French, 58 percent of Germans, 47 percent of Italians, 45 percent of Mexicans, 51 percent of Spaniards, 38 percent of UK citizens, and 62 percent of U.S. viewers.

No doubt numerous reasons exist for the public's holding this view. One reason for public discomfort is the fact that in addition to 57 percent of TV programs in the mid-1990s containing violence, 73 percent of the violent acts went unpunished.[10]

A second reason may have to do with the poor judgment exercised by some broadcasters, whose obsession with the need for ratings causes a lapse in common sense. For example, a suicide in Los Angeles was considered so important, so newsworthy, that it broke into afternoon children's programming, leaving many parents scurrying to explain the facts of adult life to their innocent and frightened children.[11]

Another example of the kind of judgment decisions made by the news media concerns crimes like the school shooting in 1999 in Littleton, Colorado.[12] For example, did the coverage of a copycat school crime in Conyers, Georgia provide necessary information or did it stimulate more copycat crimes? Different media dealt with the event differently. Some made it a lead story with top billing or front-page coverage. Others broke into regular programming to cover the story. Barrie Smith, an Emerson College media arts student just past the teenage years herself, says, "I think the news is more at fault for copycat crimes than TV entertainment programming and music videos. Every time you turn on the TV, all you see is the coverage of the awful tragedy in Littleton, Colorado. This kind of attention gives the wrong message to the kids watching. There are kids out there who think these two assassins are famous now. Kids today feel like they are nothing and don't get the attention they long for. So, when these two kids get all this attention, some may feel this is the thing to do."[13]

Another example of how the judgment of those in the media influences societal violence is the flurry surrounding Oliver Stone's 1994 film, *Natural Born Killers*. Whether one likes or hates what Stone did, there is no doubt that his film is a centerpiece for conversation. One media student observed,

"Natural Born Killers is such a powerful pipe for the conveying of messages to a mass audience because of Stone's crafty manipulation of character paradigms, empathy with these twisted characters, and the subtle creation of a sense of self-disgust in the viewer. When one watches the film, one walks away realizing that we are all *Natural Born Killers*. By getting our adrenaline flowing, Stone allows us to think insightfully about the animals we are. The role of this film, put plainly, is to act as food for thought. . . . It is a clear social commentary. But we only pay attention to the film because it shocks and thrills us."[14]

That is one reaction to the film. On the other hand, there are those who think the extreme violence was unnecessary, did not prove anything, and was the model for copycat crimes. Do we just assume that 95 percent of the viewers are mature enough to know better than to copy so heinous a crime? Or are we frightened into believing that we might be misfortunate enough to encounter the copycat criminals? The fact remains that, while the public can interpret Stone's art either way, overall crime statistics are down, and there is still some violence "out there." The film contributes to raising the perception that violence is everywhere and increasing the fear that you may be caught in the crossfire.

Just as there can be two ways of interpreting the basis for producing a violent film or interpreting TV programming about violence, there can be differing views about who is at fault for the outbreaks of violence in the United States.

For example, Christopher Leiden's radio interview program, "The Connection," afforded the opportunity for Doug Richardson to suggest that Hollywood may not be totally to blame for the violence.[15] Richardson is the scriptwriter and novelist who has written some of the most violent film scripts, including the *Money Train*, in which the subway token collector is torched, *Bad Boys*, and *Die Hard II*.

He cites a number of situations to validate his view that the media are not responsible for violence in society. Richardson noted that Detroit is one of the nation's most violent cities, yet right across the border in Canada, where the public consumes the same media, the crime rate is much lower. Richardson asked, "Where were mom and dad in Littleton, Colorado, when the kids were building bombs in the basement? " He emphasized, "I never said that Hollywood reflects culture. As a writer, I'm not trying to reflect something. I'm trying to invent something." He said, "People like violence in film. Why do they like roller coasters? It's a thrill. It's like a cliff. It takes people to the edge, but they're safe."

Is Richardson's approach one that adds credibility to the charge that professionals in the film and television business are to some extent responsible for the violence in society? Are not apologies and rationales for such violence deliberately self-serving?

Others minimize the violence in the media by saying it serves a social function. They claim that violence in entertainment acts to suppress violence in real behavior, much the way organized sports is said to substitute for warfare.

After the Littleton school shootings, parents across the country have let their outrage be known to Hollywood. The American Medical Association and the American Psychological Association studies do show a link between youthful aggression and violence in the media. In planning the 1999–2000 television season, programmers reduced the violence somewhat.

For example, Arsenio Hall asked his director to reduce the level of violence in an upcoming episode of CBS's "Marshall Law." He also refused to use any publicity photos in gun-wielding poses.[16]

At the WB network, executives have urged producers to explore themes of teenage alienation. Dick Van Dyke, star of "Diagnosis Murder," told writers and producers to cut the AK-47s, no mass murders. "Falcone," the 1999–2000 mob drama, had an ice-pick murder in its pilot show. It was later edited to show only the public reaction to the murder.[17]

David E. Kelley, producer of "The Practice," "Ally McBeal," and "Snoops," said, "I'm always wary of condoning any kind of censorship. But I'm just as wary of stapling 'censorship' to a flag and then wagging it over your head as an automatic license to do whatever you want."[18]

Mark Potok, director of public affairs and information for Klanwatch and Militia Task Force, Southern Poverty Law Center, tracks the nation's domestic violence perpetrated by a mix of organizations with Aryan racist, militia, religious right, and Holocaust-denial interests. He wishes the media would better inform the public about the physical threat these groups pose.

For example, he notes the following. The so-called "Patriot" movement was fueled by the U.S. government interventions at Ruby Ridge, Idaho, and Waco, Texas. Ruby Ridge was the home of an armed survivalist group headed by Randy Weaver. Weaver's wife and son were killed when the federal agents stormed the facility in 1992. Waco was the home of the Branch Davidians, a heavily armed right-wing extremist group, and the place where many people died when the government stormed and fire-bombed the compound in 1993. On the anniversary of Waco in 1995, the Patriots bombed the Murrah Federal Building in Oklahoma City, killing scores of innocent people. In 1998, in Jasper, Texas, white supremacists dragged a black man behind a truck to his death. Supporters of the Patriot movement are suspected to be responsible for the bombing at the 1998 Olympics in Atlanta. The Littleton High School massacre in 1999 was undertaken by two young men influenced by right-wing extremist media, committing their crime on Hitler's birthday. A 1999 killing spree targeting minority people in communities near Chicago and in Indiana was undertaken by Benjamin Smith, a member of the far-right hate group World Church of the Creator. Later in 1999, Buford Furrow Jr., a representative of the far-right Aryan Nation groups, killed a U.S. Postal Service employee because he was Filipino and a government employee, and then proceeded to a Jewish community center in Los Angeles where he opened fire on a number of people, including children.

The public often fails to understand the danger from these factions of our society because the media reports do not elaborate on what is behind the violence. Tight time requirements for media reports, lack of training that would encourage inclusion of context, and the pressure for sensationalism are some reasons the news terrifies the audience, but offers little information useful to overcome the terror.

Mark Potok offers yet another view:

> I think the major drawbacks are that the news is still driven by sexiness. I don't think that will ever change. It's people's taste. Until everyone goes to college, there will people who want to hear about the guy who keeps his kids in the closet. Yes, it's true more people are informed than they were twenty years ago, but I'm always amazed how little people know.
>
> These bombings are pretty high profile and people have no idea who Eric Rudolph is, and many haven't even heard of the Olympic bombing in Atlanta. I suppose I believe this business about competing for people's time. This is the justification for the media to write shorts and to make 'rockem-sockem' stories. There are drawbacks, however. Numbers count when they shouldn't. Most people are poorly educated. Even most colleges are pretty unimpressive. Most people are really not educated even when they are educated. People come out of school and may know how to run a company, but they don't know how to read a book, and they have no interest in society's issues."[19]

The so-called Patriot movement usually has a low profile in mainstream media. This does not mean its numbers are shrinking. In fact, while the number of organized groups may be fewer, their Internet sites are multiplying rapidly as the movement tries to become part of mainstream America. Racist hate, anti-Semitism, Christian Identity, and conspiracy theories about the United Nations' influence on the United States appeared on 179 web sites in 1997, and one year later on 248 sites.[20] Aside from the Internet presence, individuals in a lunatic fringe find their way into mainstream America through groups like the Council of Conservative Citizens, groups whose true nature the media generally ignore.

At present, hate groups are most popular in Texas, Michigan, California,

Ohio, Florida, and Tennessee. This fact, however, is not just of passing interest. These states together represent a powerful block in both the U.S. Congress and in winning the White House. These six states are home to 149
House members in Congress, 34 percent of the entire House of Representatives. They are home to 12 senators, 24 percent of the entire Senate. To win
election as U.S. president, a candidate needs 270 electoral votes. These states
carry 161, or 59.6 percent of the total number needed to win the White House.
Of course, one cannot say that there is a monolithic viewpoint in these states
regarding the political philosophy of the extreme right. However, if there are
a sufficient number of supporters in these states to tip the scales even a bit in
their direction, then the entire culture tips, just a bit more, in their direction.
Is that a price that mainstream America is willing to pay?

Is it not in our self-interest at least to be informed by the media so that we
can decide for ourselves how much mindless apathy may be too much? So
we can decide whether it is time to counter this viewpoint before fascist
history repeats itself?

The media do not always ignore the story. While their coverage may not
provide sufficient context for the many Americans with no understanding of
civics to know how they can counter the so-called Patriots, some networks
do make the effort to provide the basic story.

For example, Mark Potok explains:

> Sometimes news broadcasts do a really good job. CNN just did a four–part
> series. Linda Patillo produced the series on the Christian Identity movement. I
> know her from covering the McVeigh trial [the Oklahoma City bomber]. They
> say (Christian) 'Identity' is the glue that binds them together. That one line got
> her wanting to do that series. She did a terrific job. Television is dependent on
> visuals. She just had to have that Aryan Republican Army underground tape.
> It's not available, but we had it. She had to have Lewis Beam on tape ranting
> and raving. [Beam, a former Klu Klux Klansman, then Aryan Nation "ambas-
> sador at large" urges the movement to overthrow the government and reclaim
> America by blood if necessary.] We had the tape. She got surveillance camera
> tapes of bank robberies and some wonderful footage that the BBC had taken of
> the Covenant Army of the Lord. I was expecting this two-hour documentary.
> What they wound up being were four seven-to-eight-minute segments which
> they promoted to death. I think more people watched it than would have watched
> a lengthy documentary. Because I'm already interested, I'd watch a two-hour
> program. I'm not sure others would. CNN has a five-news-cycle format, so it
> was five times eight minutes every day for four days."[21]

What is the harm of the media scaring us to death? Surely, all of life is not
sweetness and roses; it would be terribly boring if the media were. Ultimately, the question comes down to whether the way some messages are
delivered and others screened out results in paralyzing us with cynicism and

depression, or whether it leaves us empowered to enhance a sense of self-esteem and self-actualization.

Surely, it is poor judgment to break into kids' programming unless the most severe crisis is occurring. To bring the most outrageous acts of violence into the lives of children is truly cruel to very little children who have no base for understanding what is happening. Older children will need to learn that life has violence, but one would hope this could be in a context where they understand that violence is not common, not rational, and not condoned.

Viewers need to feel that violence is controllable, is punished, and—perhaps most important—is prevented. Very little in the media goes beyond laying out the problem. They could examine real crime statistics and the trends. And they could focus on both crime prevention successes like community policing.

The media could also look at what is happening in the prisons across the nation. Are we rehabilitating people or simply increasing the anger of prisoners against the system? This aspect of criminal justice policy directly affects the public well-being. It also informs the public about the use of their tax dollars to fight crime. Seldom is it covered.

For example, some say that privatizing prison systems results in more wealthy system owners and more hardened criminals. Little attention is paid to mixing petty criminals with hardened killers—the best crash course imaginable in creating more hardened criminals. One of these private prisons had a prison riot over the fact that the warden's girlfriend, who had been hired as cook, did not know how to cook. The day she served the largely Hispanic population bologna burritos, a riot broke out. The lives of guards as well as members of the local community were at risk because of extremely poor management practices. Are our tax dollars being spent wisely? Will the ex-convicts be more dangerous to society than when they started their prison term? The media would give the public useful information if it covered some of these matters. To leave the public with scary stories where there is no recourse, no opportunity for empowerment, is to instill depression, hopelessness, isolation, and—one way or another—to scare people to death.

Drugs

The media have indeed raised the issue of drug use in both entertainment and news coverage. Some of it is scary. Some of it is just confusing and unsettling because the message is mixed.

For example, according to some critics, the movie *Trainspotting* made using heroin look like fun. Others thought the film graphically showed the horrors of using heroin. Adam Goldberg, Emerson College researcher, describes one scene where a baby is crawling on the floor in a messy room where people are shooting up and another scene where a man is waking up in pile of his own feces. "By being very graphic about the horrors of drug use, the viewer becomes shocked into thinking about these issues," he writes.[22] Should the media make the message clearer or leave it up to the audience to decide?

Aside from movies that provide examples of a lifestyle on drugs, the media ads often send a confusing and unsettling message to kids. For example, Emerson College researcher Denise Gorman says the real issue is that "anti-drug ads don't offer kids any alternatives for solving their problems."[23] She cites a WB network commercial that suggests that kids turn to drugs out of anger, frustration, and despair, and then simply concludes that anger, frustration, and despair will be the result of drug use, too. Gorman says, "What they are really saying is that drugs will make your already miserable existence even more miserable—if that's possible. We need to stop telling kids what they shouldn't do to make things worse, but rather tell them what they can do to make things better."[24]

TV has a double standard about drugs. Antidepressants are big business. Prozac ads are pitched as if everyone can use it. The ads boast that over 17 million Americans use Prozac.

So the message to kids is that drugs are bad and make your life worse, except for those drugs that make your life better. Confused? Gorman notes that "throughout the good drugs/bad drugs debate runs a unifying problem: the messages fail to include alternative solutions other than drug use, whether it be illegal drugs or doctor prescribed drugs. They tell you drugs are bad, but we don't know how else you can deal with your problems. Then they tell you drugs are good, but we don't want you to know how else you can deal with your problems."

It gets even more confusing for kids. The FDA recently approved two drugs for dogs that suffer from "behavioral problems." Drugs are good for your dog, but bad for you?

One young woman said, "My 18-year-old cousin was in therapy, suffering from depression. Prozac was prescribed. Shortly after, he got a girlfriend. He was miraculously cured. He didn't need the Prozac. His new happy state of mind continued, as did his relationship. He didn't need drugs, he needed an ego boost."

Other programs on TV have taken on different drug issues. CBS's "Murphy Brown" smoked marijuana to alleviate the pain caused by her cancer. The TV episode generated a massive uproar. Clearly it was provocative enough to stimulate thinking about pain relief, if not about the good drug/bad drug confusion. The "Murphy Brown" episode is a good example of the power of the media to stimulate discussion even while—or maybe because—it scares us to death.

Some television programs have tried to send clear messages to those using drugs. People get these messages into the scripts through the writers, the researchers, and the actors. Writers have most control over the ideas in a script. Producers and directors have the most control over what remains in the production and how it is presented. An example of this is "Beverly Hills 90210." This television program has a character named David who is addicted to pills (uppers) to keep him awake. Rather than having him look preppy and neat, he looks tired, awful.[25] The message—drugs ruin you. The program also showed a friend trying to help him stop—a message to kids that it is okay to accept help from family and friends.

A problem has arisen with antidrug advertising and how it is targeted. Some commercials are targeted toward ethnic groups; for example, a frequently seen anticrack ad featuring a Latina girl. You are left with the impression that the problem of crack is a Latino/a problem. Ads like that can contribute to racism. For example, there is another ad where a black father is seen trying to sell drugs to a young black man. "Try it, you will not get hooked," the man pleads. The boy keeps refusing. At the end of the commercial, the black man looks at the youth and, acknowledging that this is his son, tells him that he handled himself just the right way to avoid the drug dealers. On the one hand, it is a convincing commercial. On the other hand, does it also send a racist message?

Couple the racism in antidrug advertising with the TV movie scripts that usually have the drug dealers be Latino/as or blacks. "NYPD Blue," "Law and Order," and "Homicide" are examples.

From the media, one would think that the severe drug problem is only a problem for "other" people—minorities. Many prominent white entertainers are among those who have become part of the list of drug overdose tragedies; for example, the actor River Phoenix and Chris Farley, the comedian seen on "Saturday Night Live." Jean Claude van Damme, the karate action actor in *Double Team*, has reportedly used drugs for a long time, and drops in and out of the professional arena. Actor Robert Downey Jr. went to jail for not following court orders to abstain from drugs. However, the media emphasis on people like these appears to be slight. Natasha Caballero, a young Jamaican woman who works in a day care center said, "If someone white OD's, the media talks about it once and drops it. If the person is black or Hispanic, you never hear the end of it."

While the coverage of drug problems is becoming more common on television, thereby increasing the perception that increased fear is warranted, Partnership for a Drug Free America says users of illegal drugs are down 49 percent since 1985.[26]

Simultaneously the pharmaceutical ads are increasing. There are big profits in getting all of America on drugs—profits for TV as well as for the drug companies.

Whether or not the media's scaring us to death about illegal drugs or about the need for legal drugs is warranted, the fact is that the increased general knowledge of the problem serves to increase the level of fear and anxiety.

What is the alternative? It might be useful for viewers to understand the trends showing a reduction of the problem. It might be useful to show that where drug problems exist, they cut across racial and economic lines. Dealing with the double standards could also be helpful to teens, especially in their attempts to understand the feelings that contribute to their decision to use drugs, and for those young people looking for alternative solutions to their problems. Such coverage need not be boring or preachy. The media could look at the psychological profiles of those who do use illegal drugs. The media could do an investigative story on why prices for legal drugs in the United States are grossly inflated compared to the cost of the same drugs abroad, and whether pharmaceutical companies are using U.S. media to push drugs for inflated profits. The messages can be woven into dramatic or humorous or horror genre film scripts—provided there is some way out that people can see as viable. News stories and even cartoons can convey messages enabling the viewer to examine the alternative arguments about drugs for themselves. The story about the antidepressant for one's pets is a good start.

HIV

AIDS first appeared in the 1980s but it took a decade before it was really dealt with in the media. This tragic epidemic has generated much fear. Has the media coverage increased or reduced the level of fear?

"ER" both talks about AIDS and has one of the leading characters, a doctor, as a carrier of the HIV virus.[27] The film *Philadelphia* is the story of a lawyer with AIDS. His law firm finds out and fires him. The law firm cares only about making money and is worried about the perceptions that might come from employing a lawyer with AIDS. These shows both deal with the societal debate about whether people who are HIV positive should have limits on their jobs.

In "Beverly Hills 90210," the character Valerie had a story line dealing with the scary possibility that she might have the AIDS virus as a result of having a sexual relationship with someone she did not know. In the end she did not have it.

These stories do what many do. They often show the characters so scared about getting AIDs from casual contact with an AIDS victim that he or she is further victimized.

Dealing with AIDS has been incorporated into recording industry releases. For example, Elton John's "The Last Song" is about a teenage boy dying in a hospital. The song tells you he got AIDS from unprotected sex. At the end you find that the song is a conversation between a gay boy and his father. It is a message of tolerance. Lyricist Bernie Taupin does a beautiful job. The words are, "I never thought I'd lose. I only thought I'd win. I never dreamed I'd feel this fire beneath my skin. I can't believe you love me. I never thought you'd come. I guess I misjudged love between a father and a son."[28]

Society's response to AIDS has been controversial. Our culture and others across the world have been slow to address the problems of this disease, which surfaced only twenty years ago. Some have held back because of bigotry toward gays and a misunderstanding that AIDs only affects gays. Young people often see themselves as immortal and do not deal with AIDs because they think that only "others" get diseases. In some places unprotected sex is essential to "manliness." Those with the power to set policy and appropriate money for AIDS prevention and cures have not seen AIDs as their problem—until it began to affect their children and until they realized that infected blood transfusions put everyone at risk.

HBO produced "And the Band Played On," a documentary on the history of AIDS. A third-world bank executive asks, "Is the CDC [Centers for Disease Control, an agency of the U.S. Department of Health and Human Services] seriously recommending the blood industry spend what could amount to a hundred million dollars a year to use a test for the wrong disease because there's a handful of transfusion fatalities and six dead hemophiliacs?" Another character in the documentary responds, "How many dead hemophiliacs do you need? How many people have to die to make it cost efficient for you to do something about it?"[29]

HIV is already frightening to society. First of all, it has been news to a lot of people that *new* diseases can come into existence. The media coverage has been handled very carefully, by and large, except for the slow start in breaking the news that blood transfusions could carry the HIV virus. The entertainment industry has provided a number of good examples of how to stimulate thought and discussion about a societal problem that already has frightened a lot of people.

Cities and Rural Places

Cities and rural places have had a hard time in the media for a number of decades now.

Little time has been spent evaluating the impact of perception of place. Nonetheless, place is an enormous factor in the quality of life for people across our culture. For reasons of stereotype more often than fact, people choose to live one place but would not consider another. They shop one place but not another. They travel to one place but not another. People's views of place contribute to the economic viability of some places rather than others. Similarly, the preexisting economic viability of a place influences people's preferences. Place can symbolize power or prestige or wealth—or lack thereof.

The concept of place is easy to understand when one thinks of the meaning behind who has the corner office, the head of the conference table, or the reserved parking spot.

Places deemed not desirable are usually portrayed in the media as somehow scary or unsettling. Cities and rural areas are frequently seen this way.

The majority of people in the media live—either physically, economically, or emotionally—in the suburbs. Cities, like rural places, are the "other places." They are the places one can say anything about without alienating the media consumers, the majority who buy the products—suburban or middle-class Americans. One would need to be careful not to alienate this constituency; it might backfire financially. Besides, it is always a bit of a hassle to deal with "other places" in that one cannot negotiate them on automatic pilot. It takes a map, planning, transportation, etc. The leap to considering them scary or unsettling is not a big one.

The negative treatment of cities and rural places in the media contributes to the fear in society about these places. It is commonplace to find a fear about cities reinforcing a self-imposed and unfortunate ghettoization in the suburbs and small towns. Those who are economic, emotional, or geographic citizens of the suburbs can easily fall into thinking of themselves as a bit "better" than those who live in cities or rural areas. Often they do have more education, better jobs, more money, and more opportunities available to them. This results in America's younger generations having little understanding of the delights and difficulties of living either in the city, where one can walk to the best museums and resources, or in the country, where one can be in the midst of all that nature has to offer. On the other hand, these places, frequently not acceptable to baby boomers' parents, become the destinations for their offspring, as exotic and exciting, in part because they are perceived as scary.

Look at how this dynamic works within the media.

Cities, unlike rural areas, get a lot of media coverage in both news and entertainment. Perhaps this is because the broadcast studios are usually in cities. Shows like "The Nanny" and "Friends" have personal storylines for the young revolving around life in a rich family in the city or a posh apartment, realistically far beyond the financial reach of the characters who occupy it. They fulfill a fantasy for the young but they are far outnumbered by those programs and films that show the city in negative terms, stereotyped as skid row and as a place of corruption and decay.

The film *Batman* featured a sleezy mayor, hoodlums, corruption throughout the city, and no hope for urban America.[30] Other examples of negative portrayals of the city include the short-lived TV show "Naked City," which tried to confront real urban problems and neglect; "Homicide," which is set in Baltimore; "NYPD Blue," in New York City; *Blackboard Jungle, Looking for Mr. Goodbar*, and countless other films.

Los Angeles is frequently misrepresented in the media.[31] The L.A. of bungalows, irrigation, quack religions, and Midwest retirees seldom makes the Big Screen. Rather, one sees Beverly Hills—sun, fun, spectacularly dressed tanned bodies, shops on Wilshire Boulevard, beaches, bikinis, BMWs. For example, the movie *Pretty Woman* (1990) shows a hooker who sells herself to get out of the dumps. She finds a lonely millionaire and they fall madly in love—rags to riches. The reality in South Central L.A. is quite different.

Then again, South Central is not what is depicted in film and on television. Kishawnna M. Terry, Emerson College researcher, says, "Depictions of life in this inner city area would put fear into anyone's heart if they thought they would be dropped off there after midnight. For example, *Menace to Society* shows young men stomping and beating each other to death. One character becomes victim of a drive-by shooting. Hispanic culture in East L.A. is portrayed in film and on television with considerable exaggeration. For example, *Mi Vida Loca* (My Crazy Life) explores the lives of teenage female gang bangers. In *Blood In Blood Out* three young Latinos who are related live as thugs while kids and then grow up where one becomes a drug addict, another an imprisoned drug lord, and the third a cop."[32]

New York City is frequently seen in film and on television. But the portrayal is all too often negative. For example, New York City Transit Authority Chief Allen Klepper notes that "crime is down 37 percent in 1994 over four years ago [1990]. Graffiti is off our cars and now we're working on numerous safety devices. Our ridership is up 3.5 percent."[33] Then why do filmmakers depict flying bullets and blood-soaked bodies to frighten potential riders away? Why are there films like *Dressed to Kill*, with would-be rapists targeting victims on the subway, or *Money Train*, where the token collector is torched? One reason is that transit is public property and one can not stop people from filming there. A second reason is that film and video is big business worth billions of dollars to New York City. Patricia Reed Scott, head of the Mayor's Office of Film, said that from 1993 to 1994 the number of films made in New York City increased by 40 percent.[34] It is big bucks.

Make no mistake about the violent and negative portrayal of the cities, however. It is not because city film offices want revenue and publicity for their city. It is because Hollywood rejects the countless stories they could tell, in favor of promoting the stereotypes of cities as violent because it sells.

Chicago also has sought film industry dollars.[35] "Before the 1970s, filming was rarely done in Chicago," says Ron Ver-Kuilen, director of the city of Chicago Film Office. "Movie permits weren't easy to get and politicians were dismayed at the Hollywood portrayal of Chicago as a gangster-ridden city." The Illinois Film Board was established to bring filmmakers to Chicago. The Illinois officials met film executives in Hollywood, went to trade shows, advertised in Hollywood trade journals. They even had billboards, one on top of the building where film permits were obtained in L.A. The angle was that filmmakers should come to Chicago because it is cheaper to work there than in New York City or Los Angeles. And Chicago has the full variety of urban to quaint rural scene locations within a relatively short distance of each other. In the 1980s, *Risky Business*, *The Breakfast Club*, *About Last Night*, and *The Color of Money* were all made in Chicago. *Chain Reaction*, *My Best Friend's Wedding*, and *Hoods* were filmed in Chicago in the mid-1990s. It is said that Illinois and the state film commissioner took in $115 million in 1996 alone.[36]

In Atlanta, in the early 1990s, the murder of a doctor stabbed in a hotel elevator coincided with the police union's collective bargaining with the city to renegotiate their contract. The union, eager to expand their numbers and enlarge their bank accounts, seized the media opportunity. They launched a sophisticated media ad campaign warning people across the nation not to come to Atlanta, which they billed as America's most dangerous city. Convention planners received scores of calls and cancellations from registered participants. The economic pressure was on the mayor and the city council to give the police a favorable new contract. The media just ran the ads and inflated their bank accounts based on the deceptive inflated coverage of one very tragic incident. It is their First Amendment privilege to do so. No amendment requires either the cops or the media to think of the long-term consequences of panning their own city. Consequently, the context for the story is screened out. Who cares if people are afraid of Atlanta if the cops get a good contract?

The news does not do much better than entertainment in terms of providing fair coverage of cities.

Highlighting only what bleeds, in hopes for the fifteen seconds that will bring increased ratings, the news usually leaves people with a very distorted view of their city.

For example, in the early 1990s there were terrible riots and fires in Los Angeles. In Hong Kong, people who had been to L.A. watched the video on the news. "What a pity to have a whole city destroyed," they commented. Why would they think that? Nothing in the news footage led the viewer to understand that, tragic as the damage was, it was confined to a very small part of the entire city.

Surveys of local news viewers[37] included comments such as "Why did they spend so much time covering a double murder when a local boy winning an Olympic medal was hardly mentioned?" "All the media does is cover crime in big cities." "The media makes the citizens feel vulnerable." People from minority and low-income neighborhoods of the city were represented by these comments from a woman living in a black neighborhood of Boston: "The Roxbury Action Program has acquired, rehabilitated, and manages 115 low-income apartments where 450 people now live. RAP opened a full service pharmacy in 1973, and in 1995 that pharmacy had $250,000 sales volume," and then she listed many more positive initiatives from the community. She continued: "But the TV news is just negatives, and our community is not represented in a positive light." Another resident said, "The news is just a circus exploiting people." And another commented: "TV news makes us out to be a community where no one would want to live." One young professional woman from Roxbury commented on the 6 p.m. TV news, "I just refuse to watch news that only denigrates my community."

When discussing TV entertainment and violence, Natasha Cabellero, a sophisticated young woman in her twenties, was asked whether any programs on television ever scared her. She thought for a moment, bypassed the entertainment shows, and replied, "The news does. That's why I never watch it. It's depressing. Murders. Deaths. Fights. Racial tension."

While the money flows into the industry, there's no incentive to improve content. It is a very short-sighted view. With some attention to content, the audience might double and the ad revenue might, too. Many local stories are compelling and entertaining. They counter the stereotypes about the city as a sea of human misery and show the local initiatives to overcome the enormous disenfranchisement and disinvestment. Those stories do not leave people immobilized by fear. They are empowering. But those stories do not get told.

For example, there is a highly positive urban story of the long cheers, applause, and foot-stomping for a new mayor speaking to an auditorium filled beyond capacity in Somerville, Massachusetts. Catcalls, boos, and shouts of "Ride 'em out of town" erupted whenever the mayor mentioned how his administration helped to expose the corruption that would win the *Boston Globe* a Pulitzer Prize. This old urban city next to Boston, like many others, is the base for an untold drama, the story of the empowerment of a citizenry no longer willing to sit passively by watching their city destroyed. It is a story of residents too angry to be apathetic. It is a story of their organizing around decent schools and safety for their kids, outraged by local government corruption, campaigning for an alternative candidate, skirting violence to prove their determination to win back the city, and finally vindication in reclaiming city hall. It is a story of how the media did function as a legitimate "fourth estate" in covering all sides of this struggle.

Cities like Somerville and stories of positive change are everywhere. They are far more captivating than most of what comes in on the police scanner. And they are empowering. But the media professionals need to know how to gather news and to hire enough staff to do that well. And the local media need to be accessible to their local constituencies, as they were before long-distance ownership made them accessible only to their Wall Street constituency.

The media distorts coverage of rural America, too. It portrays it as a place where only "hillbillies" live, or people who are simple, likely bigoted, and probably stupid. These areas are not seen as overtly frightening, like cities. Rather, there's a dark unspoken personal evil attached to rural stereotypes.

For example, the movies *U Turn* and *Deliverance* both have characters who experience serious crises in rural areas. Perhaps they are just part of the plot line, but the setting in a rural environment adds a dimension of suspense. It is hard to identify why, unless it taps into an understanding that this "other" place is different from that which the mainstream suburban viewer knows. On the surface, rural areas are places for a pollyannaish innocence. But somehow the "other"—the unknown—can always be perceived as evil.

How are rural areas portrayed on television programs? In entertainment there were popular series such as "Ma and Pa Kettle" and "Beverly Hillbillies." They fulfilled every rural "yokel" stereotype. "We'll Fly Away" was a more recent series, dealing with racial issues in a rural southern town. This storyline did a fine job of showing the cultural conflicts between the old rural South and modern conventions. "Northern Exposure" was set in rural Alaska. It also was a major step away from some of the negative rural stereotyping in earlier programming. On the other hand, the depiction of rural America in TV horror movies certainly leaves one with insomnia.

Most of today's entertainment programming, like most of today's news, simply ignores the rural areas of the country. Police shows, hospital programs, and "twenty-something" sitcoms rarely have any reference to rural America.

The news might better serve us all if it did deal with rural issues, many of which affect us all.

For example, says New Mexico resident John Davis, "The 'water wars' are very serious business. Las Vegas, like many western communities, has no more water. Yet development is resulting in rapid growth of populations and industries that require more water. The Colorado and Rio Grande Rivers are subject to legal agreements between the regions' governments apportioning the scarce water supply. In addition, the West continues to support agriculture that is inappropriate for desert areas, only further adding to the water problems. The economic boom could, with a sustained draught, easily become an economic bust creating repercussions across the entire country." We rarely, if ever, hear about this on national TV news. Beyond that, we certainly never hear about the alternatives—to rural land use and water conservation. The media could cover the efforts to establish and enforce growth policies, and to address the ranchers' desire to preserve a way of life that wastes water.

Another story never told is how rapidly the vast expanses of the West are disappearing. No one gives much thought to the fact that this vast expanse is being lost. Davis continues, "Ranches the size of the state of Rhode Island being subdivided by developers. The new technologies make it possible for someone who works in New York to buy a laptop and live in Montana. It's great for developers. Just don't plan to take the family to see the vast expanse of the American West. Don't take for granted that it will be there. The miners are engaged in the same activity as the developers. Only the miners make their profits from the taxpayer, not in private transactions. Laws from the mid-1800s permit anyone who wants to stake a claim on public land and mine it to do so. Major mining companies are making bundles doing just that while neither are the taxpayers being reasonably financially compensated for the use of their public lands, nor will their wilderness be preserved."

Just as in the city, the media rarely tell about the important issues, either in news reports or in entertainment story lines. In city reporting they usually only tell us what is on the police docket. In rural reporting they usually only tell us about spotted owls. Meanwhile, like lemmings, in our ignorance, we merrily make money while moving steadily toward the edge of a cliff beyond which our culture will never be the same.

Why are the true stories of the city and rural areas not told? Maybe it is because the media indeed lives in a mindset where the country consists of an east coast, a west coast, and nothing in between. Maybe, in addition, it is easier for media writers and producers to sit at their desks far away from the script locations and imagine what it is like out there. Doing the research to really learn what is going on, and then turn that into energized, appealing scripts takes work and time, as well as talent. It is harder, frankly. It is more costly to produce, although it may recover the cost in higher revenue. Media owners may be too busily engaged in Wall Street fox hunts to stop long enough to redirect company resources toward this kind of creative programming. It is easier, after all, just to follow formulas that "scare them to death." It brings viewers and ratings. And it is safe—if most of the paying customers live in the physical or mental suburbs of the middle class.

Many a young screenwriter grew up in the suburbs where the very existence of the neighborhood was based on Henry Ford's memorable phrase, "We shall solve the problems of the city by leaving the city." The same adage could be applied to the rural areas. Leave them. Leave the isolation. Income variations clearly illustrate the economic difference between urban, rural, and suburban America. In 1997, the median household income for those living in rural areas and small towns was $31,110. Those in center cities had a median household income of $34,282. And those in metropolitan areas (suburban and urban together) had a median household income of $41,576. Disposable income is the key demographic target for the media.

It is logical, given the way our media is financed, that the media's focus is on their biggest spenders. It is probably logical that their entertainment programs often deal with "other" places. "Other" worlds bring opportunities for viewers to escape their day-to-day life and to fantasize about their options. It is logical that the news, to the extent that it is not fluff entertainment, focuses first on things of concern to their dominant audience, the affluent. But it is not logical for places—cities and rural areas—to be dealt with as they are in the media because it is counter to the self-interest of the media owners. The small effort required to cover both adequately could expand both their markets and their profits. They could increase the nation's productivity and preserve its environment for their own families and communities as well as for the abstract "society" by addressing the major issues that, if not addressed, will bring catastrophe to all, including the American middle class. What is scary is that the media hold the only megaphone powerful enough to reach us all, and they are controlled by people who do not see that they are acting counter to their own self-interest and to our collective national self-interest.

Media Techniques That Heighten Fear

As the competition for ratings and profits has intensified, media professionals have found numerous techniques helpful to "heighten the tension" for the viewer—making the programs more exciting. The most common techniques include: (a) a content shift, (b) a style shift, and (c) a shift in the identity given to the audience.

These shifts are facilitated, in part, by the arrival of the new communications technologies that have enabled media ownership consolidation and more centralized operations from remote locations. The new technologies have increased some operating costs, but mostly they made possible the human resource cuts that have increased profits. Business has become more competitive.

Part of the tone set by news broadcasts arises from the "feeding frenzy" of journalists all clamoring for the one sound bite or photo that will make them famous—like the photo of the fireman carrying a small child from the Oklahoma City federal building bombing. One example of this frenzy of activity is the clamor following the crash of John F. Kennedy Jr.'s plane in July 1999. James Hall, chair of the National Transportation Safety Board, added his voice to the criticism of media behavior. "Modern news today is driven by the portability of satellite technology, instant up-close and often monotonously over-dramatized and continuous around-the-clock coverage."[38] Technology replaces thinking. Certainly high-pressure demands for statements that are only speculation rather than solid investigative reporting serve little use.

The perspective of news producers has changed from one of social responsibility to one of marketing. Likewise, the perspective of entertainment professionals has shifted from one of maximizing creative talents to one of cutting costs and maximizing profits. Writers and producers must, now more than in the past, think of whether or not they might displease the owners and advertisers whose first priority is profit in a competitive market.[39]

Content Shifts

Content shifts are occurring in both news and entertainment programming. In a study comparing news program content in 1976 with that in 1992, it was found that "hard" news coverage was down from 64 percent to 19 percent. On the other hand, human interest news and sensationalism increased during the same period from 10 percent to 41 percent of the news stories. Late-evening newscast time shrank from 13 minutes to 11.8 minutes. During this period, stations began to use the Nielsen ratings to evaluate news programs as they had been evaluating entertainment. The pressure is on the broadcaster not to inform, but to reap profits. The arrival of FOX TV as a fourth network, plus the proliferation of cable networks, heightened the concern about staying profitable. Survival ranks higher on the priority list than does full coverage of the issues.

These pressures result in decreased creativity within newsrooms because there is less money and staff to cover real investigative journalism, and it increases the anxious sense of producers that they need to stick to the formulas that have worked in the past. If it bleeds, it leads. No one has time to determine if this is always the case.

Much of the news content has drifted away from information people need to know to covering scandal and crime—police blotter coverage. It is easy to do because the police department and the courts have easy-to-access material. Fifteen years ago "CBS Evening News," "NBC Nightly News," and "ABC's World News Tonight" together were watched by 41.2 percent of all American

TV homes. In 1996, they were watched by 26.1 percent.[40] The question is, how much of the fall in news viewership is because of industry diversification and how much is because people are simply disgusted by the program content's failure to provide real news?

One of the victims of the shift in news content away from news for the enrichment of society overall and toward police blotter coverage is the arts. Actress Jane Alexander, former chair of the National Endowment for the Arts, comments on what she sees happening in news coverage. "In times of hard news and sound bites, those things that people in the media perceive as 'soft' will not fly. I have not worked at a newspaper or on TV in that capacity, so I can only guess at the decision-making process, but I do feel that there is discrimination in this regard. When I was chairman of the National Endowment for the Arts, art was definitely 'soft' news and was relegated to the Style section or the Arts section of papers. Sometimes there was no coverage of arts events, particularly if they involved the elderly or the disenfranchised of any sort. However, whenever we were mired in scandal (alleged or real, grants that might involve sexual depiction, particularly homosexual, or religion), we would surely be covered, and not always fairly."[41]

We claim to be in a global economy, a global village. Yet the news one receives in this country about the rest of the world in the high-tech era at the turn of the century sometimes seems to provide less information than one might have gotten at the turn of the last century when news was sent in penned manuscripts via sailing ships.

Rajesh Sawhney, chief manager–corporate, *The Times of India*, commented about trying to find news about India in the American media: "I could not find a story on India for many days. When there are stories, they draw on the worst events of the country—earthquakes, a shooting. There are a lot of normal people living in India and a lot of good things happening. Most people will find coverage of India very negative. In terms of the percentage of time on television for international stories, the time in the U.S. is much less than we devote to international news. The emphasis here is on North America—the self-sustaining end of the population. Then you create news through sound bites. That creates problems. It leaves very little space for international stories."[42]

Dr. Minoru Sugaya, professor of media policy at Keio University in Japan, commented on international news in American media versus Japanese media: "In Japan we cover more news from the U.S. than does the U.S. cover news from Japan. Maybe it's because the U.S. consists of people coming from all over the world, and you'd need to cover Europe, Asia, etc. If news from Japan affects the U.S., it's covered. Otherwise you just get the Nikkei average and the exchange rate. CNN does very good international news coverage; but network news doesn't cover much. Maybe it's because they only have 20 minutes."[43]

The content of U.S. political coverage has also shifted. The amount of coverage has decreased and the topics rarely cover the important policy issues of the day. Rather, the focus is that everyone who runs for public office is rotten, so the media's job is to "dig up dirt." Besides, that will no doubt bring better Nielsen ratings than informing the public about credentials and positions. The message to those running for office is that a principal way a politician can get on the evening news is to be caught on camera with a prostitute or a drug dealer.[44]

While TV news is often not the news people need to know, but is simply "infotainment," news magazines and talk shows have taken on the challenge of providing even more infotainment in the guise of expanded news programming. The number of these shows has increased greatly in recent years because they are cheap to produce.

Facts have given way to commentary. The news, if it even is news, does not deal with what is happening nearly as much as it deals with what you think and how you feel about what is happening.

"Dateline NBC" was the first evening newscast to experiment with flair. Their target audience is younger, more educated, and more economically motivated than the TV viewing median. NBC West Coast president Don Ohlmeyer told *Time* that he intended to run "Dateline" seven nights a week because the profits could not be matched by sitcoms or feature movies. News magazine programs take less than half the money to produce, and they result in almost the same income. "Dateline" Executive Producer, Neal Shapiro, told *Broadcasting and Cable* on July 13, 1998 that "part of our success has been to figure out, not just good stories, but stories that work in good time spots. You don't have to be a genius to realize that on Monday nights, most men are watching football, a time when "Dateline" creates a softer, more featurish show aimed at women." One part of "Dateline"'s success is that the show has pull with the advertisers who usually go to CBS because it can reach affluent older buyers. According to Zenith Media Figures in April 1998, "Dateline" gets more for a thirty-second spot than the flagship news magazine *60 Minutes*.

The news magazines' high-profile guests, because of their jobs and because of the format, say nothing. Some say it is just another way to compete with a sitcom.[46] The problem here is not the format. TV magazine formats, like "Dateline" and "Prime Time Live," offer a good forum for telling about issues in some detail. There is much more time than on a news program, and if you have a sexy topic, like terrorism or school killings, you have people's attention. A range of diverse views can be presented. The problem, all too often, is that the infotainment drives the news rather than the reverse. There is nothing wrong with people becoming captivated—almost entertained—by real news, real stories that exemplify the problems, and real alternatives posed for solutions.

Aside from news and news magazines, another example of an alternative "news" show is the television talk show. Here, too, the content is different from a few years ago. In the past, Phil Donahue and Oprah Winfrey chatted with guests about personal issues. Nothing outrageous happened on a regular basis. The top two talk shows in 1998 were "The Jerry Springer Show" and "Oprah."[47] Who watches? The Simmons Survey of Media and Markets says daytime talk audiences are 58 percent female, half forty-five or older. The shows attract viewers who have an income below $30,000; 4 percent are unemployed and 9 percent are employed part time. Six in ten viewers have less than one year of college.

The demographic for these programs places their audiences close to the center of the U.S. population. The percent of viewers that is female is slightly above the national percent of the population that is female. The age of viewers is nearly a decade older than the median age of the population. But the education and employment figures are near the U.S. median. In 1998, 77.6 percent of the population over age fifteen had a high school degree; 18.3 percent had some college but no advanced degree; 20.9 percent had a B.A. degree or more. The unemployment rate has ranged between 4.6 percent and 4.3 percent of the workforce over 1998 and the first half of 1999.

Talk show formats have changed over the 1990s. In 1993 Ricki Lake added confrontation and her show ratings peaked. Imitators followed.[48] Jerry Springer readily became the squire of scandal. News magazines ran exposes on Springer's guests which—coincidentally or not—appeared the same time as the spring ratings sweeps. Springer stayed at the top of the ratings chart.

It is said that the Springer show is watched by 750,000 twelve-to-seventeen-year-olds. He is number one with "gen-xers," those between 18–34, and number two with those age 35–49.[49] In daytime Springer's May sweeps ratings in 1998 were more than double his 1997 numbers. What is interesting is that while he is way up in ratings, major advertisers shun his show and he can charge only one-third the amount "Oprah" can charge.[50] Thirty seconds on "Oprah" costs $85,000 and on Springer $30,000.

"Oprah" was the second highest rated talk show in 1998. It is distributed by King World Productions and brings in some $200 million in revenue or 40 percent of King World's revenue annually. "Oprah" and "Jerry Springer" are very close in ratings, but very different in content. Both figure out not just good stories, but good stories that work in good time spots.

Regular news shows, news magazines, and talk shows have shifted the news content away from the real news toward that which is a bit bizarre, or unusual, that which is entertaining.

The new technologies contribute to content shifts in entertainment programming. First, the multiple media outlets—vastly expanded in the last decade—are constantly in need of being fed with programs. This means heavy reliance on program reruns. It means sticking close to proven successes and replicating them, rather than risking time and resources on the new or the different.

In addition, recent years have seen an increasing popularity in the horror show genre. These run the gamut from "slasher" movies to programs about natural horrors such as *Fatal Twisters*. Lines at the theaters were very long the summer of 1999 to see *The Blair Witch Project*. The story line revolves around footage purportedly left by a trio of students who went to a remote wooded area to film something horrible. They were never seen again. Dread is the primary emotion evoked, lots of it. This low-budget film from Artisan Entertainment brought more revenue per screen than any other film ever shown. It had theater owners caught in the dilemma of cutting the run for a major money maker and angering major distributors like Disney, Warner Brothers, and Paramount. The major companies threatened to block distribution of end-of-summer releases if the theaters did not get rid of the independent upstart.[51] Meanwhile *The Blair Witch Project* developed a cult-like following (partly due to Internet promotion) that resulted in thousands of cars descending on the small town on which the story is allegedly based.

One can only speculate why horror genre films became so popular at the end of the century. Perhaps it is because of the bland existence resulting from such a good economy in the United States in the late 1990s. When the status quo is the best of all possible worlds for many people, there does not appear to be much real excitement. This is especially true if one is totally screened out from hearing about, or dealing with, the real national and global challenges because the news shows do not broadcast the information. Perhaps the horror genre flames were fanned by the countless myths circulating about Armageddon coming with the dawn of a new millennium. A subconscious yearning for the archetype of apocalypse or monster shadow evil might also spark excitement for these films and television programs.

Style Shifts

The priority now is style, not content. The new technologies provide a wide range of techniques that allow pictures and sound to be manipulated to enlighten the excitement. The camera itself makes rapid movements. The tape or film is projected at a faster-than-life pace. Clips are short, with frequent jump cuts editing in new material. New material is about a totally different subject, thereby ensuring that the viewer cannot think too long about any one topic. The pace of the programming matches the pace of the fifteen- or thirty-second commercial. The result is to feel "hype" excitement. Just do not ask about what. Trivia has totally smothered reality. Context does not exist. It is next to impossible for the viewer to understand what is happening and how to deal with it. But, then, nobody cares about that anyway. Feel good today. Tomorrow takes care of itself.

The style for newsgathering has also changed. Pressure for ratings usually results in the same lead stories being carried on all the stations in a market. Local stations have less and less control over their own programs.

News program time demands and station staff reductions mean one does not see much substantive investigative reporting. Scenes like tracking OJ's white Bronco down the California freeway or views of Monica Lewinsky coming into a courtroom with a sound track recounting the lab test results on a semen-stained dress or shots of the Clintons house hunting in New York are just played and replayed to increase the ratings—and the profits. Besides, it is cheaper than shooting new footage.

True investigative reporting requires quite a different style. Its first priority is to act as a watchdog for society, not to make money for the company. It usually does make money, but as a by-product. In recent years we have seen these objectives reversed. The result is an end to real investigative reporting. Watergate investigative reporter Carl Bernstein said, "We're not arbiters of guilt or innocence. That's a judicial function. But certainly we should be exercising the tremendous charter that we were granted under the First Amendment."[52]

Perhaps the biggest style shift in newsgathering has been the relatively new and growing practice of accepting puff pieces from public relations firms promoting their clients. This make-believe news—a video news release—is a large part of the content in news broadcasts. It is the result of a symbiotic relationship of the corporate PR representative with the station that does not want to send staff out to gather real news. The result is the deliberate broadcast of slanted information that is labeled news. It has been called the "take-out food" of journalism—no preparation required.[53]

Another style change has been to restrict alternative views to only those that are presented by establishment experts. Of course, it is less work to maintain a Rolodex of potential "experts" from a government or academic position. Perhaps it is rationalized that because they come with the label of an establishment institution, they can be considered "authentic." The style does, however, screen out huge blocks of the population.

Actress Jane Alexander said, "As an activist in the peace movement for decades, I have noticed a definite decline in coverage of alternative thinking. It's as if the wind went out of the sails somewhere back in the '70s and no one trusts alternative thinking anymore. I cannot figure it out."[54]

Shorthand imaging is used increasingly to communicate messages that, under other circumstances, might have contained complex material, diverse views, and a thoughtful assessment of what is to be done and how. News programs frequently flash the face of a policy maker and then, instead of letting her or him speak his or her own words, the reporter gives a personal thirty-second synopsis. Kennedy means liberal and Helms means conservative and exactly what is being discussed never is allowed to surface.

The development of computer graphics increases the possibility of shorthand imaging. Sometimes it proves a marvelous tool to convey material that was difficult to communicate on television in the past. For example, it is always difficult to communicate numbers and the trends in costs for something. Graphs can turn that into a picture and produce a shorthand that is most helpful. On the other hand, playing with the toys at the expense of the content is more common. One could hardly watch the All Star baseball game in 1999 without the cute little computer graphics bursts of stars that had no useful function other than to obstruct the view of the game and give the viewer a headache. That kind of shorthand turns information into a cartoon.

Politically Correct: Politically Incorrect Pendulum. In the last thirty-five years, mainstream America has become aware of the issues that had been raised by human rights advocates and others for decades. Their awareness comes not from a change of heart, but from laws and regulations. Racial and gender harassment and discrimination are no longer legally sanctioned. One may wish to smoke, but others have the right to breathe clean air. By the late 1980s these new practices had become categorized as "politically correct," PC by those who had trouble adjusting to the concept of equality and by college kids who liked the jargon. By the late 1990s the military was expected to be blind to gays. In 1999, a Fortune 500 company (Hewlett Packard) named a woman CEO for the first time. A woman commanded a space flight for the first time.

Things have changed. One is not allowed to harm other people's health and has to stand outside to smoke a cigarette or cigar. The racial, gender, and language minority population in the United States is not only growing, but it is beginning to develop a middle class of people that the majority find as peers in professional environments. Once it became clear that this adjustment really did mean a lifestyle change for those who were not interested in being PC, the cultural shift became threatening. Most Americans are pleased with the changes, think they are long overdue, and that, in fact, we even have some more distance to travel before equality is a fact for all Americans. Others feel at risk and are triggering a backlash. This backlash comes in the form of repealing affirmative action laws, claiming that we have already solved the country's racial problems. The backlash is also manifest at one extreme in the right-wing Patriot movement, and at the other, but nevertheless harmful, in those who think it is funny to be as crude and un-PC as possible in the media and in life. Movies like the 1998 film *Something About Mary* are an example. Young audiences found it hilariously funny that, through a series of bizarre events, Mary ended up with semen as a hair conditioner.

Another example is *American History X* released in 1998. This movie's lead character first conveys his bigotry through the symbolism of smoking. He blows smoke in the face of the black characters. This racial gesture is just the beginning. The lead character has a huge tattoo of a swastika on his chest. He takes off his shirt to show it whenever he wants to show power. At the end of the film, there appears to be some shift of position taken in a scene in the bathroom where he covers the swastika on his bare chest and seems to ask himself what he has done. But what message is left with the viewer? The more important question is to what extent the new generation of entertainers, eager to prove that they can be novel—that is, politically incorrect—is fueling fascism with fashion.[55] In 1999 MGM released *Tea with Mussolini*. The film is billed as a money maker.[56] What if flirting with fascism moves the mindset from fantasy to fact? And the media never tell us it is coming. What happens then to our culture?

Another manifestation of the backlash to political correctness is to want instant justice and to blame the government if it does not happen. Part of the price we pay for a democratic society is the constitutional right to be considered innocent until proven guilty. In cases where people lose patience, this principle is sometimes forgotten. Accusations are seen equal to guilt.

According to Mark Potok of the Southern Poverty Law Center, "The public doesn't know some of the news about the radical right's intent because of the fact that, in our judicial system, you're not guilty until the crime is committed. Before that, it's an idea, not a story. I think an instructive case is the Oklahoma City bombing. If Timothy McVeigh had been caught two weeks before that bomb went off, he would have been in every city in this country, save Oklahoma City, a story on page B4. Maybe he wouldn't have been on television at all. That's the reality of the news business."[57]

Potok adds, "I just finished putting together for this past April 19 [1998] a list of 24–25 major terrorist conspiracies. These are conspiracies that have not gotten much press out there. Probably half of those cases contemplated the murders of 100 to 1,000 and, in one case, probably 10,000 people. These were real conspirators. They were amassing the money and weapons to do the acts they talked about doing. Obviously it's not news until it happens. It's much more difficult to make a conspiracy case than it is to make an actual violation case. So at the beginning of this year, there was a very large plot taken down in Illinois. It stretched to three other states to blow up the building I work in, and to assassinate Morris Dees, the SPLC's executive director. It got some press. It made the national news on one network for ninety seconds or so. There were a few other stories—mostly local news. Those men were charged with weapons violations—a conspiracy to illegally possess a machine gun. In fact, what they planned to do and were in the middle of doing was to arm a nitrate bomb or use an antitank missile to blow up this building where seventy people work, to assassinate Morris, to blow up the Anti-Defamation League, to blow up the Wiesenthal Center in Los Angeles, and they were talking about poisoning with cyanide the water supplies of four cities. They were on the way to acquiring all the materials they needed to do this. The FBI and the U.S. Attorney's office were faced with a difficult choice. Were they going to let these people go any further? When it became so dangerous that they decided that that wasn't ethical anymore, these people were arrested—on a weapons charge.

"What's happening now is that the leader has pleaded guilty to a weapons charge and if that person serves three to four years, I'll be surprised. The prosecutors are asking for twelve to fourteen years. The defense is asking for two years."

The public should know about situations like this. But with the current system for news, it falls between the cracks. That is scary.

A Shift in Identity

A shift in the identity given to audience by the media has also occurred. There are four reasons for this: (1) Reporters, as well as producers, screenwriters, editors, actors, and some media executives by and large, are not provided a rigorous liberal arts education useful to understanding the context and consequences for society of their work—socially, economically, or politically; (2) In addition, most members of the media have little experience living abroad in countries run by fascist dictators; consequently they have little appreciation of their role as a fourth estate in democratic culture; (3) The ego boost available to those in the media who see themselves as friends of the "powers that be" eclipses any understanding of the importance of addressing and empowering the public as citizens rather than anesthetizing them as audience; (4) Finally, the pressure to conform and to support the industry norm of treating the public as consumer (shopper), hopefully "super-consumer," is constant in an industry financed by advertising. Unfortunately, this results in magnifying one aspect of public life while screening out other aspects important to critical thinking, creativity and self-government.

As early as the mid-1970s, Nicholas Johnson, former FCC commissioner, highlighted this aspect of broadcasting. "They are selling you a way of life that involves consumption of goods; that is called, in a word, materialism. Perfectly respectable philosophy, and one that I would give one hour a month, like First Tuesday or something. I think American business ought to be able to go on television and expound the virtues of materialism, hedonism, and conspicuous consumption, and looking for value and meaning in life in things outside of yourself. I just don't think they ought to be on twenty hours a day doing it. Most of the issues involving TV news, and therefore investigative reporting by networks or local stations, come back to this commercial quality. The pressures or expenses; the pressures on what items can be covered, the fact that the news is busted up every few minutes, the length of time that's devoted to it."[58]

The constant bombardment of the public with commercials, the clever product placement, and program-length commercials aimed at children as well as adults reinforce the audience, essentially propagandizing. The end result is to create a compliant public whose principal goal in life is to buy. Family gatherings discuss what one plans to buy, or did buy. Work days are spent earning the money to buy. Every free hour is spent at the mall. Should one sit down by the TV (or now the Internet), be assured that you will be provided with a multitude of new commercials and invitations to buy things you are convinced that you need. There is no time left to be a citizen, and surely no time left to think through what the obsession with consumerism might mean for the rest of life. For example, there's no room to be creative because earning money is the bottom line. Not a problem, though, because one's brain has been so bombarded with disconnected strobe light bits of information that thinking is hardly understood, rarely practiced. Don't worry, the media will do your thinking for you.

Conclusion

What are the public reactions to being scared to death—traumatized by the media?

Some just turn it off. Ignore it. No need for a common microphone through which we can speak together. Kill your television. If the public view of the kind of news we get from the media is measured by what we turn on and off, studies give some sense of what is happening. In April 1998 Princeton Survey Research Associates did a phone survey and determined that 59 percent of adults watch television news on an average day. Media Dynamics also published a report in 1998 saying that the average family watches sixty hours of TV each week, of which 7.3 hours are talk/info/news magazines—that is a little over an hour a day. So nearly two-thirds of the American population sees a need for news and information programming on television. They will not kill their TV.

Others are becoming more aggressive in taking various media to court, daring to talk back to the industry. For example, a Michigan jury found "The Jenny Jones Show" negligent in the murder of a guest on the show when the guest was identified as a secret admirer of another guest, and three days after the taping in March 1995, the guest killed the admirer. The case was made that the television show provoked the incident.[59]

Perhaps a line between free speech and manipulation or maliciousness is being drawn. The difficulty here is that the media must be free from the manipulation of government and the courts. Finding the line between a responsible free media and one that shows no responsibility toward public interests is very difficult—and a matter never resolved. Little has been done yet to seriously address the major cultural problems resulting from a media that immobilizes the public. Books are written on the topic. Action within the industry or within the society to change the practice has not yet occurred.

Writer and producer Nat Segaloff cautions, "I would much rather have news shows that scare the public than news shows that calm the public. After all, news, by definition, is what's happening to change our world, not keep it the same. That is why I have no problem with CNBC's 'All Monica All the Time' coverage (although I didn't watch it) or Charles Grodin's obsession with O.J. Simpson. Dictators rise to power because nobody scrutinizes them while there's still time to stop them; for that, we depend on a free press."[60]

Segaloff continues, "If people shut down their mental system these days, it's because newsgathering is so much more efficient and we are able to see so much more about our world that we find ourselves unable to process it all. Dr. Helen Caldicott—the Australian pediatrician who was a leading anti-nuclear activist in the '70s and '80s—called it "psychic numbing," and although she has fallen from sight, the syndrome has not."

Being anxious and fearful about the "real world" contributes to the psychic numbing that has us believing that we cannot counter these negative influences on our culture. Will Americans just remain immobilized and numb? Will we sit idle, or will we rise to the occasion and insist on an end to the media gatekeeping that poisons our system?

Chapter 4

Why Is This Happening?
Who Is the Gatekeeper?

> The concentration of broadcasting power now in the hands of
> so few people is unhealthy. . . . The fact that there are
> no regularly appearing broadcast news sources from the left
> and very few from the center to counteract the scores of
> those from the right is not only un-Amercian,
> it's just plain stupid programming.
>
> *Nat Segaloff, Hollywood writer and producer[1]*

Stealing our future! Killing our culture! Scaring us to death! It does not just happen on its own. There must be something or someone behind such unwise use of our airwaves. Once it is clear how this happens, we can set our own course for a more responsible media future.

Gatekeeping is basically determining who does and who does not get to exercise freedom of speech in the public media, and who hears or is deprived of hearing all points of view on topics aired, all available information and ideas.

It is determining what does and what does not make it onto the public airwaves. It is making judgments about what is good and what is bad. It is allowing the dissemination of what one likes and censoring what one does not like. It is those in power restricting the airing and exchange of ideas, philosophies, and information. Sometimes it is overt and very obvious. Sometimes it is very subtle and based on bigotry. Sometimes it is due to apathy. Sometimes it is based on greed.

It colors the bottom line of what people believe to be true.

There is a wide range of culprits who might do the gatekeeping. (Actually, one can blame us all as individuals if it comes down to not always acting to support what is fair and oppose what is not—that is, not speaking up by calling the media and advertisers. Maybe more important than dealing with broadcasters and advertisers, we as individuals have forgotten how to make democratic government work. We just give all our rights away without any objection.)

Let us look at the actions taken by principal institutions in our culture to screen out a segment of reality for the general public and, as a result of that action, to control our culture.

Some people blame the media professionals themselves. Others, the consolidation of ownership. Others, the government. Others, the advertisers. Others, the rating companies. Others say it is the public's own fault that programming is stealing our future, killing our culture, and scaring us to death. Let us look at each of those culprits. There are six major gatekeepers.

Media Professionals

Hundreds of thousands of people work to keep various aspects of the media afloat. They fit into some general job classifications and have a wide range of views on the state of the industry. It is not uncommon to hear views like the following:

New York theatrical producer Arthur D'Lugoff says, "The media only likes to cover the people with the most famous names. They give an enormous amount of space to sports—free. For theater, they give nothing. For movies, they give plenty. A lot of stuff just doesn't get out as it should. All in all, I think the emphasis has been wrong on how we try to communicate with people. It all has to do with making money. The bottom line is greed. Greed has been here since the beginning of time. It's gotten so far out of hand that it's ridiculous."[2]

Nat Segaloff, comments, "Let me raise the issue of whether the television industry is interested in producing creative work in the first place. I've always felt—and have seen little to change my mind—that the whole purpose of programming is to keep people from going to the bathroom between commercials."[3]

Janine Jackson, research director of Fairness and Accuracy in Reporting in New York City, noted, "Misrepresentation and distortion is happening more in the topics that are reported than in the stories."[4] She feels that many important issues are going unreported while more sensationalized reports are being told. "There is a major conflict between the goals of media and the purpose of journalism. The goal of media is to make money. The purpose of journalism is to provide a public service."

Let us examine some of the gatekeeper positions in entertainment and the news media.

It is not uncommon for filmmakers to use their craft explicitly to make a point. This invariably generates controversy, more publicity, and likely more success for the film. Some are more obvious than others. Some try harder to touch the chords of the culture more than others. Michael Moore, creator of the series "TV Nation" and of the film *Roger and Me*, said, "The best way to air one's convictions is to produce high-quality films that carry the message."[5] Moore explained in the interview that art should be about entertainment, but that maybe some art can be about doing good and changing things. Moore said, "With *Roger and Me* I made a conscious decision to make a documentary that people who don't go to documentaries would watch, and I don't know if that had been done before." Moore has surprised the establishment. They never believed he would get his films distributed. The people he interviewed said things they would not ordinarily have said in public. For example, Phil Knight, CEO of Nike, let Moore interview him. Knight rambled on about how he didn't care if fourteen-year-olds worked in his factories in Indonesia. Moore refused to cut the segments, saying, "I'm not going to take anything out of the film. I didn't tell him to say those things."[6] The result is that the negative PR has caused Nike to reform its policies on child labor.

Another example of a controversial filmmaker is Oliver Stone. In *The Devil's Disciple*, one of playwright George Bernard Shaw's characters, General Burgoyne, notes that history will say whatever the victors want it to say. In the high-tech media culture, one might add that the interpretation of history is whatever the dominant media artists say it is. Stone has a significant impact on how the public views a number of important cultural and historical events. For example, consider his films *Born on the Fourth of July*, *Platoon*, *Nixon*, *Natural Born Killers*, and *JFK*. Stone's *JFK* is particularly revealing about who he thinks plotted the assassination of President Kennedy. The establishment has lambasted him for this portrayal. He has been criticized by many for the stark antiwar, anti-Vietnam venture influences of *Born on the Fourth of July* and *Platoon*, and for the devastatingly negative picture of Nixon and his Republican cadre in *Nixon*. Nonetheless, many in the public interpret and understand the people and events of the twentieth century as he has portrayed them in his films. Interpreting contemporary history has always proved more difficult than the interpretation of ancient history, which may explain why Stone has become such a lighting rod. Then, again, if visual artists do not deal with contemporary history, who will, in an era where the visual certainly carries more weight than the printed?

An example of Stone's underlying beliefs inserted into his films is the statement he made to the National Press Club about his Vietnam War film, *Platoon*. He said, "The ultimate corruption was, of course, President Johnson sending only the poor and the uneducated to the (Vietnam) war—in fact, practicing class warfare wherein the middle and upper classes could avoid the war by going to college or paying a psychiatrist. I am sure to this day that if the middle and upper classes had gone to Vietnam, their mothers and fathers, the politicians and businessmen would have ended that war a hell of a lot sooner."[7]

Steven Spielberg is another prominent producer who has messages in his films. For example, he has used *The Color Purple, Schindler's List,* and *Amistad* to tell parts of history that have generally been omitted from the textbooks. *The Color Purple* and *Amistad* both bring life to African American history, presenting materials omitted from the history books and novels written by those mirroring the dominant culture. *Schindler's List* is the story of a German industrialist who saved scores of German Jews who otherwise would have died in Nazi concentration camps, just one of a number of similar events overlooked in most mainstream historical works. The power of Spielberg's films gives life to these untold stories.

Tom Kingdon, producer of popular and award-winning documentaries and sitcoms for the BBC, describes the typical producer who has not reached the stage where it is possible to exercise the independence exercised by Michael Moore, Oliver Stone, and Steven Spielberg. He described this common practice: "A producer does not gauge your idea on whether it is 'good' objectively. A producer judges it according to whether or not it suits their needs, and if they, subjectively, are excited by it. And, there are the industry executives to whom the producers are accountable. Progressive ideas, especially new and untried ones, are subject to a great deal of supervision by these executives."[8]

Nat Segaloff describes the death or life of program ideas in television as follows: "I have never found that there is any eagerness to produce new and creative work anyway. TV is all about giving people old material in a new form. After all, anything that is new or creative may take a while to find an audience, and the competition for viewers is so intense—what with a hundred channels—that shows today have barely three weeks to prove themselves before being pulled in favor of something else. Not only is the attrition wasteful, but TV executives no longer have the luxury of allowing a program to stay on the schedule until it attracts viewers. And even if it does, they will then change its night and time in order to bolster some other show that's in trouble. In that case, both shows generally drown. The appalling thing is that everybody knows this, but nobody stops it."[9]

Segaloff continues, "In my experience, program green lights are granted by programming executives who look at six things:

1. Will the show fit into our schedule—that is, do we have enough similar shows that we can create a prime–time programming block that will keep viewers watching for three hours?

2. Will it attract the audience that advertisers want?
3. Can the show be produced for the license fee that we can afford, or will it have to be deficit financed?
4. Can we charge advertisers enough to pay for it?
5. If it is a hit and runs several seasons, will it become too expensive to produce, causing us to lose money (as happened with "Seinfeld," "Cheers," and "ER")?
6. Does the show have spin-off, merchandising and ancillary media potential?"

"Notice how none of those has much to do with whether the show is any good."

So, is the writer or producer the gatekeeper? Or might they themselves be screened out by the industry's criterion for making money?

In key positions in the news business, things are not all that different.

Local television program directors now have limited choices to make other than those involving the news. Most of their programming comes in directly from their network. Valerie Sheehy, program director at WHDH Channel 7 Boston, notes, "From a news perspective we try to abide by a dicta of good taste and journalistic integrity. In this day and age 'almost anything goes.' I would almost wish there were more restrictions. I'm talking about the industry overall, not necessarily WHDH. I don't feel restricted. We do try, obviously, not to schedule adult oriented programs when children are likely to view them, but that's more common sense than restriction."[10]

The first hurdle in local news coverage is the person who decides whether or not something will be covered. A 1990 study of local news gatekeeping examined how stories are selected for the TV news from a pool of potential stories. The first screening is done by the assignment editor. Some 77.5 percent of potential stories never made it past that point; 57.8 percent of those that survived did air—56.6 percent of them issue oriented stories, 66.7 percent unexpected event items, and 53.7 percent entertainment items. Many times the ones that aired did so, in part, because they required less preparation work—less research, less expertise.[11]

For example, law enforcement stories are easy because everyone is already at a specific site where there are likely good visuals and not just talking heads. Politicians set up events complete with photo ops. Issue stories are more abstract, require more knowledge from the reporter, and require more time away from the newsroom to gather facts and shoot the video. It is always easier to be passive and put on the stories that are the easiest. Besides, there are many complications if one takes initiative, including the lack of institutions like the police or the courts to hide behind if someone wants to sue for liability.

Local TV station management still sets the overall guidelines for operation, but they do this in close consultation with their financial advisors. This sets an overall tone. Management does not monitor each individual story. The producers usually decide how to cover a story—who should be interviewed, what questions to ask, what camera shots to take. Sometimes a reporter decides those things.

The reporter gets the interviews and writes the story. Producing the news involves collaboration. The editor must put the reporters' video footage together in the right sequence to support and capture the producer's story in a cohesive and aesthetically satisfactory way. Deadline pressures are constant. Because the editor was not actually at the shoot, inaccuracies can creep in. Many media professionals make the decisions that contribute to broadcasting the news. Obviously, each person's opinions are inevitably a factor.[12]

A producer/writer for local televison news explained that when out on a news shoot, the reporter is aware of the "angle" given a story by the station director and that guides the questions. However, this view may conflict with that of the producer. The producer has final say in the editing room. Every story contains someone's personal bias. For example, at one New England TV station, a reporter was directed to find a doctor who would say that homeopathic medicine is for a bunch of quacks. The reporter found that most doctors interviewed said that homeopathic medicine can be good when used in conjunction with scientific medicine. The program director did not accept the answer and the reporter was told to keep looking for the predetermined quote.

All these constraints—financing pressures, management views, producer and reporter views, editor ideas on a story's content or slant contribute significantly to screening out the full information. In addition, deadlines must be met if the news is to be broadcast on time. Anything taking too long to research or shoot or edit will not work. The segments must be brief and provide good visuals. If the point of the story cannot be made in a few brief sentences, it will not work, nor will talking heads work. Controversy that might produce a lawsuit is sometimes deemed too risky to cover. Some things should be screened out; after all, viewers have limited time too. The problem lies in the rationale behind the judgment calls about which information is included and which excluded. Sometimes these calls are based on what the public needs to know to maintain a high quality of life in a quality environment for living and working. More often they are based on what brings the highest ratings and biggest profits to the TV station. And other times they are based on what can be produced most easily and the fastest to convenience a pressured staff or to meet a tight deadline.

The change in the self-interests and values of the journalists themselves no doubt contribute to changes in news quality. Only in recent years have journalists moved directly from graduate school into jobs in major newsrooms. In years past, they came up through the ranks, gleaning a lot of experience and some wisdom along the way by working on local papers or in local radio and TV jobs. They covered local and state government. They shared a common experience with most Americans in local communities, watching, experiencing, and learning how a democratic system can work. Often today's young professionals come with upper middle-class biases and little understanding of how the stories they cover fit into a larger cultural and global context. For example, in 1993 President Clinton proposed to raise taxes some $305 billion. Most of the tax increase came from the very wealthy. In this country, the wealthiest 10 percent of the population holds some 90 percent of the nation's wealth. The 15 million poorest Americans got a tax break through an expanded earned income tax credit. The middle class paid no more than $200 per family in increased taxes. Yet, based on the media coverage, 70 percent of Americans thought Clinton had raised taxes on the middle class. Why? Two reasons: First, the reporters didn't understand the demographics of the country because nothing in their educational program had given them this background. Second, the national anchors, top reporters, and producers determining the orientation of the story were nearly all earning salaries well over $75,000 themselves, placing them in the wealthy category whose taxes did increase. Because they believe themselves to be middle class, (not realizing that median household income was less than $40,000 in the late 1990s) it is easy to totally fail to see the extent of their privilege in comparison with those around them. Only 15 percent of American households earned over $75,000. They had no sense of how far their income was above the median household income. The problem lies with the journalists' education.

The university programs that educate the next generation of media professionals have changed over the last two decades. As liberal arts education has fallen out of fashion in the United States and complex and hypnotic new technologies have been created, students of journalism and media arts no longer follow the footsteps of many of the journalists and creative artists who have preceded them. Their interest is to "play with the toys." A solid grounding in public policy and sociology and history and economics had fallen by the wayside in favor of a superficiality that should embarrass many of the institutions turning out the graduates. Without being educated to understand the big picture, how messages fit within a context, and how one creates and sustains a desirable quality of life for one's community and one's world, these young professionals miss 90 percent of the opportunity placed before them as communicators.

Teaching the techniques of writing and producing is insufficient. It is not enough to know how to produce a high-rated headline story that has impact, is timely, and is close to home. It is not enough to ferret out the conflict, the unusual, the current. It is not enough simply to remember the five "ws" and the one "h"—who, what, when where, why, and how. Learning the little tricks of how to write well are but a small part of learning to assume a job carrying out the responsibilities of the fourth estate. Of course, the story must have a dramatic unity—be a completed circle of climax, cause, and effect. Of course, it is essential that there be good writing—clear, concise, simple, to the point. Use strong nouns and verbs. Of course, top-quality production is essential. Of course, understanding the technology revolution is essential. But even if you accept the notion that the job is to inform, not explain, and that the audio and visuals must impact, this is all fill, presentation, form.

There is very little content.

Certainly the First Amendment requires that there be no censorship of content—but we are mistaken to interpret this as "no content." For media professionals to decide what content goes into their programs, they need some understanding of the role of the fourth estate in a democratic system. They need some examples from history and contemporary global situations to illustrate when a democratic free press functions, and when it does not. They need to understand the consequences of having media who ignore their charge. Their syllabus needs to introduce both journalism students and students heading toward entertainment media to the social, economic, and political world in which they will operate. Students need some understanding of how history affects the present, of how major themes—like environmental changes or hazardous materials— affect contemporary life. To report on most topics today, students need to understand that the present situation is the result of laws and regulations—and these are political decisions. Consequently, they need to understand how the democratic process is designed to operate. They also need to understand where it does not work right, and exactly what mechanisms exist to change things. Students who will work in a global economy need some understanding of what exists beyond the borders of the United States. They need to understand cultures, economics, and politics of different parts of the world—at least at an elementary level. They need to understand how individuals have brought about enormous changes globally—from Martin Luther King Jr. to Bill Gates. Students need to understand what kind of substantive and process information an informed citizenry needs to know. It would be useful to provide them examples of how such information can be contained in news, entertainment, and advertising. Mass communication students today often leave school knowing a great deal about technique, but little or nothing about the standards and criteria for selecting program content.

The result is contentless news, and contextless entertainment. It is sabotaging the First Amendment. What good is free speech if the speech has no content?

What the young reporters are taught is important because 45 percent of today's journalists are young—between twenty-five and thirty-four. By contrast only 28 percent of people in other professions in the civilian workplace are in this young age bracket. Other professions have an older workforce.[13] Women account for 53 percent of new reporters hired, but 65 percent of long-term journalists are men. The same is true for editors. Part of the problem of dumbed-down news is that the young news gatherers, doing their very best, are acting on their experience. They just do not know how else to do it. It is not their fault that their education is, all too often, pitiful.

Those who survive long term in the profession are in much better shape, because they learn along the way—unless they are too quickly cocooned into the Washington press corps or one small corner of Hollywood.

To be sure, change comes rapidly in today's world. A good reporter (and a good entertainment professional) has trouble mastering all society's topics. No one could possibly master every subject that they might encounter: things change too quickly. For example, former *USA Today* reporter Mark Potok looks back on his experience. "I don't see it as any kind of conspiracy by the news gatherers or even as an irresponsibility. I was very interested in the topic [the radical right and hate group movement] as a reporter, and I was not able to stay on top of what was happening all across the country, even with the power of *USA Today* behind me. There was a full-fledged library. Money was no object. Any kind of research was fine. Maybe if I had been assigned to cover the radical right and nothing else. . . . I was running around after tornadoes. I was a fairly high-profile reporter and was in the media a lot."[14] Even with a defined interest and experience in the business, the pressures to cover whatever arises, coupled with the deadlines, means it is not possible to do in-depth investigative reporting as things are presently structured.

Covering elections in the media also falls short of its potential, because pressures and deadlines make it easier not to do the substantive work. Just fall back on some commissioned polls indicating who is ahead—who *was* ahead when the poll was done.

Yet, with all the easily accessible materials on the Internet, and the speed of communicating both video and voice, one would think a top-rated educational curriculum could make it possible to ease these burdens for the next generation of media professionals. Concurrently, educators could demonstrate how both newsrooms and entertainment professionals might access whatever is needed to cover timely subjects intelligently.

In 1991, when the Soviet Union split apart and the former Eastern Bloc countries became democratic countries, representatives came to a New Century Policies conference sponsored by the John D. and Catherine T. MacArthur Foundation held in the Netherlands to learn how to cover democratic elections. The seminars were led by representatives from the media in England, Germany, the Netherlands, the United States, and Australia. The debate among the participants highlighted the difficulty in sorting through the volumes of events and piles of information to provide the appropriate coverage. All too often, "appropriate" is based on the stereotypes that may appeal to an audience, rather than on the substance of the events.

For example, as alluded to earlier, election coverage is often reduced to "horse-race coverage." The media will tell you who is ahead. Unfortunately, you will not know nearly as much about the contestants as you would if they were, in fact, describing horses in a race. The reports are issued in polls. Margaret Douglas, chief political advisor to the BBC, told the East European journalists to look closely before relying on polls. "When you report on polls, you must bear in mind that all they tell you is what someone said they might do yesterday. They never tell you what they will do tomorrow."[15]

In addition to the judgment calls debated by the journalists concerning polls, the issues surrounding an "advocacy press" were also debated. In Eastern Europe as in the Soviet Union, the custom was for a particular station or paper to openly advocate a given political position. For example, in Russia's first-ever election of a president in 1991, the television was still state-controlled and did not offer broad and equitable coverage of all the candidates. The print media, experiencing a taste of freedom, was delighted to choose sides. *The Independent*, a new paper paid for by the Moscow City Council, displayed a bar of photos of six candidates. The photo on the left, the largest photo, was of Boris Yeltsin. As one glanced to the right across the page, each photo was smaller than the last until you got to the tiniest, least-popular candidate on the far right of the page.[16] That is advocacy! The U.S. media coverage, grounded in the First Amendment, in theory is objective in covering all candidates in elections. One scarcely sees bias displayed as overtly as in the Russian paper. However, the same gatekeeping makes it difficult for the public to reach decisions on self-government matters. Often the horse-race coverage totally obfuscates the real election issues, leading the public to forget that important issues will be decided by whoever is in office. At other times, some candidates are covered and others are either omitted or addressed by label ("activist") rather than title ("deputy attorney general" or "state Democratic committeewoman"). Journalists nearly always fail to focus on the credentials useful to the specific office. For example, to be elected to an executive position, one should be able to listen, then make decisions, delegate, and monitor performance. To be elected to a legislative position, one should be able to be a compelling public speaker, to organize support, to lobby, to argue well and persuade colleagues. The press corps has, in recent times, missed much of this, just as it has missed the essence of positions on pending legislation and past performance. It has missed the assessment of where a candidate stands based on where their major contributors stand. It sees election season as scandal hunting season. Certainly, some public behavior is atrocious and must be exposed, but, in the last analysis, it is the American people who are hurt if government and the media are focused only on the sideshows. Journalism schools less and less teach the difference between reporting news stories and covering the democratic process—talking not to an audience but to participants. The journalists themselves may not know how candidates are selected and how campaign budgets are developed. They likely do not know how government budgets are developed, or how bills become law. It is little surprise, therefore, that journalists do a poor job of informing the public when, where, and how to have a say in forthcoming policy decisions. Journalists have been pushed toward covering the infotainment that obsesses about sex scandals and personal lives. Sometimes the entertainment media's coverage brings more information to the voter than does the news media. For example, films like *Wag the Dog*, *Primary Colors*, and *The Insider* all convey messages to the audience. The result is a total eclipse of coverage about very important decisions that are made by the departments of government every day.

Lives have been lost over the right to vote in many countries of the world. Too many Americans have not been motivated by the media to appreciate our opportunity to directly participate in the determination of government leaders and policies. Some of us would not understand why, in the spring of 1999, an MIT student from Israel left school for two weeks so he could fly home for the election and stay for a runoff if one were needed. He knew every vote was important because the leadership of Israel can determine the direction of peace in the Middle East. In the United States the problem is worse than whether there is too much horse race coverage. It has become whether the media will even cover the elections. As stated by Dave Berkman, host of "Media Talk," a talk show in Milwaukee, "Arguably, the most significant senatorial race in the nation (two of four congressional seats in their [the Milwaukee TV media market] coverage area were in tight play, along with both houses of the state legislature and [there was] a gubernatorial candidate raising significant issues about the conduct of his incumbent opponent. No legitimate news operation would have reduced campaign coverage to the peripheral significance it was accorded on Milwaukee TV.

"Case in point: On the 6 PM Channel 4 newscast the Saturday before the election, the clueless—but ever perky and always smiling—Lynise Weeks and Ann Ballentine gave no indication a state and national election was looming just three days later. There was, however, sufficient time allotted to Bill Taylor, who told us about a successful teenage-run Halloween charity event."[17] The problem is not the Halloween event; in fact that is good local news. The problem is ignoring the events crucial to our common future. Those elections determine such policies as whether schools or stadiums get priority, whether highways or the environment are funded, whether cost of prescriptions or subsidies to industry are protected.

The excuse of "having no choice" between two bad candidates is made out of ignorance. Similarly, the excuse that the subgovernment deals with media moguls and others with big money, thereby making the voters superfluous, is also unacceptable. The comments, all too often, are true. Nonetheless, things will never improve if voters—who still have the law on their side—abandon ship. The ship will sink, and the population will be left with anarchy, or—worse yet—power grabs by media moguls and the like.

Other practices influence the journalist's coverage of news.

Paying journalists huge fees for speaking engagements colors their judgment and ability to report stories independently. Howard Kurtz, the author of *Hot Air: All Talk, All the Time*, says, "The public has a right to expect that those who pontificate for a living are not in financial cahoots with the industries and lobbies they analyze on the air. It's become common for journalists to think the speaking circuit is their dessert." When a journalist receives $20,000 for a lecture to the Group Health Association of America, or $15,000 from the Amerian Medical Association, it should be known by the public. Some journalists do very well on the lecture circuit. For example, Rush Limbaugh earns about $25 million a year, Howard Stern $7 million, and Larry King $2 million. Sam Donaldson and Ted Koppel earn about $2 million a year in fees, Howard Kurtz wrote in *Washington Post Magazine.*[18]

Deciding what to cover and how to cover it all depends on whom the journalist sees as the client. Is it their employer, the subject of the news coverage, or the readers and viewers?

Dr. Peter Phillips, professor at Sonoma State University in California, is director of an advocacy project called Project Censored.[19] The project has, for some years, produced compelling studies of what is not covered in the news. Among the stories screened out are those about powerful people in both public and private bureaucracies, about those who are making important decisions that affect millions of people, about important issues such as socio-economics, the national economy, environmental issues—and decisions taken about those issues by the major corporations. Phillips cited three main reasons for misrepresentation and distortion:

- There is a tendency for media outlets not to want to cover news stories that negatively affects their major advertisers. In addition, the news story selection process tends to focus on news stories that appeal to upper-middle-class spenders. These are the target market for many advertisers. So the stories that fit the interests, biases, prejudices, of upper middle-class people will tend to get more coverage than news stories that would threaten, upset, or in any way cause these target markets to tune out.
- Newsrooms have been downsized with corporate mergers. With fewer reporters covering stories, while working under intense deadline pressures, there is a trend building that requires journalists to contact PR offices of government and business to get stories. Half to two-thirds of news stories today are pre-written by public relations specialists.
- Eleven major corporations control the majority of radio, television, and the print media in the United States. The people who run these corporations have a point of view. It is only natural that they will tend to favor news stories that tend to agree with their own views. These eleven corporations have about 150 director, the media elite of the world, who have interlocking directorships with thirty-six other Fortune 500 companies.[20] (And the AOL/Time Warner merger announced in January 2000 further consolidates media control adding the new element of control of computer outlets.)

Aside from the jobs in the media and the opportunities for gatekeeping available as people make the judgment calls necessary to do their job, there is another kind of gatekeeping in the media. It is stems from the obsession with image—images as portrayed in people and in format.

For example, in the news business, the latest fad for stations is to hire consultants for their news programs. Increase the ratings. Make the news more appealing. WCVB Channel 5 has long been the Boston media market's news leader. Natalie Jacobson, along with Chet Curtis, are the news anchors. Natalie Jacobson revealed how strongly she feels about the changes in news coverage in an interview with the local newspaper. "There's pressure for stories to be quicker and shallower. Crime stories have elbowed aside exploration of issues."[21] Jacobson believes there are two factors contributing to this change: One is consultants whom she describes as "the chief villains . . . and . . . the worst things that have happened to television." Consultants now advise news directors across the United States on how their newscast should look. A

Boston Globe story on TV news stated, "Under the sway of consultants, newscasts have gotten glitzier in Boston and across the country."[22] The second influence Natalie Jacobson cites is competition with another local channel (Channel 7 WHDH, with a new management team that came in from Florida). That channel's belief appears to be that success is based on image, not content.

Over the last couple of decades, network station representatives have assumed more important roles, largely because program strategies have changed due to changes in revenue sources, regulation, program supply, and station competition. A package of research, promotion, and full marketing services provided by one network to its local affiliates advises that "rep programmers" from the network will come to present stations with a programming list ranked according to Nielsen share performance averages for a show. The list is finely tailored to eliminate anything for the "wrong" market demographic, and to evaluate those deemed most appropriate for competing with what the other channels run during that time slot. Along with this list, the rep gives the client audience projections. In this way, the networks offer "guidance" to local channels.

News consulting is something additional, to be financed by the local channels. The consultant suggests ways for the station to improve handling the behind-the-scenes work of gathering and processing the news for delivery. In addition, consultants advise on set design, camera presence, voice and delivery of the anchors, graphics, format, photography, and editing.[23]

The consultant's priority—image—is the vessel that supposedly holds the content—assuming, of course, that any room remains for real news content once the image game is won.

The obsession with image got its start in the entertainment end of the business. Whatever is critical to creating an image serves to make the success of some people and programs and destined to oblivion those who are just talented or have a message, but have no *image*. Access to local newsmakers is effectively screened out.

The impact created by lighting or music or camera angle is another part of image creation—in film as well as on TV. The effect is different depending on whether color or black-and-white film or video is used. Does one use grainy film or high-quality film? How are characters dressed? What are the little symbolic gestures that contribute to image creation—blowing smoke in someone's face? What is done with costuming and hairstyle? What archetypes and symbols and images are evoked by the media artist at every step of this process?

A very obvious but less discussed aspect of image creation is format. The industry pays deference to those formats seen to bring high ratings, which are the definition of success. In entertainment, for example, it was reported in *Entertainment Weekly* that one of the most successful formats (in 1998) was group comedy.[24] There is something about a group of people—friends, family, coworkers—that makes us laugh. One of the most successful shows currently on television is NBC's "Friends." For the week of December 14–20, 1998, "Friends" held tightly to the number three spot with a total of 23.7 million viewers.[25] The program targets the twenty-to-thirty-plus age group, people who lead similar lives either as affluent young urban professionals—"yuppies"—or as those who aspire to this lifestyle (in a fictitious New York where not one nonwhite lives).

One of the most striking TV entertainment formats at present is the sex and terror shows targeted toward a teenage audience, including programs like the slasher flick *Scream* and "Buffy the Vampire Slayer" on the WB network. WB targets all its programs toward teens.[26] "Felicity," a show about a young woman just off to college, follows "Buffy" on WB. On January 20, 1999, the night of the president's State of the Union speech, the Nielsen ratings report indicated that "Felicity" combined with "Buffy" to generate the biggest Tuesday audience for the network since the start of the 1998–1999 season.[27]

Many young artists see the process of being turned into images, or icons, as the key to their success. For example, if a band wants to "make it," the image-making process gives them the exposure they need to rise to the top in popularity, and, of course, to be a revenue maker for the industry that sells stars. James Chiello, a band leader completing his university degree in media arts at Emerson College, says about the image factory, "They're no different from fast food. We have real food at home that our moms cook. It takes time and preparation with careful ingredients. It's rich and thick with nutrients, different from the fast food market, where it's made to give the same effect, but processed and comes out of a can."[28] The Spice Girls are a prime example of a band who was given an image, music to sing, clothes and makeup to wear, lines to say, and perhaps some silicone to sport. The result was huge success with albums and a feature film, making them a successful product for the industry. Chiello continues: "Music and film are the two most powerful mediums. One can express anything they wish to express. They have the ability to attack one's emotions in a most powerful way, more powerfully, perhaps, than reality itself." He sees "image making" as the best way to have one's message heard. He continues, "Ideas and concepts bring us together. Regional music scenes across the nation become common. Large companies push everything all over the country and the globe. Image is very important."

If he can be remade into an image, James Chiello will become the rock star he has always wanted to be. If you are transformed into a star, then you may see image making as a positive form of gatekeeping, selecting you from all the rest. If you are not so transformed, you may view gatekeeping as a way of screening out talent without the luck to be noticed.

The art of creating and packaging images is what the media emphasizes today. And this promises to be an infant stage of the industry. Imagine the potential for symbol and image creation and manipulation when digital imaging reaches its full potential. The clever animation and image creation portrayed in "Ally McBeal" and TV commercials is but the tip of the iceberg. Virtual-reality theme parks already exist in Japan—fake beaches, for example. The media have created fake sex, fake airplane flights with crashes, fake travel. Such fun, the toys through which one can recreate and redefine reality. The decades ahead promise rapid expansion of this kind of image making. The technology is ready. The technicians are eager. The industry sees new and lucrative possibilities for entertainment.

Where will people go to find out about the reality of the real world—the one with hopes and dreams for opportunity in society, for absence of war and oppression, for education and family? How can the next generation distinguish between fact and fiction, ideas and images? Can the news be counted on to really tell us what we need to know is happening because it affects our lives? Will entertainment tell us about the amazing things human beings really have accomplished and the full dimension of the worlds we can explore? When we want to be entertained by a romance or an adventure or a mystery, will we have any ability to segregate the messages that are fantasy from the world one must return to when the set is switched off? Or will all that be screened out?

The answers to many of these questions will depend on whether those with the power to ensure that these new vessels being created for communication become an end in themselves, or whether any space is left for content, of all sorts. It is a question of whether free speech remains possible or just the symbol thereof in the form of a giant microphone through which nothing travels.

We have dealt with media professionals as gatekeepers. Let us examine the gatekeeping roles of media owners.

The Owners

The owners of stations and networks increasingly are blamed as the principal gatekeepers. There are two ways in which owners might influence media access and media content by screening out some of the viewpoints represented in our culture. First, the owners themselves might approve or veto certain content—or their employees might self-censor programs, anticipating trouble from the top. Second, media ownership is now so concentrated that there is very little opportunity for diverse viewpoints to be presented.

It is true that owners sometimes pay little attention to the programming decisions for their networks or stations, choosing to focus their attention on the financial health of the corporation. This, of course, means that only shows that command high advertising rates are acceptable. In itself, that is a form of censorship.

Rupert Murdoch, the owner of News Corp whom "Frontline" called a modern–day global media pirate, for example, has a reputation for finding the lowest common denominator in programming in order to attract the maximum number of readers or viewers and therefore make the most profits. His approach has been to reach people's emotions and to catch their attention with the bizarre. He has worked hard to personalize his links to those in power, and his media have been used as a tool both to elect rulers and to throw them out of office in Australia, the United States, and Great Britain. He placed expediency before free speech when he threw the BBC news off of his STAR satellite northern tier coverage over China because the Chinese government disliked the BBC version of the news. No problem. No controversy. Play mandarin music instead. This heavy-handed ownership illustrates one way in which owners exercise their power to screen out what they do not wish aired—or what people whose power they depend on do not want aired.

Another example of owner gatekeeping is the way the ABC network handled a story on Disney's lax screening of employees for child sex offenses. Disney owns ABC, which dropped the story.[29] Critics point out that if this had been a story about the Catholic Church or a school district dealing with pedophiles, the story would have gotten top billing. The question is, who made the decision to drop it? Was it Disney telling ABC to drop it or was it ABC employees who, remembering who signs their paychecks, deciding not to offend the parent company?

On the other hand, Mark Potok, formerly a reporter for *USA Today*, did not feel the heavy hand of owners in his work.[30] "I've never had an experience of being censored. I've had a hard time getting things into the paper, but the considerations were either legal or entertainment considerations—it wasn't interesting enough or it was your talent, you hadn't pulled it off well enough. The new *USA Today* managing editor is out of Stanford Business School and there are more high-earner interests—not much interest in poor people's stories. On the other hand, the paper is weirdly progressive about diversity issues. That paper has a virtual rule about photos on front page—it will not only be white males on the front page. They put out a people of color experts' guide, so you quote all kinds of people. Gannett, the owner, also has a reputation as a union buster, sucking life out of small papers, but at *USA Today* the policy is as I said."

Potok makes another point about the perceived gatekeeping by media owners. Discussing the view that the media are scaring us to death, he said, "I don't know who said that 'frightened people are easier to govern'—it might have been Murrow. But my sense is that the media barons are not going out of their way to scare people. They are only doing everything they can to get attention from a jaded viewership. Tom Johnson of CNN told me that their ratings spike during world crises and that their problem, as programmers, is to keep people watching when there isn't a world crisis going on. A CNN salesperson later told me that the real problem is how to charge advertisers the same high rates they charge them during news spikes when there is not a news spike ["spike" refers to a ratings jump, not killing a news story as in print journalism]. Frightened people do not buy big ticket items like cars or computers or houses. They blow it on Coca-Cola and McDonald's." And of course, there are lots of advertising dollars for Coca-Cola and McDonald's.

As the examples illustrate, owners have the capability to mold their companies to fit their interests. Sometimes they exercise these powers, sometimes they do not. The heaviest influence weighs in when the financial profits are affected. But sometimes gatekeeping is based on the personal views of owners. When there are fewer owners, there are fewer views.

The consolidation of ownership has increased dramatically in recent years. The nation's major corporations have owned the major media outlets for some years now. General Electric and Westinghouse, both major nuclear weapons contractors, are at the top of the list. GE owns NBC and CNBC, Bravo, American Movie Classics, A&E, the History Channel and E! Westinghouse owns CBS. The Walt Disney Company owns ABC, the Disney Channel, ESPN, and Touchstone Television. Time Warner owns CNN, Cinemax, HBO, Comedy Central, the TBS Superstation, and TNT. In January 2000, a new kind of communications industry monopoly was launched. America Online acquired Time Warner in a merger worth some $350 billion. AOL, the Internet company with about twenty million subscribers bought access to consent delivery. Time Warner enters the rapidly growing realm of E-commerce.

The consolidation that has occurred in recent years even screens out many who once could afford to own media outlets, not to mention the general public who must yell and scream and behave in bizarre ways to even hope for a few seconds of access to their airwaves. Since the public owns the airwaves, legally, perhaps the full spectrum of public views are entitled to a voice, legally.

Critical to operating a democratic society is multiple media ownership. When the Soviet Union dissolved and the Russian republic came into being in 1991, one of the first efforts rigorously pursued was to make certain that multiple ownership of the media existed in Russia. Multiple ownership makes it much more difficult to shut the media down in a coup, or to provide distorted views of events. Curiously, those of us in the West who have seen the values of multiple ownership in twentieth century history are the very ones who are tolerating the reverse in our own culture.

Publisher Bernard Mann of Mann Media Inc. talks about the experience he and his friends had owning radio and television stations in the past:

> A lot of companies got out of the business because they didn't like the fact that it wasn't very predictable. A lot of companies became public companies because the volatility was gone. There's much more predictability. From the listeners' standpoint, it means that the companies that own these large stations are changing the face of what they're providing. They now are much more profit-oriented, not investing in the local market, trying to do as many things on a mass basis.
>
> More and more stations are now programmed not from the community they're located in but from some central location. So (on radio) instead of more news, there's less and less. The news departments are something that cost and they keep trying to shave costs. The owners of the stations are not susceptible to the community. They're susceptible to Wall Street. Wall Street doesn't care if there's a story that happens in Greensboro. They just want to know what the profit is and how is the next quarter is going to be.
>
> So, what we're seeing is a slow ebb of sets in use. Radio is now about the rating of 17 percent of sets in use. [On average, 17 percent of the public listens to radio at any given time.] It's slipping and may go down to 7 or 8 percent. Network television has gone from maybe 90 percent to 50 percent because of cable. The other factor is the amount of time people are willing to give to these media. There's a lot of other things to do."[31]

Mann points out that the trends in radio and television are similar. The ownership consolidation and the distance programming are all efforts to cut costs and increase profits. Satellite programming is not intended as an improvement but, now that the infrastructure is largely in place, as a cheaper way to do business.

Owner gatekeeping is economics driven. Coordinating stations with the least cost for staff, the least cost for talent, and the least cost for management is the goal. Coordinating it from the top rather than having lots of duplication of people in small markets cuts costs.

Former Massachusetts governor Michael Dukakis speaks of dealing with the media owners in Massachusetts:

> In Boston some years ago, we weren't dealing with absentee ownership. Channel 2 (public television) was locally owned, as were Channels 5 and 7. Channel 4 was not, but it was the flagship of a small chain of

.inghouse stations, and they always had their best people at WBZ. We
/ local boards for two of the three stations, and the other board was
ıte accessible given the importance of the station to them.

Who owns Boston television today? Channel 7 is owned by a Massachusetts native but he moved to Florida. Channel 5 is owned by Hearst. Channel 4 is owned by Disney.

Aside from the arrival of absentee ownership, we no longer have federal regulation which requires them to do community-based programming. In the 1980s the President and Congress changed that. In the past, each station had to do an assessment periodically and interview local leaders to see if the public felt they were serving the community. They don't do that any more.

They say it's about competition. They say it's ratings. Look at this garbage mouth Howard Stern. Can you imagine putting this guy on CBS? In a country of 270 million people, you'll always find 10 million or 5 million who want to listen to somebody talk dirty—and show women disrobing. There are some people who want this garbage day after day. Part of it was lifting the government requirements for these public franchisees. And part of it was a very warped sense of what it takes to be competitive. A lot of people who work at public and commercial stations are well informed. They know. They just get into this world terribly dominated by large corporate owners.

"The media say to you, well, people aren't interested in positive stuff. I don't believe that. I think people respond positively and well to stories about people doing good things. You turn on your television set at 6 p.m. around here and it's not a fair reflection at all of what happened that day. It's whatever bleeds. These days, unfortunately, we don't have much bleeding around Boston. So we get the news from Tulsa where somebody's bleeding. I don't get it. It's lousy journalism. Furthermore I don't even know if it's profitable journalism."[32]

Reminded that the data indicates the number of news viewers dropping, Dukakis says, "Who wants to watch the stuff?"

Government

Government also has responsibility in media gatekeeping in that in a democratic society, the principal controls placed on greed are laws enacted and enforced through government regulation and sanctions.

The Federal Communications Commission, an independent agency, is responsible for regulating communications. According to Dr. Robert L. Hilliard, former FCC chief of public broadcasting, the FCC's jurisdiction includes mass media, common carriers (like telephone companies, cell phones, and domestic satellites), and private radio. Mass media includes AM and FM radio, broadcast TV, direct broadcast satellite, instructional television fixed service (ITFS), and cable TV. It licenses stations; develops policies, rules and regulations; and administers international treaties regarding communications.[33]

How the five commissioners regulate is invariably influenced by the politics of the era. For example, the proconsumer attitudes of the Kennedy era resulted in years of strong public-interest regulation. Subsequently, the marketplace theories of the Reagan-Bush era resulted in massive deregulation.

For example, in 1984 the Cable Communications Act eliminated almost all regulatory control of cable. On two occasions the courts upheld cable companies arguing against the "Must Carry Rule," stating that it was no longer required that they carry local broadcast stations on their cable systems.

FCC rulings, past and present, that have affected the public's access to media and that indicate some aspects of government gatekeeping include the following:

- *Banning subliminal advertising*, or the flashing of words and pictures not consciously noted by viewers is barred as not in the public interest.
- A *Duopoly Rule* existed for some years, prohibiting one media owner from having more than one TV station, or one AM or FM station in the same market. This was later deregulated.
- The *Fairness Doctrine* was eliminated by the FCC in 1987 after Reagan vetoed a Fairness law. The doctrine had required that a station presenting one side of a controversial issue provide those on the other side of the issue the opportunity to reply (not necessarily with equal time).
- The *Political Equal Time Provision* (Section 315 of the Communications Act) provides that any station that permits a legally qualified candidate for office to use its facilities, paid or unpaid, must provide "equal opportunities" for use to other candidates for that office. News and public affairs programs are exempt, thus allowing owners to give visibility to candidates they support and not to others.

Congressional law and FCC regulation are crucial to the existence or demise of cable access and local origination stations, and crucial to regulating the extent to which cable TV prices regularly increase. A 1990 Cable Act, for example, gives the customer the right to have twenty-four hours' access for customer complaints and to have broken cable service repaired within twenty-four hours.

The FCC also regulates the licensing for low-power television stations (LPTV) and for microradio stations. LPTV is authorized in the form of up to 10–watt VHF stations and 1,000–watt UHF stations to serve local community needs. Costs of getting a license and starting a station have ranged from $20,000 "mom and pop" spare-room stations to over $1 million for professional studios. Low power microradio stations were just legalized by the FCC in early 2000. For several years prior to that, numerous small groups across the country were operating such stations and challenging the prior ruling prohibiting such stations. Low power stations were prohibited over twenty years ago on the grounds that they interfered with reception of larger stations. It takes less than $200 to start a microstation making it easy for growth in a movement to legalize microradio. This movement has its roots in the view that people are being denied the right to communicate on public airwaves because radio is limited to large, wealthy FCC licensed stations. The National Association of Broadcasters (NAB) opposes the FCC legalization of such stations.

Those wanting to start microradio stations find empty frequencies and adjust their transmitters to those. Their broadcast range is approximately six miles to ten miles from the point of transmission. The microradio advocates argue that the U.S. Constitution allows the federal government to regulate interstate commerce and make treaties with other nations, but that the federal government cannot interfere in the right of people to communicate at a local level. The NAB contends that such use of frequencies will result in interference with other stations, thus causing chaos on the airwaves.

The Telecommunications Act of 1996 was passed to update the law in light of the many new communications technologies. Media coverage of the draft law was minimal during the period of debate over various versions of the bill. Journalists made little effort to translate it into nontechnical terms that the public might understand. It is not clear whether the media owners would have wanted to minimize the coverage of the legislation to avoid divulging their huge gains in the legislation. Since the journalists give priority to murders and sex scandals, the issue of owner discomfort had no need to be addressed. The public, effectively screened out of the democratic decision making, had little reason to know about the issues at stake in the 1996 Telecom Act, and largely ignored it.

Writer and producer Nat Segaloff summarizes the changes in the communications law:

> I don't consider television and radio to be free press—not since the elimination of the FCC regulation and the relaxing of the 'sevens' rule [the old FCC rule that one entity could not own more than seven television stations, seven AM stations, and seven FM stations nationally]. The concentration of broadcasting power now in the hands of so few people is unhealthy—as anyone whose views differ with those of News America, Time-Warner, Viacom, TCI, Disney, GE, AT&T, etc. well knows. The fact that there are no regularly ap-

pearing broadcast news sources from the left and very few from the center to counteract the scores of those from the right is not only un-Amercian, it's just plain stupid programming.

Since 1981—when Reagan appointed Mark Fowler to head the FCC—we have seen a calculated conspiracy to destroy America. Maybe I am being a little fanatic about that. By deregulating broadcast at the same time they enlarged the 'sevens' rule, the FCC created a situation in which station owners could acquire more holdings at the same time as station management no longer had to offer news and public affairs, seek license renewal through conducting community ascertainments, and didn't have to be responsive to communities. In other words, Reagan and the FCC purposely cut off any access by the individual to a broad audience. At the same time, the rise of the cable industry and its requirement for public access channels gave the illusion of redress where, in fact, it further fractionalized the audience.

What happens when you tell the American people that they can make a difference, yet you devise a construct that denies them access? You set in motion two extreme reactions: one, in which the individual feels he cannot do anything, so he stops trying (the definition of Generation-X) and the other in which the individual feels he has nothing to lose, so he tries anything (the rise of gang violence and the culture of hate)."[34]

Former FCC commissioner Nicholas Johnson comments on the relaxation of ownership regulation in the 1996 Telecommunications Act. "If they relaxed any more, they'd be dead. How much can they relax and still stand up and walk around? Look at it another way. Say that nobody can own more than one broadcasting station. I never did see what's wrong with that idea. As long as you've got more people that want to broadcast than there are stations out there, why have these multiple owners? I see how it serves their interests, but I'm damned if I can see how anybody can make a finding that it serves the public's interest."[35]

Publisher Bernard Mann explains how the regulation change transformed the entire landscape that he and his colleagues in radio and television once enjoyed:[36]

To be a good entrepreneur, one needs to anticipate fads and trends. I bought stations that were not doing well, built them up, sold them, and bought others. You could take a radio (or TV) station which was doing poorly and, through your own inventiveness, ideas, hard work, make it profitable and make it a service to the community. Those days are gone. They are gone because the regulation has changed. The competition, the landscape has changed.

When I was in business, up to a few years ago, you could own seven radio stations and that's all—one FM in each market and one AM in each market. That's all. Now it's not unusual for companies to have in excess of 40 percent of all the radio stations in America. Some cities only have two owners. This market [Greensboro, North Carolina] has twenty-five radio stations that are owned by three companies. The change makes it very difficult for an individual to own one radio station and make a difference. Now, you're not competing one on one with someone, you're competing against four or five stations. On the other side, it has taken the volatility out of radio and has made it a far better business for large companies. Large companies now can project income. They are not so dominated by the ratings. If they have five stations in a market and one station loses ratings or the morning team leaves, they'll make it up in another. There's still only so many people who listen to the radio, so if they don't listen to that station, they'll listen to another, and the same company will own that one too."

When asked how one might revisit multiple media ownership in the United States, Mann commented, "Well, right now it [monopoly ownership] has been permitted by the FCC. How do you undo that? The paste is out of the tube. It's hard to push it back. The FCC is the gatekeeper that permitted the ownership of multiple stations. That was the crucial thing. It was a wonderful business for a long time. You had to be part of your community. Licenses were often granted based on the ascertainment of the service you were going to give to your community—whether you were going to live there. If there were two applicants, the one who proved they were part of the community often got the license. That's gone. Future demand won't change it. People will just turn it off and go to something else."

Is the government the gatekeeper? If so, in the interests of the public or the interests of the powerful? Have the media moguls hijacked our government—and our culture?

The Advertisers

Advertisers can play a major role in screening out many entertainment and news media messages. Why? The principal function of television has evolved into that of delivering consumers (sometimes called audiences) to advertisers with products to sell.

Television programming runs like a Swiss watch. No one pays much attention to what is on so long as it delivers money, through the conduit of advertisers, to those who get paid to keep the station running and to those who expect profits from their ownership or investment. And, of course, the advertisers who pay to keep it running expect the consumers to buy their products. Then they can spend more money advertising, keeping the station happy and selling new products.

Where does the public fit into this equation? It is simple. Its job is to spend, not to think or to be entertained or educated—and not to share in the use of the airwaves it owns.

The phenomenal growth of the advertising industry has brought us to the point where the ads and the power behind them screen out many other uses for our public airwaves. In 1940 advertisers spent $16 per person in the United States. In 1980 it was $260 per year per person. In the late 1990s, it is over $600 per person to provide to the average American 300 to 1,600 ad messages each day.[37]

Overall industry financial figures provide a base for understanding its impact. In 1990 the government spent $171 million on the National Endowment for the Arts, less than that spent for military bands. Since 1990, even less has been spent on the arts. In 1996, $39 billion was spent on federal medicaid—health care for low-income people, most of whom are elderly and the rest largely children.[38] In 1997, $179 billion was spent on all forms of advertising—358 percent more than is spent on health care for the needy, and over 1000 percent more than the amount spent on the arts. TV stations now have about forty ads per hour. TV is the largest player in the advertising market. In 1996, advertisers spent $43 billion on TV alone—80 percent of U.S. TV stations are commercial or accept ads. Now, with diminished funding for public broadcasting, even the public radio and television stations are needing to expand their underwriting or advertising funding.

Because advertising is the lifeblood of the industry, it is to be expected that the media owners take advertisers' concerns seriously. Usually this concern is simply about placement on programs with high ratings—a topic to be discussed here shortly. There are, however, two other ways in which the advertisers can influence the viewer. One is when they have a direct confrontation over program content. The second is in the content of the ads themselves and the messages sent in those ads.

Examples of advertiser influence on program content are numerous. Sometimes this takes the form of the requests from airline advertisers not to have their ads placed on programs about plane crashes. One supposes this does not result in lost revenue because the ads can be placed elsewhere in the program schedule, and, hopefully, it does not result in curbed coverage of any accident. One example of advertiser influence on program content is when NBC invited Coca-Cola to preview a documentary with segments about how Coca-Cola exploited migrant agricultural workers. NBC acceded to Coke's request to cut certain segments from the documentary.[39]

Advertisers boycotted the final show of ABC's "Ellen" in 1997, the show in which Ellen announced she was gay. Chrysler, JC Penney, and Wendy's all backed out of the final program. Chrysler said it did not want to be part of "a polarizing issue." They feared a backlash from conservative consumers and they called the decision to pull their ads dealing with priorities, namely, corporate survival.[40] The impact of their decisions on the viewing public was to ensure that free speech is limited to only the dominant "60 Minutes" viewpoints and to push those with other messages out of the arena of debate.

An example of advertiser gatekeeping in news programming is the story in late 1995 that there was evidence the tobacco companies knew the dangers of smoking—the story of Brown and Williamson Corp.'s whistle-blowing employee Jeffrey Wiegard. CBS chose not to air the story. Mike Wallace, veteran journalist on "60 Minutes," said, "It was the first time that I really felt . . . let down by my company. It became so obvious that . . . we were simply dead wrong, that we were caving in." Other networks covered the story. Emerson College media arts research Matthew Barone points out that "after this fiasco, journalists are bound to tiptoe through interviews." Phillip Morris controls food and insurance companies as well as tobacco and their pressure can be enormous. A boycott on their part would be a serious financial problem for the network.[41]

Tobacco has not just waited to "yea" or "nea" a controversial program. It has been proactive in getting its message out. In 1985, the former CEO of Phillip Morris detailed the tobacco giant's strategy with the media to "exploit . . . ad agencies and media proprietors," noting that "Rupert Murdoch's papers rarely publish anti-smoking articles these days." And, in another memo "a number of media proprietors . . . are sympathetic to our position—Rupert Murdoch and Malcolm Forbes are two good examples. The media like the money they make from our advertisements, and they are an ally that we can and should exploit."[42]

Another example of advertiser influence on programming has a bizarre twist when one considers the inconsistency in Phillip Morris's views. Keep in mind the morality of their own product: It kills people. Steven Levingston, former director of the business and economics journalism program at Boston University, writes about several advertisers who pulled their ads from the Fox cartoon sitcom "The Family Guy." The cartoon humor is based on bigotry, hate, and total lack of respect for all people not conforming with the designated "majority." The ads were withdrawn because, as Phillip Morris told the *New York Times*, it "is not consistent with our values as a company." Hypocritical? The logic for joining Kentucky Fried Chicken, McDonald's, Pepsi, Sprint, Chrysler, the Gap, and Coca-Cola in withdrawing their ads was that "an offended viewer is a vengeful consumer."[43]

The argument for "The Family Guy" cartoon was the argument that free speech should not be silenced. A difficult line to draw in our culture is the dividing point between free expression of diverse viewpoints and spreading hate that results in physical harm to people. Some may argue that "The Family

Guy" should stay on the air. It is free speech. Others say it sinks below a decency standard expected in the United States and should be removed. Still others say that while many find it offensive, it should remain on the air because all views deserve to be heard.

In the early 1980s, similar advertiser intervention occurred over "The Lou Grant Show." The sponsors, led by Kimberly Clark, the manufacturer of Kleenex, joined the manufacturers of Peter Paul Mounds candy bars in pulling their ads for the show. They had been pressured by groups led by Charlton Heston, the actor who in the late 1990s was president of the National Rifle Association. Ed Asner, the lead actor in "The Lou Grant Show," had been involved in providing medical supplies to the El Salvador rebels seeking to overthrow the dictator ruling their country. Asner had twice defeated Heston for the position of president of the Screen Actors Guild. Heston was eager to attack Asner. The timing was perfect in that the Cold War was still hot. Heston called Asner un-American. The sponsors were scared of controversy. CBS, frightened by adverse reaction from their advertisers, arbitrarily canceled the show.

These are just a few examples of the heavy hand that advertisers can play in determining whether or not shows are on the air.

Advertisements in themselves are designed to be memorable. But they can bring their own form of gatekeeping. The question arises of whether the real American culture is more memorable than the ads designed to influence young Americans. The Colonial Williamsburg Foundation and the Annenberg Public Policy Center, mentioned in Steven Levingston's *Boston Globe* article, have made studies testifying to the impact of both advertising and the absence of information important to one's self-interest in keeping a society democratic. More kids recognize Budweiser frogs and the tobacco industry emissary Joe Camel than recognize the vice-president of the United States Similarly, 79 percent of American adults can identify the Nike slogan, "Just do it," while only 47 percent recognize that "life, liberty and the pursuit of happiness" is a guarantee written into the U.S. Constitution.

Some argue that it is not the job of television to teach the public about things critical to preserving their culture. However, the evidence clearly shows that television is teaching and is redefining our culture. The calculated genius behind selling products to consumers through advertising may prove so seductive that the same technique is effectively reprioritizing our culture.

What about the content of the ads themselves? TV is the largest player in the nation's advertising market. Indeed, their messages sell the products. But what else do they sell at the same time?

They sell attitudes and values. For example, while the standards for appropriateness of content constantly shift, the issues of AIDs and abortion have helped make sex an open-discussion topic, changing the definitions of acceptable over just a few years in the mid-1990s. Calvin Klein's 1995 campaign of "provocatively posed young models" reflects the recent trend in the television industry of a relaxed sexual atmosphere, and was intended to spark a "look twice" appeal. Klein hired photographer Steven Meisel, known for sexually charged images, to create this campaign. *Boston Globe* writer Pamela Reynolds article describes the ads. "The television spots are filmed in a paneled basement. There's harsh lighting and an old step ladder, slyly suggesting that these pictures are being shot in the privacy of someone's home. The young models, reminiscent of scraggly runaways, wriggle uncomfortably as the camera rolls. A voice off camera asks a skin-shy model to take off a shirt, or pull down her pants. In the print ads, a slice of underwear is sometimes visible beneath a mini-skirt or cut-off shorts."[44] The ads produced such controversy that they were banned in many places. Klein eventually took out a full-page ad in the *New York Times* apologizing for the "misunderstanding." But some say that the ads were specifically designed to generate the controversy that would increase publicity and boost sales.[45] Despite boycotts, sales remained stable.

Some ads promote "good values" as well as products; for example, Nike. One Nike ad does not talk about the sneaker it sells, but about girl athletes saying such things as, "If you let me play sports, I will be less likely to stay with a man who beats me." On the other hand, never doubt that opportunism thrives. The same company boosting sales to women athletes in the United States is said to exploit child labor in the countries where shoes are made by people in poor working conditions who are paid very low wages.

Another example of ads that promote human creativity as well as their product is Apple Computer. Apple's "Think Different" campaign was created by TBWA Chiat/Day. Its objective was to make clear, as Apple CEO Steve Jobs said, that " 'think different' celebrates the soul of the Apple brand— that creative people with passion can change the world for the better." The ad campaign was launched in September 1997, during the ABC Sunday night movie *Toy Story*. It was shot in black and white, honoring heroes like Albert Einstein, Mahatma Gandhi, Pablo Picasso, Martin Luther King Jr., John Lennon, and Alfred Hitchcock. The phrase "Think Different" has since become a part of pop culture.[46] The ad is spoken by actor Richard Dreyfuss, saying: "Here's to the crazy ones, the misfits, the rebels, the troublemakers, the round pegs in square holes, the ones who see things differently. They're not fond of rules and have no respect for the status quo. You can quote them, disagree with them, glorify or vilify them. About the only thing you can't do is ignore them, because they change things. They push the human race forward. And while some may see them as the crazy ones, we see genius, because people who are crazy enough to think they can change the world are the ones who do."

Benetton, the Italian clothier, since 1985 has an ad campaign dealing with the good values of racial equality, preserving dwindling resources, preventing violence, curing AIDs, safe and adequate food distribution, and ending Mafia murders. The campaigns have drawn considerable attention. They have won awards and they have been boycotted. Luciano Benetton hired prominent Italian fashion photographer Oliviero Toscani to develop these new messages. The ads were praised when they focused on the clothes, which were worn by kids from different racial and ethnic backgrounds—the "United Colors of Benetton." But using images that stir social consciousness in the "United Friends of Benetton" campaign triggered controversy. Thinking about "issues" proved too much.[47] Some later ads were said to be of questionable taste, resulting in mixed messages, and making audiences nervous. Jennifer Arkin, a young woman from Boston University who is just entering the mass communications field, raises an interesting point. "The issues covered in the Benetton ads should be more widely discussed. The majority of the stories covered in the news are about murder and violence. That is considered normal. But when you take the same photo out of the news and put a Benetton logo on it, individuals will get angry if they can't come to terms with it. When journalists focus on strange and serious topics, nobody criticizes them for trying to sell their stories to the media. Yet, when an advertisement touches on a real problem, everyone protests that it is in bad taste. An advertisement which misleads the consumer with deception and lies is considered more correct."

"Got Milk?" These ads were common in 1999. They provide another example of messages in advertising. How could one argue with the Dairy Association ad campaign? Maybe one cannot argue with the basic message, but the story is different if one sees the full picture. The supply of milk has increased because scientists have found a way to increase production through administering the Bovine Growth Hormone (rBGH). The drug causes increased cases of various diseases in cows. It is not clear yet what this might do to humans. Indeed, it results in over a quarter million tons of surplus milk each year. Much of that is thrown out.[48]

Another "harmless" ad is one for Breast Cancer Awareness Month, a campaign initiated by Zeneca Pharmaceuticals, a leader in cancer research and treatment. Zeneca limits its ads to detection and treatment of breast cancer, not prevention. This may be because it is also among the world's largest manufacturers of pesticides, plastics, and carcinogens that are alleged to cause breast cancer.[49] Does its primary activity mean that one should disregard its PSA for Breast Cancer Awareness month? Of course not. On the other hand, does the public have a right to know about preventing breast cancer or only about treating it? Can we expect companies not to be opportunistic? Probably not. Can we expect them not to harm the public and not to be hypocritical? One would hope so.

Aside from product ads, public interest and political ads are intended to sway public policy.

For example, in President Clinton's first term of office, a comprehensive effort was made to revamp U.S. health insurance programs. The health insurance industry's lobbyists created one simple TV ad—"Harry and Louise." They spent some $50 million on this campaign. Their strategy was very clever. With the help of Republicans who opposed health care reform, a relatively small amount of that money was raised in order to place the ad first on stations in the Washington, DC, media market. The next step was to send copies of it to reporters across the United States, illustrating what was shown on the air in Washington. These opposing health care reform then benefited from an estimated $300,000 worth of free air time covering their position as "news" on stations across the United States. The campaign worked because the ad was fuzzy enough not to be an overtly political ad in opposition to the Democrats. A subsequent part of the sponsor's strategy was to put ads on TV in the small media markets whose members of Congress were considered swing votes. This again was picked up by wire services, which carried the ad as news. Seldom was there any accompanying discussion of who sponsored the ad or whether the "facts" presented were accurate. By designing the ad campaign this way, ads reached the news, which then reached legislators and more reporters. It is a very clever multiplier technique to maximize the dollars spent on the ad campaign. No opposition voices were heard.

The public made its decision about the health care debate, effectively having been screened out from access to full information on both sides of the issue. In addition, the media did nothing to increase public awareness of the role big money was playing in buying off Congressional votes so that health reform would never happen. The media moguls protected their friends—the wealthy in other industries. Public opinion polls and calls to legislators led Congress to understand there would be no problem if they sided with industry against consumers. Today over 40 million Americans are without health insurance.

One cannot look for a villain behind every video produced by advertisers. Some industry efforts are important to our cultural growth. The Ad Council coordinates the pro bono ad campaigns for the industry. The responsibility for producing pro bono public service ads is rotated among the ad agencies. Examples include "Friends Don't Let Friends Drive Drunk" and the United Negro College Fund's "A Mind Is a Terrible Thing to Waste." NBC program stars are featured in ads like those in the "The More You Know" campaign to persuade kids to stay in school.[50]

An example of an ad that woke up the audience to some of our culture's gender stereotypes while selling its product is the Kellogg's Special K ad campaign "Reshape Your Attitude." It was devised by Leo Burnett, the eighth largest advertising agency in the United States. The campaign uses humor, shock, and play on words. It debuted at the 1998 Super Bowl in black and white. Men sat at a bar saying things about their bodies that women typically say such as, "I have my mother's thighs. Do these make my butt look big? I will not let my dress size determine my self-worth." The announcer then comments that men do not obsess about these things, why do women? This is a major strategy shift for a leading advertiser. It is another approach to targeting a youth audience. According to Seattle-based Eating Disorders Awareness and Prevention (EDAP), half of all teenage girls are on a diet; 81 percent of girls, say, ten to eighteen have a fear of being fat.

One might ask who acts on the citizen's behalf to regulate advertising. Largely, the industry is self-regulated—doing what the market will bear. The Federal Trade Commission (FTC) can, in some circumstances, intervene. It regulates unfair, misleading, and deceptive advertising. The FTC Policy Statement on Deception says: "The commission will find deception if there is a representation, omission or practice that is likely to mislead the consumer acting responsibly in the circumstances, to the consumer's detriment." In addition, other federal organizations exist to represent the citizen's interest. These include the Federal Communications Commission (FCC), the Food and Drug Administration (FDA), the Bureau of Alcohol, Tobacco and Firearms (ATF), and the Patent and Trademark Office. Private-sector advocacy organizations include Better Business Bureaus and the National Advertising Review Council. Whether the organizations are effective defenders of citizen interests depends on whether a substantial base of citizenry actively communicates with them, supports or decries their actions, and whether or not they have funding sufficient to do their jobs in the public interest rather than in corporate self-interest.

The advertising industry is very much a world of its own—as is the case with most specialized industries. Ad agencies compete to be the largest in terms of revenue, to list the top corporate clients, and to win international, national, and local awards for creative excellence. For example, the 1998 "Best International Ad Campaign" award went to Arnold Communications for its Volkswagen New Beetle advertisements.[51] Arnold incorporated VW ideas with Arnold's creative design and built in some humor with the intent of giving the consumer a brand identity. But the bottom line is that the purpose of public relations and advertising is to generate product sales.

Once one is completely ensconced in the world of creating advertisements and finding the ideal way to sell products, gatekeeping and screening out some aspect of messages is often not even a matter of thought. The rationale is that the company is just doing what is needed to compete effectively. That position will likely stand unless some sea change causes the public to object and the broadcasters and advertisers to take a more proactive stance on the impact of the corporate sector on American culture.

Are the advertisers the most effective gatekeepers? Or might the principal gatekeeper be the high-speed train to which both broadcasters and advertisers have hitched their fortunes—the Nielsen ratings?

The Ratings

The ratings are considered by some to be the fuel that drives gatekeeping.

Others say that ratings are just the tool of the advertisers and broadcasters to maximize the profits each will generate. The bottom line is that Nielsen Media Research Inc., the company that has dominated the ratings field since the beginnings of television ratings, plays a very large role in deciding where $45 billion per year of advertising money is spent.

The purpose of ratings is to help broadcasters know who their audience is. This in turn enables them to set the price tag for advertising. Erik Barnouw, media historian and author of *The Sponsor*, wondered as early as 1961 if programming would become the by-product of the advertising.[52] The ratings system, more than any other factor, makes this happen. Today, most honest programmers will admit that the only value of any given program is how many rating points it gets.

The result of paying deference to ratings is that genuine media creativity has given way to paint-by-number creativity.

TV networks go after the audience that the advertisers want and, thus, stay in business. Advertisers prefer audiences of both men and women between ages eighteen and forty-nine. Their second choice is women between eighteen and forty-nine. Their third choice is to reach an audience of men and women between twenty-five and fifty-four. These are the most profitable demographic groups. For example, if advertisers want the eighteen to forty-nine-year-old demographic—the demographic where half of all TV advertising dollars go—the programs are likely not on CBS, whose the average viewer age is 52.5. The numbers hunt is further refined by studying the total numbers of hours each potential consumer might watch TV. For example, a Nielsen Media Research Study shows that men eighteen to twenty-four watch twenty hours and forty minutes a week of TV, while people over fifty-five watch thirty-five hours and seventeen minutes.[53] The search for younger audiences is based on studies that prove that younger buyers change brands more often than older buyers do. Other studies seek to contradict this accepted wisdom, pointing out that older consumers have more disposable cash and are a growing segment of our overall population. Time slots preferred for advertising on U.S. television are Monday through Friday between 8:00 and 11:00 P.M. Eastern Standard Time, 7:00 to 10:00 P.M. Central Time, and Sundays between 7:00 and 11:00 P.M. Sunday is the heaviest viewing night of the week.

According to Nielson, "the number of persons per TV household has remained steady at approximately 2.6 following a decline in household size from 1970 through 1990. The number of homes with TV has increased 63 percent from 1970 to 1998, the number of adults 18–49 has grown by 56 percent and the number of adults 50+ has grown by 51 percent. . . . Children and teens only just began to reverse a decline for their age group, and have grown only modestly over the past seven years."[54]

Overall television usage has remained fairly constant throughout the 1990s. Because the options have changed now that the average home receives at least forty-five channels, the major networks have lost viewers. In 1997, the prime-time viewing rating was allocated as follows: 33.1 percent network affiliates, 6.8 percent independent stations, 2.2 percent public television, 3.8 percent pay cable TV, and 20.5 percent basic cable.[55]

Most network commercial advertising time is sold on the basis of a guaranteed rating delivery. Of course, it must be delivered to the right audience for the product. The illustrations above provide only an introduction to the complex ongoing search for the numbers that generate the biggest profits.

Nielsen Media Research Company services the ratings needs of the nation's broadcasters and advertisers almost without competition. Nielsen services more than 1,000 local TV stations, hundreds of cable systems, and in excess of 2,000 advertisers and advertising agencies. In late summer 1999, VNU NV in the Netherlands, the publisher of *Billboard* magazine, announced it would buy Nielsen Media Research for $2.7 billion. In 1998, Nielsen made an alliance with NetRatings Inc. to monitor the popularity of Internet online sites. The VNU NV deal includes the new Nielsen Internet service, the beacon indicating the route ahead for Internet communication.[56]

The Nielsen television numbers come from surveying a statistical sample on a continuing basis. Approximately 5,000 households throughout the United States (some 11,000 people) constitute the national sample used to measure the television preferences of our population of some 99.4 million TV households in the United States. In addition, 18,500 households are monitored in forty-four major local media markets.

Nielsen uses the U.S. Census Bureau's decennial count as updated annually for a count of housing units in the United States. They randomly select 6,000 small geographic areas intended to represent a cross–section of the demographics of the country. Surveyors go to each area to enumerate housing units. Housing units are then randomly selected from this list within each sample area. Each occupied unit is a household. Those identified are asked to be part of the Nielsen measurements.[57]

The forty-four major markets in the United States include 63 percent of all the TV households in the United States. "People meters" are used to gather data electronically on what channel is tuned in, what time, and for how long, as well as who watched. The meter electronically scans the TV, the VCR, and the cable converter every 2.7 seconds. Every night the results are transferred by modem to the mainframe in Dunedin, Florida. Every morning, the numbers are available to broadcasters and advertisers.

At intervals during the year—periods in November, February, May, and July called "sweeps"—paper diaries are distributed for a cross-check of viewing preferences in each of the 210 television markets in the United States. It is no accident that there is better programming available during those months. Nielsen processes some 2 million household diaries annually. The diaries give more refined data for each of the local television markets.

In recent years, the data gathering has become more complex because of the addition of new stations. Now there are seven English-language broadcast networks, two Spanish-language networks, plus over 100 national syndicators and more than 1,000 stations. There are fifty cable networks and hundreds of cable systems.[58] As digital television and convergence with the Internet occurs, Nielsen sees its services as even more vital to it is customers, and probably even more challenging to collect.

The data gathered breaks down into categories: homes using television (HUT), people using television (PUT). The rating extrapolated from the sample is the percentage of the households tuned in to a particular station at a particular time.

In some households a new scanner device has been added, with viewers asked to scan the bar codes of products purchased in order to more specifically link household product preferences with television program preferences.

The data tabulated becomes a bible for programmers and advertisers. The accuracy of the numbers is not questioned because, after all, no alternative system of quantifying data is available. The numbers determine which shows stay on the air and which do not. The ripple effect is that any new shows are designed to copy the currently successful formats that bring high ratings. The financial risk of experimenting with anything new is too risky. If people stop watching, no one asks why. Those people just are not counted as part of the potential customer base for the advertiser. Potential customers are not part of the equation. In fact, despite the advertiser interest in a young adult demographic, viewers in college dormitories are not counted. It is a very rigid, backward-looking system designed to serve the advertiser first, the broadcaster second. It has nothing to do with the public's interests, either programatically or culturally.

According to John A. Dimling, president and CEO of Nielsen Media Research, "The Nielsen TV ratings are the currency for more than $43 billion in transactions between sellers and buyers of commercial TV time. The ratings also are vital to program buying and scheduling decisions on both the national and local level."[59]

One of the many areas of controversy challenging Nielsen's system is the counting of minority viewers.

For the moment, African Americans represent the largest block of minority households—12 percent. Nielsen has determined that this population segment watches 75 hours of television per week, compared with 52 hours per week for the rest of the population, and their viewing behavior differs from the rest of the population.[60] The Nielsen data show African Americans watching TV two hours more per week during prime time and five hours more through the whole week—more daytime TV than the population in general. One implication, is that watching daytime TV is a racial characteristic. In fact, it is an economic characteristic. Poorer people have more unemployment and fewer dollars to spend on alternative entertainment, and therefore tend to spend more hours at home watching TV. The Nielsen program preference comparisons noted that of the fifteen top-rated shows in African-American households, only one show, "Touched by an Angel," appeared on the top fifteen list for all other viewers.[61] Beginning in the 1990s, Nielsen began to work with advertisers to target the buying power of the African-American community. One wonders if the consumer product assessments take into account the economic differences between middle-class and affluent black households and poor households?

The Latino/a population will soon become America's largest minority. There are 30 million Latino/as in the United States. It is said that the United States will be 20 percent Latino/a by early in the twenty-first century.[62] Nielsen estimated there were 7.74 million Hispanic TV households in 1997–1998, an increase of 3.1 percent over the previous year.

It is not clear that this subset is appropriately represented in the sample frame Nielsen uses. In 1992 Nielsen began to use a separate sample of 800 people-metered homes to monitor viewing in the fifteen television markets with the largest number of Hispanic viewing households. It is called the Nielsen Hispanic Television Index. In 1994 and 1998, the monitoring was expanded to include Spanish cable and syndication. Nielsen's general conclusions are that while Hispanic households are larger and their viewing greater than the general population, the adults watch less TV than does the general market. Teens and children watch more. Again, some sources attempt to explain this by stereotyping the viewers. One legitimate reason is that children of newcomers to the United States, not yet part of the mainstream, are not engaged in the wide range of after-school programs as other children are, so they come home and watch TV. Perhaps adults watch less because almost everything is foreign to their language and culture. Spanish-language networks are growing rapidly. Nielsen ranks the viewing on the principal Spanish-language networks, Telemundo and Univision, as well as attempting to measure Latino/a viewing of English-speaking network programs.[63]

Perhaps if Nielsen tabulated more than the simple data it gathers, the results would benefit the viewers as well as the broadcasters and advertisers.

Apparently those broadcasting and selling products in some of the communities with the largest Latino/a markets are not happy with Nielsen's measurements of this rapidly growing consumer market. Miami, for example, is the nation's third largest Latino/a market, following Los Angeles and New York. There are an estimated 450,880 Hispanic TV housholds out of a total 1,385,940 TV households in the Miami media market, or 32.5 percent. Sunbeam Television Corporation, the owner of WSVN in Miami, canceled its contract with Nielsen because it believed the data undercounted its viewers.[64] This demographic count is very important in a media market because it is the key to station programming in ways that can increase ratings, and it is the key to advertiser marketing to potential consumers.

Other criticism of Nielsen revolves around its sample selection. People in the households selected are asked to host a "people meter" or take a "diary" to record their viewing preferences as volunteers, giving them occasional gifts. One of many problems in getting a representative sample of the public is the self-selection that occurs after the sample is identified. There has been a 22 percent decline from 1994 to 1998 in those agreeing to fill out the diaries. The level of cooperation in agreeing to take the electronic people meters was, in the late 1990s, down to 45 percent of those asked.[65]

Other forms of self-selection also distort the sample. It is easier for Nielsen to find willing participants in rural areas than in urban areas. Households representing ethnic minorities are harder to include because people are less receptive to taking part in the sample. The poor are often not included; one reason is lack of a phone. Households composed of older people are more likely to decline offers to be Nielsen homes, perhaps because they do not like letting strangers into their homes, or because most of the programming does not appeal to their interests. (Remember, they are not part of the advertisers' preferred demographic.)

The Nielsen sample becomes a sample of those who are the easiest to reach and to convince that participation is worth the effort. This may not be the same as the most accurate sample.

Other complaints about the ratings system exist:[66]

1. Errors occur in tabulating data, especially with the manual diary method, but also with the electronic people meter. The errors include response errors, nonresponse errors, operational errors, and sample errors.
2. Serious undercounts for people under age 18 and failure to count students in dormitories are cited.
3. People meters tell what sets do, not what people do. Sometimes sets are on, but people are not watching.
4. You cannot expect people to do data entry when they sit down to relax.[67]
5. Nielsen reports that the passive people meter does not work 40 percent of the time.
6. The new technologies are not only expanding the media options with cable, satellite and digital TV, but they have expanded the information-gathering systems, making possible enormous improvements over the present system.

Let's face it. Skepticism about Nielson increases when the CBS drama "Judging Amy" is reported to have an audience of 72,000 at a time when the TV screen is blank for twenty minutes due to problems with the fiber optic cable.[69]

Look briefly at other points local television executives raise about the Nielsens. Ross Kramer, programming director at WBZ-TV 4, a CBS affiliate, thinks the quality of the data would improve greatly if the audience sample size in the Boston market were stable. Out of 400 people meters used in this media market of about 5 million people, roughly 80 percent are in use at any one time. That means that only 320 households are recording data at any given time. Jack Mullaney, research director at Boston's WFXT Channel 25, a Fox affiliate, says size sample does not matter if the margin of accuracy is within the acceptable range. Mullaney says that to double the accuracy, you would need four times the sample size because the accuracy does not increase incrementally but geometrically. Nielsen is willing to increase the sample size if stations are willing to pay. Kramer also says that the Boston market has 80 percent cable users, and this market fragmentation demands a more accurate sample than the present one. The swing caused by only one or two meters can make a difference for a program in recording it with a good rating or a poor one. Kramer also points to problems in using diaries to cross-check the electronic people-meter data. Nielsen sends out at least 400 diaries, but gets back only about 30 percent, and consequently the sample received does not represent the market.[69]

One of the most amazing things about a profit-oriented industry relying on Nielsen's ratings is how it undercuts their potential for new revenue. It offers no hope for increasing program audience by measuring what people would prefer to watch, that is, no delineation between quality and quantity. It is used to judge what will be the scope of new programming, but includes no measures that might indicate areas for future market growth. New programming basically mimics last year's successes.

As early as 1988, a passive infrared device was suggested to measure commercial viewers rather than program viewers. It was suggested as an alternative to Nielsen's people meter. Preliminary tests indicated that about 17 percent fewer people are in the TV room or tuned in to the station when commercials are on air. Nielson has begun work on its own "passive" meter, which uses heat sensors to register body size—a joint effort with the David Sarnoff Research Center. A system called an Active/Passive Meter (A/P) is now patented by Nielsen. It is intended to read video and audio codes in programs. The viability of infrared meters is yet to be determined. How costly are they? Is there a health risk to those sitting in front of them? Will the public accept them in their homes?

The Markle Foundation, believing that high numbers does not necessarily reveal people's appreciation or involvement, has funded a qualitative diary-based measurement service as an alternative to Nielsen. Its thinking is that if a quality program with low ratings has an avid attentive audience, its commercial value and the likelihood of program survival might increase.

Statistical Research Incorporated (SRI) funded a study in Philadelphia called SMART (Systems for Measuring and Reporting Television) ratings. Their plan relies on an electronic coder buried within the programs, coupled with an identification of all the people in the room with the TV set.

For an alternative to Nielsen to succeed, it requires a solid list of subscribers and it is difficult to gather such subscribers because most broadcast stations cannot afford to subscribe to both Nielsen's service and another one. Nonetheless, twenty-four Nielsen clients—four main networks, three cable networks, a syndicator, thirteen ad agencies, and three major advertisers (Procter and Gamble, Kraft Foods, and Coca-Cola)—signed letters of intent in 1998 and 1999 to support SMART.[70]

TCI and Media One, the cable companies, are experimenting with systems to measure every channel viewing at every minute, but this system will not measure what people do while the set is on or what the 24 million non–cable homes do.

Writer and producer Nat Segaloff notes, "If Nielsen gives a breakdown of what kind of shows historically do and don't do well in numbers, that's another whole ballpark. Golf and professional wrestling pull huge ratings, but how many TV series or TV movies are built around those wacky guys who yell 'Fore' or those rugged guys who deliver body slams? We see a lot of 'reality based' shows ("America's Most Wanted," "World's Greatest Police Chases," "When Animals Attack," etc.) not only because they attract voyeuristic viewers, but because they are cheaper to produce ($400,000–$500,000 per hour) than dramatic shows ($900,000–$1,200,000 per hour). So there's now a kind of financial hedge to creativity.

"In any event, Nielsen is the proverbial snapshot of a flowing river—it's of some value, by consensus, at least, on the moment it is taken but, after that, you're on your own."[71]

One can summarize the criticism of the Nielsens and question the broadcaster and advertiser reliance on them by reading Elizabeth Jensen's comments in *Brill's Content*, "Four Viewers Equal $50 Million."[72] She describes the situation giving an example of rating one show on one date—November 9, 1998. That day "Ally McBeal" rated second in prime-time shows among adults 18–49 with an 8.2 percent rating (i.e., 8.2 percent of all adults in that age group). The show drew 10.2 percent of all women age 18–49. How was that conclusion reached? Nielsen shows that in its 5,000–home sample, there are 6,352 adults between age 18 and 49, of whom 3,303 are women. During this particular week, fewer than 85 percent of the sample were "in-tab," or returning data. That means 5,259 adults, of whom 2,764 were women, registered their opinions. "Ally"'s 8.2 rating came from 431 sample viewers tuning in. For the 10.2 rating among women, 282 women tuned in. Three women would make a 0.10–point rating change—a number considered significant. If the big four TV networks lost 0.10 point in ratings across the entire prime-time schedule over a year, they could lose $50 million in ad revenues.

Surely there is a better way to count potential consumers for advertisers. There must be a better way to generate broadcaster revenues. Such improvement would be culturally useful, and maybe even profitable. It might be based on paying more attention to what the public really thinks and why.

Nat Segaloff states:

> The odd thing about the Nielsens is that they are applied *after* the fact; that is, the ratings as we know them have not, as yet, been applied to program pitches

or pilots, but only to shows that actually air. Not to worry: there are *other* research organizations that hold focus groups to strengthen the flaccid spines of programming executives before they commit to a show.

The two primary instruments which, in my opinion, limit creativity are something called 'Q Ratings' and 'Network Approval.' 'Q Ratings' is a list which circulates among programming executives containing names of entertainers ranked according to their popularity with the TV audience. If you're near the top, you work; if you're not, no matter how good an actor or actress you are, you don't. A lot of it has to do with whether you've ever been on a successful TV series. This is why, for example, Ted Danson or Jaclyn Smith will always find work, but God help Jeremy Irons or Dame Judi Dench. I once asked a friend of mine at NBC whether 'Q Ratings' really existed, and he said with a smile, 'There's no such thing as a Q list, and I have a copy right here in my drawer.' The Q scores are developed by Marketing Evaluations in Manhasset, NY.

Then there's something called 'Network Approval,' which is a status conferred upon writers or show runners (experienced producers who can get a show up as opposed to managers or executives who assume the name 'producer') who have previously been hired by a network. If a writer, for instance, is not 'Network Approved,' he or she cannot be hired to write the script—even if it was his or her proposal that sold the show to the network! What the producer does in that case is hire a 'Network Approved' writer to rewrite the nonapproved writer's script. This explains why the same people are always writing the same crap—at least until a producer evinces the guts to demand new writers. I have been told by producers that they have watched their shows fold under them because the network wouldn't let them hire the creative personnel that they wanted, and then get blamed by the network for the show's failure."[73]

Out of fear that they might lose money, the owners and the advertisers have created systems for evaluating program decisions that force them to repeat yesterday's successes. It is as if the auto industry never had a new car model but kept advancing the Model T because it was a big success at some point years ago. It is as if the printing industry only printed manuscripts written with quill pens and never moved on to typewriters and certainly did not dare venture into word processing or computers. The absence of vision is astonishing, especially since those who worship the ratings god are acting contrary to their own self-interest when they screen out creativity and diversity. Why should one be surprised if the results are mediocre for both the audience and the industry? Throughout history, those who actually did what the broadcasters and the advertisers want to do—make money—understand that it is necessary to take risks to do so. From Columbus to Calvin Klein, Bill Gates, Jerry Seinfeld, and Steven Spielberg, all went ahead with ventures that challenged the status quo—and conventional wisdom in their fields.

Some say that the ratings systems are not the gatekeepers, rather the gatekeepers are the people who use the ratings—the programmers, owners, and advertisers. It is a chicken-or-egg debate. Only people can change the shells we build that lock us into prescribed behavior.

The Public

The public is sometimes called the gatekeeper. When the finger is pointed at the industry, the industry often diverts attention back to the public. Charges that the media are killing our culture or scaring us to death are frequently met with the reply that "we only give the public what it wants." The scapegoating continues. Members of the public reply that blaming them is like telling kids to reform their alcoholic parents. No one appears ready to assume responsibility for their own actions. The Swiss watch just continues to operate in the same fashion.

How could the public be a gatekeeper?

1. Failure to become media literate is a major cause of gatekeeping. People simply are taken advantage of when they are not media literate in much the same manner that print illiterates in our society have not always been able to protect and provide for themselves.
2. Failure to become "civic" literate is another major cause of gatekeeping. Even an aware public does not provide for its own interests when it does not understand that a democratic society is, by design, created to respond to the pressures of a supporting or opposing public. It does not work when there is public apathy. Our government works very well in that respect; unfortunately the public, by and large, has dropped out and exerts no pressure to counter the pressure from wealthy corporations protecting their self-interests. Because the public has virtually dropped out of the debate, policy makers and wealthy corporations can, and often do, consider them irrelevant. We give our rights away.

The public might have influenced such policies as: (1) what is included in the 1996 Telecommunications Act; (2) imposing a tax on advertising revenues in order to curb greed and finance public-interest programming on commercial as well as on public stations; and (3) more aggressive antitrust reviews of the corporate monopoly grip on free speech and public airwaves. Challenging the media moguls is indeed a David and Goliath battle, but that is no excuse for avoiding the battle. There is too much to lose.

The 1996 Telecommunications Act was passed with ample input from industry, but minimal interest from the public—no counterpressure. Consequently, monopoly ownership is legally sanctioned. Now a single company may own as many TV stations as it wants up to coverage of 35 percent of the U.S. public. Civic leaders were unaware or unable to get access to the media to inform the American public of the enormous risk to a pluralistic and democratic society when multiple owners are screened out. The tip of the iceberg is that cable television is free now to increase its bills to the public, every month if it wishes. The more severe problem is that only those with messages approved by corporate owners have their viewpoint aired. In the twenty-first century corporate monopoly does what Fascist and Soviet governments did in the twentieth century—eliminate choice, expression of diverse views, and access to public airwaves. Public ignorance is resulting in no opposition to these corporate monopolies.

Former Senator Robert Dole lamented in the *New York Times* about the government's giving more airwaves to the existing media industry.[74] The summary of his view is that networks and station owners are fleecing the taxpayers by getting spectrum for digital TV with virtually no fee. There is not even reciprocation in the form of allowing free time for legally certified political candidates. Free time would greatly reduce the cost of campaigns and ease the obsession with fund-raising, thus allowing more focus on campaign issues and increasing the likelihood that ability, not money, would win elections. The public is a gatekeeper. It is either ignorant of how corporate lobbyists buy Congressional votes, or it is ignorant of the consequences of losing control of our culture by failing to counter the industry pressure.

The issue of taxing advertising is not even raised in Congress. Similarly, the issue of providing free communication on the air for political candidates is not seriously addressed. Why? Members of Congress need two things for self-preservation: money and votes. The advertising corporations will give candidates money so long as they protect corporate interests once elected. Free media access is opposed by the broadcasting corporations. It is partly an issue of station profits, but in large part the media opposition to free time coincides with the self-interest of both corporations and incumbents not to give opponents any opportunity for a successful campaign. The public either has no understanding of the consequences of current policy or it does not care. The public does not act to protect its own self-interest, then it complains that nothing can be done to change a corrupted system.

The public is an unaware gatekeeper.

For example, media researcher Chris Bastien says of news programs: "The problem is that most people who consume news don't even know that misrepresentation and distortion occur." [75] Problems include:

1. not reporting news on certain issues
2. not reporting accurately on certain issues

3. reporting only the views of one side of an issue
4. stereotyping certain sectors of society
5. providing public relations information instead of real news
6. not having a cross-section of the public on news reporting teams
7. not reporting on who makes decisions, when and where, or how the public can have a voice.

But the public is not totally apathetic. Some people have assumed responsibility for influencing the policy decisions that concern them by joining together in advocacy groups. They may be very sophisticated about media gatekeeping. For example, Susan Shaer, executive director of Women's Action for New Directions, says, "I think everything on the media has to fit into a sterile band that's acceptable. To go past the edges of that band is to have so small a market share that you can't make any money. There are small radio stations that do have a market. I think we should find markets where we can get in. Your own people believe that if it's not on CBS, it didn't happen. The media has sold us on the notion that prominence is preeminent. Why? It serves the corporatization of America. It serves their bottom line. The bottom line has to be a big wide line. It's not a narrow line. When you try to appeal to the largest audience, you end up looking like mashed potatoes."[76]

The Conservation Law Foundation (CLF) is another very sophisticated public advocacy group. Robert Russell, an attorney at CLF, thinks that "most reports are on topics and issues that are dangerous and immediate in nature, those that can have somewhat quick solutions."[77] He points out, for example, that there are many reports on El Niño storms and few on climate control. He also says that many environmental issues are ongoing problems, like global warming, which require a great deal of complex information to explain correctly. Issues like global warming are also very slow to see any progress, so it becomes much more difficult for news outlets to keep reporting on it. Russell adds, "Stories about transportation and land use planning are usually reported in the business and real estate sections respectively. They should be reported as environmental stories because they affect things like clean air and water. The public doesn't realize the environmental impact caused by land use and transportation."

Members of the public active in advocacy organizations and civic and political efforts are trying to self-direct their futures with some success. Real success usually only comes when they find a way to get media access. Then they are able to exert the pressure to counter the moneyed interests. However, what if the media is not serving the public, but rather is representing the self-interests of the industry?

Media access is, for the citizenry, what money is for corporate interests. Many points have already been discussed illustrating the tightening noose on media access—executed by the industry in the name of free press.

Janine Jackson, research director of the premier advocacy organization promoting democratic media, Fairness and Advocacy in Media, explains the problem that misrepresentation and distortion causes for the public: "The media is the dominant method of socialization. It shapes people's opinions. It makes people believe what they are hearing."

As noted earlier, the average family watches sixty hours of TV each week, of which 7.3 hours are talk shows, information programs, and news magazines. Since the public legally owns the airwaves over which these programs travel, one wonders what it will take to wake us up—to so outrage the U.S. public that we will break through the powerful gate of complacency? How long will we tolerate the imposition of an anticonsumer viewpoint and practice at the expense of the real intent of the First Amendment?

Chapter 5

What Can Be Done?

It seems to me that the problem is not coming up with wonderful ideas about how the world could be better. The problem, is how do we get from here to there?

Former FCC Commissioner Nicholas Johnson[1]

The public is the greatest stakeholder in the communications realm. In a society like the United States, public access to the media and free exchange of ideas is the cornerstone of our system. The viability of our society depends on informed citizens who act to set the tone for the culture and the nation, through their votes, their opinions expressed in polls, their priorities expressed in how they spend money, and through their advocacy for or against issues. The public must have access to the media to express its grievances with the status quo in order to keep the democratic organism alive and healthy. If media gatekeeping causes this access to be denied, the entire democratic system is at risk.

In today's society, the new technologies can be a great help toward accomplishing the objectives of access for all to free speech. People receive timely information constantly. Background material is easily available on the Internet. Access to offer one's views on the media is now technologically easier to do than ever before.

It is easier for both news and entertainment media to provide us the communication essential to overcoming the hatreds and parochialisms that have plagued humankind throughout history. Mass communication is a tool mightier than the sword in winning the battles that have divided, destabilized, and destroyed both people and nations.

Could the media live up to these expectations? Or must one be resigned to the manipulation and gatekeeping by big corporations and wealthy individuals designed to serve their own interests rather than the public interest?

All too often, the media end up stealing our futures, killing our culture, or scaring us to death. So many gatekeepers twist or screen out free expression.

For example, in exercising *their* First Amendment rights of free speech, the owners of the media provide us with news containing speech but little information.

In an attempt to increase profits, media owners and advertisers all too often abandon democratic processes and principles in order to invoke techniques of both content selection and production that are designed to frighten the public, immobilizing rather than empowering it.

In an attempt to increase profits, the media owners and the corporations that advertise on the media advocate and lobby for laws and regulations that bypass the democratic processes by almost totally ignoring the public.

In a lapse of logic, educators and the public ignore the need for media literacy and for sufficient civics studies to enable the average citizen to understand how the system works. As a result, both the public and the media often fail to comprehend the impact of what is placed on the screen.

In an attempt to be clever, creative people are encouraged to only produce the bizarre and the shocking. News people are encouraged to provide only the cynical and the scandalous. Rarely do the media show the best of the human spirit.

Can the media do a better job for our culture and still remain profitable? Yes.

Below is a listing of many specific improvements that could be made— some, in fact, were once law. A litany of suggestions for how to get "from here to there" follow. Some past models for turning ideas into reality can work now; in other areas, new solutions must be found. This chapter deals with what can be done and how it can be done.

What can be done?

Robert L. Hilliard, former chief of public (educational) broadcasting at the Federal Communications Commission (FCC), focuses the question. "While one entity may play a greater role in gatekeeping than others, all major gatekeepers—owners, stations, advertisers, government, and the public itself—contribute to the restriction of fair, full, and objective dissemination of information and ideas over the media."[2]

Hilliard continues. "The question is, what can be done to curb the power any one group has to control the public's right to hear and see without trampling on that group's—and by extension, all of our—First Amendment rights. The key lies in recognition of the fact that the airwaves belong to the people. The government, through congressional law and the FCC rules and regulations, represent the people in making sure that the airwaves serve, as stated in the Communications Act of 1934, 'the public interest, convenience, or necessity.' The owners and the stations are licensed for specified periods of time to serve the public interest with their programming. The advertisers have no more right to usurp the public interest than do the owners or the stations. The rating systems are simply there to serve the stations and the advertisers, and are only another link in the chain serving the public."

Who determines the public interest?

In order to determine what specific actions might be taken to improve the quality of media, one must first know who holds the power to create and sustain policy innovation. There are a number of important power bases from which to launch initiatives for change—power bases responsible for the public interest: (a) The first and most important is the federal government, specifically the Federal Communications Commission and the U.S. Congress. (b) Second, administrators responsible for journalism and mass communications school curricula play a role in whether or not those creating programs understand public interest. (c) Third, managers responsible for providing public access to the media on existing stations, or through new outlets, increase access. (d) Fourth, administrators responsible for public education are the ones responsible for creating a media-literate society. (e) Fifth, administrators and public officials responsible for operating and financing public media determine the extent to which it services the public. (f) Finally, rating company executives are responsible for devising the criteria and standards for ranking media success.

The Federal Communications Commission and the U.S. Congress

"Officially, it's the government—the FCC—whose job it is to protect the public interest. In no case is the owner or stations or advertiser or rating system authorized or entitled to override the public's right to regulate the airwaves through their elected representatives' appointees, the FCC commissioners," Robert Hilliard remarks.

This is why the government's action, or inaction, is crucial to implementing any changed media policy.

Hilliard continues. "Given the above, then we must rely principally on the government—Congress, the president, and the FCC—to regulate gatekeeping. What are some of the factors that have led to ever stronger gatekeepers and ever-weaker public interest? Principally, the trend toward deregulation, serving the interest of the industry first and the public second, which began in the latter years of the Carter administration, escalated during the Reagan and Bush administrations, and continued, although to a slightly lesser degree, during the Clinton administration."

The specific examples of rulings and laws that contribute either to media gatekeeping or to serving the public interest are many. Some are listed below.

According to Robert Hilliard, "Gatekeeping has been increasingly con-centrated in the hands of the few by Congress's and the FCC's virtual *elimi-nation of the anti-monopoly rules* that marked the 1960s and 1970s. With no further restrictions on the number of radio or television stations that one entity may own—with the exception of some limits on stations owned in one market for radio, and the percent of the U.S. population covered for television—fewer and fewer owners have obtained more and more stations and programming power, thus narrowing the choices of information and ideas the American listening and viewing public have. Solution? Simply for Congress to reinstate multiple ownership [the number of stations any one owner can be licensed for nationally] and duopoly [the number of sta-tions any one owner can be licensed for in the same market] rules. Concommitantly, efforts could be made to stop the current trend toward elimination of the cross-ownership rule, which bars common ownership of a daily newspaper and broadcast station in the same community. Without strong antimonopoly rules in all of these areas, a few owners are becoming ever more powerful, and the traditional First Amendment rights of the pub-lic to hear freedom of speech and press are severely eroded because media freedom of speech and press are effectively practiced by only one or a few individuals in any given community."

Hilliard cites rules the FCC could make. "Another area of preserving the rights of the public is to return the media to principally news and entertainment programming. During the Reagan administration, the FCC *eliminated its pro-gram-length commercials* rule. The rule forbade commercials of five minutes or more. Now we have the airwaves cluttered with full hours of nothing but com-mercials, whose only purpose is to exploit the consumer and which reduces the amount of noncommercial time available for information and entertainment. Further, the FCC has eliminated strict limits on the amount of commercial time permitted per hour, resulting in some programs—watch a TV movie with a stop-watch sometime—having more commercial time than program time.

"Another rule abandoned by deregulation required stations, depending on size, is to *devote a minimum percentage of airtime to news and public affairs programming*. This rule should be reinstated.

"Also in the 1970s, all stations were required to do *a formal ascertain-ment of community needs*. Then, at the end of each year, they were required to prove to the FCC that the station had addressed in some of its program-ming the ten most important issues the members of the community had cho-sen as significant to that community. Restoring that rule, which was eliminated during the Reagan administration, would do much to restore some say in programming to the public interest, rather than allowing it to be totally based on the beliefs and, sometimes, prejudices of the stations and owners."

Hilliard continues, "The elimination by the Reagan administration of the *Fairness Doctrine*, which provided time for spokespersons from opposing views when a station presented only one side of an issue that was controversial in that community, also strengthened the hands of the owners and station gatekeepers. Congress could do much to lessen the gatekeeping stranglehold by passing a Fairness Law." The Fairness Doctrine had been disliked by some broadcasters who claimed that it infringed on First Amendment rights of broadcasters. However, in 1969, the *Red Lion* court decision said otherwise. The U.S. Supreme Court ruled that the Red Lion Broadcasting Company in Media, Pennsylvania, was wrong in opposing the Fairness Doctrine. The Supreme Court ruled that these regulations "enhance rather than abridge the freedom of speech and press protected by the First Amendment." The Supreme Court ruled that stations "must give adequate coverage to public issues . . . and coverage must be fair in that it accurately reflects opposing views."

Nicholas Johnson's response to the question of what can be done is, "There are really two questions here: Can anything be changed? And is it worth trying? It's always worth trying.[4] Johnson was FCC commissioner during the strongest proconsumer period of the century and was responsible for putting many ideas on the policy table at that time. Unfortunately, today we live in a world of corporatized media resulting from the Reagan-Bush era's repeal of many of the public-interest protections adopted in the 1960s and 1970s. Our current situation, consequently, requires that ideas for improvement in laws and regulations be accompanied by sophistocated strategies for providing sufficient resources for fighting for the public interest to hold their ground when doing battle with those fighting for corporate interests. More on that later.

Johnson's list provides numerous examples for changed rules and laws. For example, "The Aspen Institute's Charlie Firestone proposed years ago the idea of 'access is fairness.' Broadcasters wouldn't have to comply with the Fairness Doctrine (now repealed) if they made time available for access by local groups." Johnson continues: "Or the idea that while broadcasters don't have to sell time to others, if they do so, for the commercial advertisements, they should not be able to refuse to sell time for ideas. The freedom to speak one's mind should not give a handful of broadcasters the legal power to censor all the rest of us—as the law now provides. This came up in the DNC, and BEM cases."

"Or we could divide the time equally among all applicants—like how Thames Television and London Weekend share the station in London. So if there are seven stations in town, and seven people who wanted to be broadcasters, each one gets one station. But if there are fourteen applicants each would just get to broadcast for a half-day everyday, or all day three-and-one-half days a week. If there were enough applicants that no one got more than two hours a day, so be it."

Johnson explains, "There are many options for funding public broadcasting. Citizens for Independent Public Broadcasting was created to take a new look at these issues. One-time CBS New President, Fred Friendly, once proposed using some of the revenue from communications satellites—a 'people's dividend' from the satellite technology taxpayers funded in the first place. Some have proposed taxes on television sets."[5]

Other rules that the FCC could change to create a more pro-consumer media would be the following:

- Reduce the number of minutes of advertising to no more than 5 percent of a programming hour and make program-length commercials illegal.
- Reinstate the provision—for which Nicholas Johnson was principally responsible—that each station must have a given percent of news and public affairs programming (depending on station size) and link it to the ascertainment of community needs. That would be the only way to define news and public affairs as relevant to local interests since the FCC is banned from legislating program content. This rule was passed in 1972, but repealed in the Reagan era.

Later in the chapter we will address *how* such changes can be accomplished.

Change involves bringing the law makers in Congress and the rule makers in the FCC to a point where they understand that their self-interest is to be more beholden to the American public than to the National Association of Broadcasters (NAB) and the media-industry special interests.

Journalism and Mass Communications School Curricula

News directors have often preferred to hire people with backgrounds in political science, history, sociology, law, and psychology rather than those who graduate from programs in journalism and media studies. The reason is that people with this educational background often have a better understanding of the relevance of the material on which they report.

For example, University of Milwaukee Journalism Professor David Berkman tells about his students in communications: "I once gave a current affairs exam, and of the twenty kids in the class, only one could identify Boutros-Boutros Gali [United Nations secretary general], and if somebody had put down 'the UN guy,' I would have accepted that. . . . I'm profoundly disturbed by the ignorance of contemporary affairs, the disinterest in it, and I let it be known. . . . The student rush to PR [public relations] is the latest symptom of the serious, qualitative deterioration which has come to beset journalism education."[6]

The rapid development of new technologies has influenced the focus of mass communication and journalism education. Increasingly, both faculty and students become fascinated with how the technologies can be used, as was the case when television replaced radio as the dominant electronic media. The problem this creates is a shift in focus away from understanding the importance and the impact of news content toward studying technique.

One cannot deliver quality programming unless one knows to whom they are speaking—that is, unless one understands the demographics of the nation and the place of this nation in the global community. One cannot address the diverse issues that the public needs to know about unless one understands the many viewpoints held by people from different social and economic and cultural backgrounds. In a global economy, one cannot understand the consequences of events at home or abroad unless one has some understanding of world events. One cannot have the vaguest understanding of the news releases read on air about public policy unless one has some experience learning about the sectors and processes of government and about those who advocate and lobby for and against various proposed policies. The best way to glean this wisdom is to serve a stint covering or working in local or state government. One would hope that the curricula in higher education programs for media professionals would afford them the opportunity to learn the meaning and implications of what they report. It is hoped, they will learn about the role and responsibility of the media as the fourth estate and that its substance goes far beyond reporting scandal and spewing cynicism.

Similarly, those educated for careers in film and entertainment can benefit from some of the same knowledge. Understanding the demographics and social and political composition of the country can be a distinct advantage. Some understanding of global cultures can also be important in a marketplace where one's art will be exported to other countries and competing with that of people who live there. Should one become prominent in their field of the arts, she or he will speak more articulately and act more appropriately when in the public limelight if one understands how to stay abreast of current events and how to interpret the meaning of those events.

Expanded Local Access Media

In recent years, media ownership consolidation permitted by government changes in laws and regulations has resulted in screening out a large section of the American public from the media. Women and minorities are greatly underrepresented as media owners. Remember that these "minorities" add up to two-thirds of the nation's population—a clear majority of Americans. In 1990 only about 3.5 percent of broadcast licenses were issued to minorities.

Strengthening the few places where media access is possible for the public is key to reducing media gatekeeping.

Mixed in with the barrage of programs coming on commercial cable television, broadcast stations, and main-line film, one finds a few places where a cross-section of the public might have free access to its airwaves.

To be sure, there are talk shows on major networks that invite public call-ins. But these opportunities for participation are rare and constrained. And in the 1990s, many talk shows have become a form of staged entertainment dealing with the outrageous—certainly not a forum for public interest communication.

Some other venues exist for media access: low-power television, microradio, community access cable television, and independent film releases.

Low Powered Television

Low powered television, or LPTV, was first authorized in 1982 when the FCC granted over 150 licenses. These are broadcast stations that operate on reduced power and reach a community in a radius from five to fifteen miles of the transmitter. The low frequency means that the station will not interfere with others beyond their radius that use the same frequency. At the end of 1998, there were 2,000 LPTV stations nationally. At that time, it was estimated that an LPTV station could be placed on the air for much less than a regular broadcast channel. Some said it could be done for between $50,000 and $300,000.[7]

Mark Pinsky described the birth of LPTV in the *New York Times:* "The concept emerged out of the counterculture of the early 1970s, when technically oriented young people began to use cheap new technologies in rural areas that, for topographical reasons, couldn't receive traditional television signals. One place this happened was in Lanesville, New York, in a small valley near Woodstock. A group of people who called themselves the Vidiofreex set up a low power station, without troubling the Federal Communication Commission for a license. . . . These populist pioneers, using the slogan, 'low power to the people,' managed to convince the FCC that, in addition to serving rural people 'off the net' of existing television broadcasting, low-power technology could aim for the fringe, providing programming diversity and encouraging minority ownership."[8]

Programming on LPTV is ecclectic, and usually seeks to reach an audience not served by the dominant channels in the media market. Original programming is common. Nonetheless, some of the syndicators, like Viacom, offer special packages with feature films to LPTV stations.[9]

Examples of LPTV use include stations serving rural communities across the country, special language stations to Spanish-speaking populations near Miami and in other geographical areas with large Latino/a populations, and stations offering services to Alaska Natives.

Microradio

Until 1980 it was legal to operate a 10–watt noncommercial radio station. The station would broadcast within a radius of six to ten miles depending on the quality of the antenna. Most of the stations existing at the time were college radio stations. The Corporation for Public Broadcasting and other segments of the public broadcasting establishment convinced the FCC to get rid of them as part of a plan to develop a system of high-powered, professionally operated stations.

In recent years, enterprising "techies" across the country have again begun to set up micropower radio stations. According to one of these groups, Radio Free Berkeley, it costs less than $1,000 to put a community voice on the air.[10] One microradio station operator indicated that it is necessary only to find an empty frequency and adjust the transmitter to it.

The problem has been that the FCC said it was illegal.

The microradio advocates argue that the U.S. Constitution allows the federal government to regulate interstate commerce and it can make treaties with other nations, but the federal government cannot interfere in this right of people to communicate at a local level.

The major impetus for the microradio movement is anger at the fact that most of the publicly owned airwaves in the United States are inaccessible to the public because of the government collaboration with industry elites. Writer Lee Ballinger notes, "In 1995, the top 50 radio chain owners controlled 876 stations, today (1996) the top 50 owners control 1,187 stations, an increase of 40 percent in just 12 months.[11]

By 1999 some voices in the FCC said microradio should be made legal. And, early in 2000 the FCC voted to legalize ten-watt stations owned by noncommercial groups with local community fees.[12] Some supporters of microradio across the nation say they should be allowed to operate without any licensing at all because the licensing bureaucracy is too complex, bureaucratic, and a waste of time. The powerful National Association of Broadcasters (NAB) lobby, the lobby for the major stations continues to oppose microradios, ostensibly fearing frequency interferance, but perhaps also because they see potential competition. NAB may persuade Congress to prohibit microradio. Nonetheless, these stations appear all across the United States carrying programs for low-income communities, ethnic music, nostalgia radio for seniors, militia radio, neighborhood activist programming, and whatever you might imagine. The National Lawyers Guild's Committee on Democratic Communications has filed amicus, or "friend of the court" briefs on behalf of microradio station owners in the cases challenging the FCC throughout the late 1990s. Microradio advocates point to Article 19 of the Universal Declaration of Human Rights stating that all people have the right "to seek, receive and impart information and ideas through any media regardless of frontiers."[13]

The microradio activists argue strongly that the big corporations and the nation's wealthiest people, through control of mass communications, are making it impossible for democratic resolution of problems affecting the mainstream population. This position is best expressed in a chapter of *Seizing the Airwaves* by Ron Sakolsky and Stephen Dunnifer, "If you can't communicate, you can't organize, and if you can't organize, you can't fight back."[14]

Community Access and Local Origination Television

In the early 1970s the FCC ordered the cable television companies to include in their franchise agreement with a given licensing community the following services: public access, local government access, educational access, and local origination programming. In all cases, the cable company was to set aside designated channels for each of these interests. Local government access provided an ongoing view of government meetings. Educational access provided a range of programs that the school department might make available. Public access provided the opportunity for anyone in a community to learn to use the production equipment in a studio provided by the cable company and then to be able to air their programs. Local origination went beyond making a channel and equipment available. In this case, the cable operator was required to hire staff to professionally produce local programming.

Now, nearly thirty years later, these services are at risk. Access channels are no longer mandated. Although they continue to operate in most communities across the nation, they are generally at lower funding levels. In addition, the Telecommunications Act of 1996 allows for competition in providing television signals. Consequently, utility companies are beginning to offer television in competition to the cable companies. President Clinton signed a provision in the FY2000 federal budget approving satellite TV companies request to offer local TV broadcast channels. This increases the competition for cable companies. It is doubtful that community access can survive this environment. It is cheaper for the cable companies to cut these services, and if the public and local government does not complain about service cuts, they will get away with it.

Independent Films

Some of the more creative voices expressed through film do not have access to the major corporate production houses and distributors. They do not have the big budgets for their films.

Consequently, the filmmaker must find a distributor to release the film, place it in theaters for the public. This has proven very difficult. Without iniatives such as that of Robert Redford, himself an actor, producer, and director, the future for "the indies," as they are called, would be bleak indeed. In 1981 Redford started the Sundance Institute in Sundance, Utah. Its annual festival has become one of the nation's best points of exposure for creative young filmmakers. The festivals are places for negotiations between filmmakers and distributors. In addition to the festival, Sundance has also established a cable network to showcase independent features.[15]

As the new millennium begins, independent film makers and recording artists are experimenting with bypassing the monopoly distributorships by releasing their work directly to the public on the Internet. Mergers like AOL/Time Warner and the increasing influence of advertising on the Internet may, if the public and public interest lawyers are not vigilant, minimize these new opportunities for the independent artist.

Internet Web Sites

Increasingly, the technologies of computer and video are merging. The venue of the Internet provides more room for public access—at least in theory. *Broadcasting and Cable* magazine emphasized this convergence in an article about video-streaming Web sites.[16] The diversity of sites is enormous and growing. The sites listed below are by no means a comprehensive list. They are simply intended to provide a small sample of one's options.

- Alternative Entertainment Network (AEN), found at www.aentv.com, also comes via RealVideo. Available are videos of a wide range of vintage shows such as *Jack Benny* and *Burns and Allen.* AEN also carries news specials.
- CNN Interactive, found at www.cnn.com, is streamed through RealVideo and Windows Media technologies. It carries current news as well as an

extensive archive and a range of special reports on given topics.

- Fox News, found at www.foxnews.com, also carries a twenty-four-hour stream of news stories, some archived material. It is provided through RealVideo. The viewer can also "cherry-pick" from current headlines to develop a personalized stream.
- MSNBC.com, found at www.msnbc.com, is delivered through Windows Media. It carries video clips of current news and also has clips that can be retrieved from recent news shows.
- MTV is located at www.mtv.com, as provided by RealVideo. The site has clips from on-air programs and background material.
- NBA.com is found at www.nba.com and is provided by RealVideo video streaming. Clips from the previous night's games and archived material are available.
- Tunes.com is at www.tunes.com, provided also by RealVideo. One can find 12,000 music video clips as well as music news and features. There is a link to the reincarnated version of "The Rolling Stone," JAMTV.
- VideoSeeker, found at www.videoseeker.com, comes through RealVideo and Windows Media. It provides clips from NBC news and entertainment. There are previews of upcoming series and special archival materials.
- WarnerBros. Online is located at www.warnerbros.com and is streamed through Windows Media. This site has clips of the company's TV series such as *Seinfeld*. It also has trailers from recent blockbuster releases.

Note, however, that while established corporate sites are present on the Internet, it is not clear whether anything will change in terms of real access to the media for the public. New mergers are announced daily with the intent of profiting from E-commerce. Nielson is now offering ratings for on-line advertisers. Home computers have difficulty delivering speedy Web service because of the volume of ads on key sites. It is too early to say whether the easy communication access for Internet users will continue as demand for commercial sites grows.

Parallel to the commercial sites, countless other sites exist to foster public interest communication. For example, the Association for Progressive Communication (APC) hosts twenty-one international member networks. See http://www.apc.org. Their networks link over 40,000 nongovernmental organizations (NGOs), activists, policymakers, educators, and community leaders from 133 countries across the globe.[17] Included in their networks are:

- PeaceNet—http://peacenet.org/peacenet/—linking people interested in peacemaking. Also see http://www.igc.apc.org/interact/Peacenet.html.

- EcoNet—http://econet.apc.org/econet/—organizations interested in sustainable environment.
- ConflictNet—http://www.igc.apc.org/conflictnet/—linking groups working on conflict resolution.
- LaborNet—http://www.igc.apc.org/labornet—exchanging news and information among those interested in democratic labor movements.
- WomensNet—http://www.igc.apc.org/womensnet/—women's resources.

In addition to this type of web site, there is a wide range of news groups. For example, Usenet, also called Net News, deals with several thousand specialized interactive news groups.

Nonetheless, being able to send one's comment through cyberspace does not mean that the messages are read or the concerns addressed by those with the power to respond with action. Communication among a few dozen or a few hundred, or even a few thousand, people is satisfactory for some special interests, but it is by no means "mass communication" in the sense that it is practiced by the major corporations on public airwaves.

Once the hype about the new technology wears down, it may become clear that the public's interest is still screened out—unrepresented on the airwaves it owns, unattended by the government officials whose salaries it pays. Until some equilibrium is established between the currency of votes and the currency of money, it is not likely that the Internet will eliminate gatekeeping. Its contribution will simply be to make it more convenient to locate what one wants to find.

Curricula for All Levels of Education

Any educated person should understand a range of topics necessary for achieving media literacy. This means achieving a level of competence whereby one can intelligently judge the messages one is receiving on both news and entertainment media. It means reaching the point where one can utilize the media to deliver as well as receive media, where one can know how to register one's objection if denied access to the media. However, as will be discussed below, media literacy must go hand in glove with an understanding of civics in order for a person to function effectively in society.

Components of such a curriculum might include the following:

- *Media literacy* (print, visual, and aural)—Understanding how words, pictures, and sounds are used as symbols that convey or bias meaning beneath the obvious message. Understanding the semiotics of how images are portrayed—images of women, of different racial and ethnic groups, of place (cities), and of economic class.

- Understanding the need for the message receiver to *cross-check sources for the truth* behind the message. Reviewing several media to validate the message. Utilizing several media when sending messages. Issues of truth, mediated truth, virtual and digitized reality, propaganda, persuasion, and opinion.

- Understanding one's *rights to use mass media to communicate within the nation's legal framework.* Knowing the meaning of the First Amendment, libel law, the Fairness Doctrine (or lack thereof), truth in advertising, prior restraint, copyright, invasion of privacy, Freedom of Information Act (FOIA), shield laws (protecting sources), free press, fair trial and Anti-Trust violations. Knowing who really gets to send and who gets to receive mass communication.

- Understanding the *basic rights provided to the citizen* in the U.S. Constitution to petition officials or one's representatives on any topic. Understanding the basic structure of government, including its checks and balances, the process for selecting and electing candidates to office, the process for making laws and for funding programs. Knowing the "sunshine" laws and regulations that require public access to information and meetings.

- Understanding the basics of *media gatekeeping*, whereby the media owners, program creators, financial backers, and sometimes the media consumers filter, mediate, bias, and omit all or parts of public messages.

- Knowing how various forms of media can be used effectively to *amplify and incorporate diverse views* into a debate around community needs, to document and disseminate community accomplishments, to empower community voices, bringing them as full partners to the policy-making table.

- *Understanding the role of mass media* in (1) mobilizing people, (2) influencing people, (3) enabling people to express their views in noticeable and memorable ways, (4) halting intrusions on human rights and violations of public trust, (5) empowering and electing leaders to champion human rights and democratic society, (6) providing "sunshine" on the policies and practices of those in power, who set popular and political agendas, (7) influencing policy changes through measurements of public opinion and through creating perceptions of reality (or portraying actual reality). Learning to effectively use the mass media to these ends.

- Understanding of the role of the mass media in Hitler's Germany, in order to identify the *ways in which mass media becomes a tool of ideo-*

logical hegemony, and understanding options for preventing such ideological dominance. Assessing the impact of new communication technologies—their pervasiveness, seductive appeal, and diversity—as tools for both fostering and for diminishing ideological hegemony.

- Understanding the *pervasiveness of the mainstream media*, its monopoly ownership, how it uses ratings and sales tools, not content, for program decisions and for limiting which artists are able to market their music. Learning to critique said practices. Learning when public and community service messages occasionally are broadcast. Examining the impact on communities when monopoly messages conquer/close the hearts and minds of the audience.

- *Understanding the U.S. and global economic classism*. Analyzing how mainstream mass media portray class within the United States and globally. What social and political forces influence the mediated reality that is commonly presented? Especially examining television and film as the dominant communicators influencing the masses. Will these messages bring increases in middle-class consumerism, or will unrest increase as people are increasingly aware of what others have that they do not?

- Understanding how *to ensure that programming is diverse and equitable, and exhibits social justice*. Techniques for use by community people with messages to tell. Techniques for monitoring and improving mainstream performance in this area by writers, reporters, artists, filmmakers, producers, composers, and so on. Encouraging awareness among both performers and audience for the entertainment media so that acceptable behavior is to show and tell entertainment messages within this value system.

- Understanding that it is *as much a self-interest issue as an ethical issue for one to become sensitive to and aware of correcting cultural biases*. Examine multiculturalism in all forms of mass media. Assessing the impact of current practices in local communities and in the larger community—a neighborhood, city, nation, or global village.

- Understanding the tendency in American film and entertainment *to focus on one hero* (often only white and male) and to neglect acknowledgment that accomplishments are usually the result of the work of many workers and organizations together in a democratic struggle for solutions. Countering that misinformation with both the senders of message and with media literacy among receivers of messages.

- Understanding that mainstream media molds societies into *consumers rather than citizens*. Examination of the role of workers and community organizations in offsetting this pervasive cultural message—not by retreating into isolation, but by engaging communities in action that is more appealing than consumerism.

- Examining media tools that promote citizen empowerment. *Empowering community people* and their organizations as makers of news, creators of all forms of messages, and not passive recipients of messages. Enabling communities to understand how not to be ignored by the major media, how to speak for themselves rather than to be spoken about by others. Engaging community organizations in the distribution of messages utilizing all forms of mass media. Facilitating community leaders in providing persuasive feedback to mass media owners and program sponsors in order to expose media gatekeeping.
- *Understanding the role that music and art play in transmitting social and political ideas* when used as background in film, video, or radio, when used on posters, monuments, and graffiti and in street theater.
- Awareness of the *changing era at the beginning of the twenty-first century* where global forces make possible opportunities heretofore unknown, and knowing that the same *global forces* may undercut individualism, free speech, autonomy, and the rights of self-determination for communities addressing their own public and community service needs.

Such a curriculum can be incorporated into any university, and should be, if schools wish to graduate adults who are capable citizens as well as capable professionals. In addition, such a curriculum should begin at the lowest levels of elementary school, tailored to fit the age of the students.

It is important to bear in mind that media literacy cannot be just about the media. Those who study this curriculum must also have some education in civics so that they can understand how policy decisions are made and what their role is in making those decisions in a democratic society.

Unbelievable as it seems, many states no longer require civics as part of their secondary school curriculum. How can one possibly have an adult public able to self-govern without an understanding of civics? It is not uncommon to find adults totally unaware of the most basic principles. As Nicholas Johnson pointed out, "The U.S. Constitution provides that any citizen can participate in almost any governing process. For example, I'm on a school board here. Anybody who wants to write a letter to the school board or come before the school board and speak can do so. Anybody can file an *amicus brief* with the FCC or with a court. Anybody can write their elected officials or chair of a congressional committee and ask to testify, send in information, whatever. That's what the 'right of petition' guarantees."[18]

Expanded Public Media

One way to escape media gatekeeping is to increase the use of alternative media. Dr. Peter Phillips, director of Project Censored, the organization that publishes the annual *Project Censored Yearbook*, "the news that didn't make the news and why," includes in the book a lengthy list of alternative media outlets—mostly print media.[197]

The most potentially effective use of alternative media could be a reinvigorated Public Broadcasting Service. The reason to look in this direction is that the infrastructure is already in place for a screen and microphone that can reach into most homes across America.

Public Broadcasting

The Public Broadcasting Act of 1967 was the blueprint for public television as we know it today. While the first non-commercial station went on the air in 1953, it was not until 1967 that a major national commitment to public broadcasting became a reality. Bill Moyers, as special assistant to President Lyndon Johnson, was key in turning this idea into reality. The law created the Corporation for Public Broadcasting from which PBS (Public Broadcasting Service) emerged. This was to be the place for the wide range of cultural, educational, and public affairs programming not likely to be found on commercial television. It is not television run by the government, as is public television in many countries. It is public television organized by and subsidized by the government, but run by independent boards of directors selected at local levels across the nation. To create and strengthen public broadcasting was a major step toward ensuring that the media can address the public interest. It is, therefore, most unfortunate to see efforts being made at the end of the twentieth century to reduce this commitment and to remold public broadcasting into just another form of commercial broadcasting.

Public broadcasting can be the place where the public interest is most protected, apart from the pressures of advertisers seeking programs that attract potential product customers. It can be the place where First Amendment freedoms actually apply to the citizenry of the United States. To accomplish this, however, would require a rather different approach to public broadcasting than what has evolved since 1967. We have a system that, indeed, provides more in-depth news and more quality entertainment than usually appears on the commercial stations, but it is elitist and not representative of the cross-section of people who are America. In addition, it is not really a point of access for the full range of alternative thinking in this country. Like its commercial brothers, it reflects the dominant views and seems frightened of ideas that bring too much fresh air.

Janine Jackson, research director of Fairness and Accuracy in Reporting (FAIR), is one of many who believe that "we must reinvent public broadcasting." She sees it as crucial to break the chains that private corporate funding use to constrain public broadcasting, and to redesign the system to provide real freedom of information.[20]

The ideas for reinvigorating PBS are not new. Robert Hilliard, when chief of public broadcasting for the FCC, was releasing trial balloons in the late 1960s. He said: "There's a difference between seeking large audiences for programs that are good and seeking programs that will draw large audiences. Some critics believe that when a principal criterion for choosing programs is to attract as many viewers as possible, there is a tendency, even an unconscious one, to gravitate toward the bland and noncontroversial. It has been suggested that public broadcasting, instead of trying to reach the greatest number of people, should try to attract the greatest number of different audiences." This may be the best forum for "providing materials to those groups whose numbers are too small to be served by the rating-directed commercial stations and whose interests and needs can be met only by noncommercial TV."[21]

Alternative Public Television

Hilliard suggested that the Corporation for Public Broadcasting (CPB) add a parallel service to that of the PBS. This service would be called Alternative Public Television. "APT would not only be an uncensored outlet for controversial programs that now fall by the wayside before they reach all of the public. It would also permit the airing of materials considered too off-beat, lengthy, esoteric, unpopular, specialized, difficult to schedule, or otherwise unacceptable for national or local distribution under the present system. It would cover live events, controversial or not, that affect the public, no matter what time they occur, breaking into scheduled programming if necessary, without concern how the ratings would be affected. APT would use satellites to link classrooms, meeting halls, and other group gathering places throughout the world, providing live forums for the exchange of views and feelings in order to achieve greater understanding among all peoples."

Hilliard envisioned this added public television service as governed by a board of people from backgrounds alternative to the traditional corporate board—people representing the broadest range of geographic, political, economic, social, political, vocational, and ethnic perspectives. The funding would come from the same mix used by public broadcasting now—government funds, foundations, viewer donations, and industry. It would operate nationally, but would promote local production.

To make such an alternative station a reality, several things would be required: (1) FCC would have to grant CPB the frequencies; (2) Congress would have to show commitment by providing the authorizing legislation for it to be created; and (3) Congress would have to provide funding for its operation.

Hilliard concludes that "the key to Alternative Public Television's success is flexibility. APT must be prepared to adapt constantly in order to effectively meet the needs of the people, not only serving as an alternative to public television, but, if necessary, as an alternative to itself."[22]

Financing Through a Tax on Advertising

Another way to improve public television is to stabilize the funding for media intended for the public interest. This might be done by denying the tax deduction to advertisers in the electronic media and using the proceeds from the tax to finance public broadcasting. This idea, recommended in *We the Media*, notes that a considerable sum would be raised if the $130 billion advertising industry were taxed, and the proceeds used to provide a major boost to public broadcasting.[23] At present, the tax law allows advertisers to deduct as a business expense all that they spend on ads on the airwaves. Considering that the airwaves belong to the people, it can be argued that the people should benefit from the commercial use of these airwaves by profit-making corporations.

Public Broadcasting Opportunities

Improving public broadcasting would help greatly to overcome gatekeeping. Nonetheless, it is important to note that there are media networks and programs already working to reach the public screened out from information on commercial television. The premier service in this area is the cable-industry-sponsored C-SPAN, which provides the public with gavel-to-gavel coverage of Congress in session and of other important policy meetings.

Entertainment programs as well as news programs shown on various cable channels provide fine examples of television at its best. Theatrical producer Arthur D'Lugoff cites an example. "I saw three hours on what's happening in Yugoslavia on the Discovery Channel. It was terrific. It was in depth. There was no advertising. It was almost like a PBS program. That's the right direction. There's just not enough of it. The amount of time taken by advertisers—and on radio it's worse—is outrageous. I just think that there isn't enough public input outside of the corporations. It's become a corporate state."[24]

Change the Rating System

So long as commercial television is financed by advertisers, there will need to be some way to measure how many people watch their commercials for products. We are at a window of opportunity for improving how this measurement is done. The convergence of new technologies with a growing dissatisfaction in Nielsen's traditional approach creates the opportunity. Simplistic counting of what channel is tuned, what time and how long, and who watched is no longer satisfactory.

Many opportunities are overlooked by so simple an audience count. For example, while a documentary may have an audience of 5–6 million people, in Nielsen terms it is insignificant because viewers may number as many as 50 million for the Super Bowl football game. Yet, any number of companies would consider themselves quite satisfied to reach the specialized documentary size of audience and gain even 2 percent, or a million people, as customers. So the top ratings may be viable for some, but too diluted for those whose money is better spent if focused on their particular clientele. Touting the numbers as broadcasters do is misleading to advertisers and unrepresentative of viewers' real interests.

Nothing in the current system tells broadcasters why the public turned off the set or switched channels. As a Washington, DC, professional woman said, "I watch because I live alone, and it's background noise in the house. Sometimes I watch to learn about the weather forecast. The news has no news, just opinions. The sitcoms are dumb and not decent entertainment."

As Nielsen challengers seek to find the ideal information base for broadcasters and advertisers, and to find perfect technology to use, the opportunity exists to refine what is measured.

For example, technology exists to easily correlate the viewing data with demographic data and to examine not what is watched, but what is not watched. What potential markets are lost because no one cares whether they are pleased with the program possibilities?

Another option would be to experiment with sweeps periods, not to find the stations with the most viewers per se, but to identify what kind of innovative programming might draw an audience. For example, more people might watch a news program if it contained information people needed to know—about funding for education, new career opportunities, health care, and similar topics speaking directly to people's needs. Maybe more people would watch national and international news if topics were covered with the same detail and rigor used to cover athletes in sports competitions—all the background information about past performance, alternative positions, backup personalities, and party positions. Maybe more people would watch entertainment that did not contain violence as an end in itself—drama and adventure taken from real-life situations, programs that empower the typical person with whom the viewer can identify. Maybe there is more of an audience than one might imagine for shows that expand the horizons and carry viewers into other worlds far from their own neighborhood—introductions to the global village in which we now live. Of course, while such creative programming may provide new profits, it will also involve new production costs. But without comprehensive research neither researchers nor broadcasters nor the public will know whether the benefit outweighs the cost.

Changes in the criteria for determining profitable programming must be initiated by the industry itself—the broadcasters and the advertisers. They simply need to understand that it is in their self-interest to do so in order to expand their markets. The technological problems are now solvable. The backward-looking criteria for program evaluation now in place are wasteful for all involved.

How Can Such Change Happen?

The matter of how to get from here to there is critical. All the good ideas are worthless if they cannot be implemented.

The hardest ideas to implement are the ones that require the approval of the largest and most complex institutions. In this case, implementing new curricula is difficult because academic administrators must approve changes. Using alternative media is sometimes easier because there is less need to move mountains—then again, there is less of an audience and less money. The most important institution essential to ending media gatekeeping is the federal government.

It is the most important because it is, by law, the protector of the public interest. That is why we finance it with our taxes. That is why we elect the people who run it. It is the hardest to get to make changes because it is so enormous and the stakes are so large. Ultimately, change happens depending on how one of two kinds of currency are spent: money or votes. Money buys those things essential to running a campaign—paid television advertising, consultants, pollsters, travel, etc. But votes buy the actual victory.

The gap between the rich and the rest of America has grown in recent decades. It is appalling enough that a democratic country with a supposedly large middle class is in fact a nation where 10 percent of the households hold 90 percent of the wealth. The fact that 1 percent of the nation's households own about half of the nation's wealth is the essence of the problem. Most people expect their concerns will be heard, and wonder why they are not. Very rich people not only expect it, but they can pay to make sure that they are heard.

Concurrent with the concentration of wealth in fewer and fewer hands, the corporate mergers that have also taken place over the last decade or two mean there is less and less opportunity for competition or for diverse viewpoints in any industry.

Overlayed on this reality is the fact that the political leadership at the federal government level has not been very proconsumer. The Republican administrations of Ronald Reagan and George Bush were responsible for dismantling scores of consumer protection laws and regulations. The Democratic administration headed by Clinton has been frequently in a deadlock with the Republican-majority Congress and therefore unable to pass virtually anything of a proconsumer nature. The capitulation to corporate interest over public interest in legislation such as the 1996 Telecommunications Act is appalling.

And the public has been told for nearly all of the last two decades by the media that government is useless. Politicians get headlines only when there are scandals. Government is special-interest oriented. Since most people have no clue about how to do anything about this predicament, fewer and fewer of them feel it is worth their time to actually vote on election day.

As a result of this sequence of events, the currency of money weighs very heavily in Washington these days. And the currency of votes is taken less and less seriously.

Nicholas Johnson summarizes the situation: "The problem comes back to how can you make government more responsive to interests other than those of the wealthiest participants, the institutional participants that have the lawyers, the lobbyists, and the publicists. One answer is that you make it more possible for public representation so that you have more parties at the table when the goodies are being divided up."[25]

Johnson continues, "I'm going to look at all the ways that you could fund lawyers doing legal work and see if we can come up with some new ones. A major part of my interest in that is in terms of public interest law. The idea of a treble damage action plus lawyers' fees in an antitrust case is already available. So if you're concerned about antitrust matters, and it happens to fall within the area that's covered by the treble damage action remedy, you can get enough to fund lawyers to do that work. There are other things that provide lawyers fees—damages plus lawyers' fees in a number of contexts. There's the private attorneys general idea. There's the provision that if a regulatory agency would certify that a public interest group had actually contributed to the resolution of the matter at hand, they would be compensated. Then Ralph Nader proposed at one time a Department of Consumer Affairs or such, an agency of government that would hire lawyers who would appear before regulatory commissions to put the case for the public."

Johnson explains why he sees the need to fund professionals to represent the public interest as crucial to effective encounters with those arguing on behalf of big money's special interests. "The right to petition exists pretty universally, even if it doesn't have much force and effect. The problem comes when the large corporations and trade associations—and folks on the right would say the unions—have the ability to bring a bunch of $300,000-a-year lawyers and publicists to bear. The ordinary citizen cannot do that.

"A part of it is also that, as consumers, the consequences for each of us is much less significant. In other words, if General Motors has an issue before Congress, it is well worth their while to run their computer data-base and identify every dealer and every supplier in the United States by congressional district and write them a letter telling them to write their congressman or senator. They pull off something like that."[24]

The major corporate petition or lobbying effort can combine the best of both political currencies. They have lots of money to contribute to the campaigns of the politicians who serve on crucial committees. And they have the money and resources to do the grass-roots lobbying that mobilizes the voters so crucial to an individual's reelection—the folks from the home district.

Johnson continues, "But if all the people who own one of the Chevrolets with whatever the defect is want to organize to lobby, there's no way they can get hold of the information of who even they are. Even if they could get the information of who else owns a defective car, none of them would find it worth their while to take the time to write a letter to Congress, let alone go to Washington to argue their case. It would be easier to buy the $2.70 device to fix the problem and forget the injustice. So that's the problem."

Funding lawyers to work with citizen groups would, in Johnson's view, take one step toward leveling the playing field where citizens trying to make their case are opposed by high-paid attorneys presenting the corporate interest.

Political innovation that codifies ideas like the ones at the beginning of this chapter is possible if the public-interest advocates can muster the resources—and if they understand the policy innovation process. Even some of the nation's most skilled experts sometimes fail, or experience enormous delay in policy innovation, because they did not orchestrate things properly.

Nelson Polsby, author of *Political Innovation in America*, sets certain criteria as essential to innovation.[27]

Polsby believes there are two causes for innovation: (1) a cultural disposition for it, and (2) a political system with incentives to put solutions in place. Many of the changes wanted by those eager to end media gatekeeping require the four key ingredients Polsby identified as key to policy innovation:

- a period of incubation,
- a crisis or perceived crisis,
- favorable timing,
- a policy entrepreneur.

The period of incubation coupled with the perceived crisis serves to create the cultural disposition for change. Timing is often critical to giving the political system the incentives it needs to enact change. Even then, without a skillful policy entrepreneur to focus the political system, things easily fall apart.

Specific ideas for innovation must be floated in the public arena, discussed, debated, reshaped, and packaged to suit the public need at the moment. They must become a common thread in the public fabric. Then their patrons will grow. Ideally, some of the nation's moneyed interests will find it in their self-interest to support a new policy, either for substantive material benefits or for the political benefits of opposing their nemesis.

When an event occurs to precipitate either a real or a perceived crisis, people in all sectors of society will be motivated to take action to solve the problem. Research will be produced. Options are assessed. The crisis gets the policy maker's attention. Again the currencies of government are carefully counted. Will votes be lost if nothing is done? Will money be lost if nothing is done? What is the trade-off?

To survive, the innovation must be proposed at a favorable time—favorable to the debate and favorable for the action needed to enact the law or regulation or appropriation required. More compelling events cannot distract the policy makers. If they do, the proposed innovation will likely return to the back burner and those advocating it will need to start all over at a later date.

If a consensus appears to be generally agreed upon, a policy entrepreneur will then be needed to shepherd it through the minefield of hearings, approvals, protocols, and votes essential to codify the innovation as new policy. The route is never a direct one. The guide can only be one well acquainted with all the logical and illogical obstacles that might block the path. The rewards for successful codification of a new policy are usually substantial, in recognition, if not in monetary gain.

Then the task is to ensure that the adequate administrative resources exist to ensure implementation of the new policy. It will require informed and emotionally supportive people. And it will likely require an appropriation of funds. Until a new policy has been in effect for several years, one can never be certain that it will be sustained or that its implementation will accomplish the objectives for which it was created. Constant advocacy and monitoring are required.

Then, as is evident by the enormous steps taken backward by the FCC in the 1980s after the long struggles to implement innovation in the 1960s and 1970s, one can never declare victory and cease one's vigilance. Creating and sustaining innovation is a never-ending effort.

It is wise to remember these criteria when taking the steps to create any one change.

Venues for Innovation

Now that the context is clear for the process of codifying and implementing new policy, let us look at some of the specific venues in which one might work to carry out the process.

Included here are a range of places for such work, including: (1) citizen-initiated "rule" changes in the FCC; (2) NGOs, research institutes and advocacy organizations; (3) starting one's own station; (4) public awareness campaigns; and (5) law suits.

All these processes can be initiated by confident and determined individuals. Anthropologist Margaret Mead said, "Never doubt that a small group of thoughtful committed citizens can change the world. Indeed, it's the only thing that ever has." The point is that, regardless of all the ominous problems one faces in dealing with big media corporations and monied interests, creativity occasionally breaks through. Innovation occasionally succeeds. Whether that innovation appears inside or outside of corporations or government agencies, it is always initiated by a small group of determined individuals persistent in their belief that they will succeed.

As we examine the places where one might work to initiate innovation, it is important to note that the FCC rule changes, new laws passed by Congress, and lawsuits challenging how laws or rules are interpreted are the specific changes that hold the power to actually change national policy. Advocacy and research organizations, alternative stations, and public awareness campaigns hold the power of persuasion. They cannot change policy, but they can develop the cultural disposition conducive to change.

Citizen-Initiated Federal Communications Commission Rule Changes

A graduate student from Ohio State University initiated a rule change with the FCC after having completed her research on the composition of the boards of directors of public broadcast stations. The research proved that the boards did not reflect the composition of the broadcast media market in terms of race and gender. She filed a petition to include public broadcasting in the ascertainment-of-community-needs requirement then imposed on commercial stations. Her petition was joined by others also interested in this ruling. The commissioners adopted such a rule.

If one wants to file a ruling with the FCC, any person or group can submit a petition to the FCC secretary. This petition must both provide suggested language for the new rule and detail the reasons for such action. If the staff in the appropriate section of the FCC decides the petition is meritorious, the FCC Dockets Office assigns it a "rule making number." Obviously, as in all organizations, before such material is tracked for a vote, there are informal discussions with the other staff and the commissioners. Once the proposed rule, or notice of inquiry, is listed on the weekly public notice, the public has thirty days in which to submit comments. After the staff reviews the comments, and subsequent "reply comments," the item goes as an agenda item to the commissioners with a recommendation. This could take the form of ending discussion on the item or a report and order for the new Rule.[28]

This process is reasonably straightforward on the surface. Building the political support to carry a proposed rule is the more difficult part, requiring an understanding of the way in which stakeholders work. One must carefully assess every point in the process at which something might be blocked and determine a strategy for overcoming each and every obstacle. A policy entrepreneur familiar with both the personalities and the politics is an essential ally from the very beginning because the novice may never know what sinks a proposal. It could be something as simple as whose names to attach to the original petition. As Nicholas Johnson said, "The problem is the subgovernment."[29]

Subgovernment refers to the informal and unofficial networking of people playing the role of policy entrepreneur. Their conversations and handshake agreements made on the golf course, in the rest room, or over a drink are often cornerstones that mark the foundation and shape for laws and policies that will later be codified. This subgovernment has no transparency and no actual legal status. Yet, because it is done by the powerbrokers who stand to win or lose depending on the wording of real laws and policies, the power of the subgovernment can be enormous. It is influenced only by an active citizenry who holds elected powerbrokers accountable and by a press whose investigative reporting brings sunshine to inappropriate informal deal making that might hurt the public.

Nongovernmental Organizations, Research Institutes, and Advocacy Organizations

Nongovernmental organizations (NGOs) are vital to persuading the policy makers that an issue needs attention. They have no power to actually enact any policy innovation that might reduce media gatekeeping. They can, however, raise both public and policy-maker understanding of the issues through their research, and they can organize a base of voter support and sometimes even monetary support.

A wide range of nongovernmental organizations exist across the country with the objective of focusing on media and the public interest. Most of them are funded by foundation grants, donor contributions, and, sometimes, program-specific government contracts.

Research institutes usually have a staff of people with credible professional and academic credentials engaged in the mission of examining and documenting activities, trends, and impacts of certain events.

An example of the research institute is Mediascope.[30] This California-based institution was founded in 1992 to "promote constructive depictions of health and social issues in the media, particularly as they relate to children and adolescents. It publishes the results of its findings for the entertainment industry, policy makers, and the general public.

According to Hubert Jessup, president of Mediascope, "Mediascope has worked in the area of media violence, the 1992 Children's Television Act, network program ratings (the sex and violence ratings), substance use in music lyrics and prime time television, and other public health issues as depicted in the media."

Jessup describes Mediascope's contributions. "One significant success story. The 1992 Children's Television Act did not please anyone. Networks and stations were frustrated by 'being told' to turn over three hours a week to children's educational programs. Producers were disturbed by the lack of definitions. Children's advocates were unhappy about the lack of specifics. Mediascope organized a neutral space for the meeting of all sides and initiated a two-year long dialogue process that brought together all sides to participate in the development of an ongoing set of processes for the implementation of this law. The results were codified in a Mediascope publication: *Building Blocks: A Guide for Creating Children's Educational Television*. Distributed to producers of children's programming, network children's television departments, local stations, and children's advocacy groups, *Building Blocks* has become an important tool in the actual use of the law. Because of Mediascope's approach during this process, we continue to be invited by children's industry and educational groups to help them plan and produce within the context of the law."

Another example is Fairness and Accuracy in Reporting (FAIR). FAIR is oriented toward both media research and advocacy. This media watchdog group does careful research to document bias and imbalance in reporting. It focuses public attention on media monopoly ownership, media allegiance to establishment views, and lack of fair coverage of women, minorities, labor, and poor people. The group goes beyond the typical research group in that it organizes support for journalists attacked for promoting the First Amendment rights of the public, and it organizes to protect public broadcasting from congressional budget cuts. FAIR operates a nationally syndicated radio program called "National Spin" and it publishes a monthly magazine called *EXTRA!*"[31]

Advocacy organizations are created to make the case on behalf of the public or a special-interest group for a specific idea. Public interest support is usually manifest in numbers of supporters—that is, voters who might support or oppose candidates depending on their position on the issue at hand. An advocacy organization might engage in a media campaign, assemble a public demonstration of support, launch a boycott, lobby Congress for a new law, or file a lawsuit.

For example, Paper Tiger Television has existed since 1981. This group creates television programs that appear on cable access channels across the country. Paper Tiger is focused on addressing the ideological assumptions and social impact of mainstream media. It looks at the communications industry impact on public perception. It offers viewpoints not usually given access to mainstream media.[32]

A group that crosses the boundary between research organization and advocacy group is the Union for Democratic Communication (UDC).[33] This group holds an annual conference for those who are concerned with media democracy. The participants range from operators of microradio stations to scholars of media literacy seeking proactive approaches to work with mainstream media. Others involved in UDC are groups that teach NGOs how to access the media: how to know the media landscape and the language of sound bites, how to stay on message, the ideal time for press conferences, and taking programming off the Internet.

Advocacy has as many faces as there are people concerned about the topic. For example, Anne Norton, Emerson College researcher concerned with the advocacy for children's TV, says, "Advocates need to reinvent themselves as public relations professionals if they want their issue addressed adequately in the media."[34] Linda Morton, writing in *Public Relations Quarterly*, says that advocates "must think of gatekeepers as more than the medium to reach the audiences. In and of themselves gatekeepers compose an important public ... [they] and others in that level are most responsible for influencing opinions of politically active citizens." To this end, Morton says, advocates "cannot assume that gatekeepers think the way that they do."[35]

Norton points out that, regarding children's television, the children's needs are being discussed and addressed within the two forums of industry and advocacy groups, but little communication about these dialogues is provided to the general public.

Starting One's Own Station

The most easily achieved ways to gain access to the airwaves were discussed earlier in this chapter in the section on expanding local-access media. In addition, one can follow the example of some of the organizations identified above that produce television programs for circulation to cable access stations, or that produce anchor programs for syndication on radio stations.

Actually, getting a license for one's own broadcast station is technically possible, but less and less realistic. Technically, the FCC has all the forms and protocol. As Robert Hilliard says, "The procedure in applying for a broadcast station (TV, AM FM) is essentially the same for other facilities such as ITFS (Instructional Television Fixed Service), MMDS (Multi-channel, Multipoint Distribution System), and auxiliary services. Any qualified citizen, company, or group may apply for authority to construct a station. They must show the FCC that they are legally, technically, and financially qualified, as prescribed in the "Rules," and that the operation of the proposed station would be in the public interest."[36] Of course, they must find an available frequency on which to operate.

But it is not that easy. The big moneyed interests have made it virtually impossible for one to finance such an independent station, even if one could find a frequency available, and then manage to get a license for it.

Public Awareness Campaigns

Demonstrations, marches, speak-outs, and boycotts are classic techniques used by those not represented at the decision-making table. These activities are never easy to organize, and unless one has built a movement of significant size, and a movement that knows how to follow its speeches with action at the ballot box and the cash register, the impact can easily be lost on the policy maker.

As with the Civil Rights movement of the 1960s, the Women's Rights movements of the early 1900s and the 1970s, the Labor movement of the

1930s, the anti-Vietnam War movement of the 1960s, the Environmental movement of the 1970s, and the Nuclear Freeze movement of the 1980s, such public demonstration of interest in change can bring innovation. The Civil Rights movement brought the legislation of the President Lyndon Johnson era that greatly increased opportunity for minorities and ended segregated facilities. The Women's movements brought women the right to vote, laws like Title IX providing for women's athletic opportunities, and some presence of women on corporate boards. The Labor movement brought decent wages and working conditions, retirement programs, and safety requirements to the workplace. The anti-Vietnam War movement brought about the end of this unpopular war. The Environmental movement brought a number of new laws to protect air and water quality, endangered species, and to protect humans exposed to toxic substances. The Nuclear Freeze Movement hastened attention to slowing the planned arms race escalation and contributed to the move away from the Cold War.

Boycotts, like the grape and lettuce boycotts organized by Cesar Chavez and the Farm Workers movement, resulted in union contracts for migrant workers and some progress toward improved economic conditions for those who pick the food we eat. The Nestle boycott resulted in some corporate changes in response to those who complained that babies across the world were dying because women had been convinced to trade breast feeding for Nestle formula mixed with contaminated water.

To date, there has been no public-interest movement or major boycott of corporate media to protest the government's and industry's collusion to deny the public media access.

The culture is ripe for such an effort, however. Frustration about the media is growing. Anger at the media's focus is increasing. Organizations like the ones cited above are multiplying.

Organizing a movement at the turn of the twenty-first century is more difficult than in the past—largely because the media has stolen our hearts and minds. Like the character in *1984* who realized he loved Big Brother, we find ourselves happy to be complacent.

Nonetheless, as Jane Alexander said, "The people of the United States are not fools, although they are easily led. They do not vote because they are way ahead of most of the politicians in their thinking. We need to address the imbalance of power that exists in arenas of decision making, especially in the corporate boardrooms, in politics and in the media."[37]

Today's effective public movement will require enormous sophistication about how best to mobilize resources. Those embarking on the movement will need to understand the difference between community organizing and political organizing. It is as follows:[38]

Community Organizing	Political Organizing
Objective	*Objective*
Feel good	Change policy
Method	*Method*
Get as many people as possible involved	Get voters organized by district, enough to swing the election away from incumbent
Result	*Result*
Make a point	Make a difference
Program	*Program*
Teach, vigils, demonstrate	Lobby incumbents before key policy votes Support electable candidates
Result	*Result*
Rally like-minded people	Create a new establishment and change policy
Timing	*Timing*
Act whenever convenient	Before key policy votes in Congress Before elections
Result	*Result*
Media policy innovation Discussed as abstract idea	Media policy innovation Codified into law

Lawsuits

If the executive branch of government (in this case the FCC) does not run a program properly, and the legislative branch (Congress) does not pass laws to mandate corrective changes, then the judicial branch (the courts) is the place to turn to mandate action that is consistent with the Constitution. Those seeking policy innovation and to redress grievances in the media constantly use the courts toward that end.

For example, WLBT in Oxford, Mississippi, was at the center of considerable controversy in the mid-1960s. The United Church of Christ (UCC) had joined with the National Association for the Advancement of Colored People (NAACP) to protest the FCC license renewal for this station. They accused the station of racist programming and failure to employ African

Americans even though the signal area for the station covered a media market that was largely African American.

The FCC renewed the license and refused to hear their petition on the grounds that outside groups had no standing. The matter was taken to court and the Washington, DC, appeals court overturned the FCC, saying that these national nongovernmental organizations did have standing and that the FCC should reexamine the wisdom of renewing this license.

The FCC met again and decided it would not change its position. Its decision to renew the station license would stand.

The court then issued a ruling that the FCC was wrong and that the WLBT license was not to be renewed.

To be effective in winning redress against media gatekeeping in the courts, one needs considerable expertise about the Constitution and the law. One needs to know how laws have been interpreted. And one needs to understand that one's opponents will likely include highly skilled and highly paid armies of lawyers from the monied firms that have much to lose by seeing pro–citizen media innovations become law.

Nicholas Johnson's and Ralph Nader's efforts to identify funding options for public interest lawyers is crucial to providing public-interest groups the needed legal support to win such law suits.

Some groups of lawyers already exist. For example, the Media Access Project (MAP) is a nonprofit telecommunication law firm. It promotes the public's First Amendment rights to hear and be heard in the media. Much of its work consists of providing legal advice for nonprofit organizations (NGOs) and it often testifies at FCC and congressional hearings. Its particular interest is female and minority media ownership.[39]

Lawsuits do not necessarily need to be initiated by public-interest groups. Another model is to have "ten-taxpayer suits" or class-action suits. In such a situation, a group of people file requesting relief from some injustice. The airline industry price-fixing suit is an example, as is the case against the manufacturers of silicone breast implants. Class-action suits against the media might be directed against a given company for a specific unconstitutional action. The results, if the case was won, might provide those who joined the suit a cash payment. It might cause the industry to change its practice. Whether it can have the effect of changing national policy is an open question.

An example of a court case intended to change policy was one initiated by a number of the nation's major media against the U.S. Department of Defense for violating the First Amendment by restricting media access to coverage of the Gulf War. Many thought the courts would say the Constitution supported the position of the journalists. The case was dismissed because the war ended before it came to trial.

Conclusion

The media is the megaphone for announcing what is reality in our culture, and for suggesting how to interpret it.

It terrifies people about crime, perpetuates stereotypes about people and places. It tells people that democracy does not require participation, but only requires attention to the latest scandal and the newest cynicism. It tells Americans that no one outside this country matters—no, no one virtually *exists*. It hypnotizes billions into believing that the only matter of importance is the latest adventure of a Hollywood star or a sports figure.

Most of the public is screened out from being portrayed in television news or entertainment. We own the airwaves but do not complain about how they are used to steal our futures and kill our culture. A few of us get angry enough to buy a bumper sticker that says "Kill Your TV." We laugh at the stupidity of such a gesture, shrug our shoulders, and move on with the day's affairs. Many of us, those under fifty who did not experience the 1960s, do not believe things can change. There is no recent personal experience of seeing systemic change happen. The role models and heroes are from another era. We seem content to be spectators while the media moguls fill the roles of modern day Horaces and Hannibals conquering the hearts and minds of billions of people across the globe.

With that little box in the living room sending the "right" message, a single ideology or propaganda, what more could the fascists want?

It does not have to be that way. TV has made an enormous difference in people's lives and has enormous potential:

- The motivation for tearing down the Berlin Wall is said to have come from the fact that East Germans saw West German TV and learned that the Hungarians were allowing refugees safe sanctuary.
- Satellite programs broadcast the Jordanian parliament meetings to Arab neighbors where parliamentary debates were unheard of.
- People in Turkey wonder why, when arrested, they are not read their rights— the way it is done on reruns of American TV dramas.

Imagine programs that showed grass-roots experiments in cooperation between ethnic groups with a history of hatred, or programs that showed the economic microbusiness successes rather than the disinvestment in areas of poverty.

Imagine ongoing news, not once–a–year features, that examined weapons sales and land mine sales or even advertisements for milk within a context of who benefits, who hurts, and who is paying no attention at all.

Imagine programs that allow the indigenous people of the world to speak for themselves. Why must the media patronize them by having journalists speak for them?

People only become partners at the human table when they describe in their own voices what happens to their ability to provide for themselves once multinational corporation gatekeeping destroys their livelihood and their culture.

There is a window of opportunity now for minimizing the gatekeeping. The ideas for how to do that are legion. A number are listed above. The window is open because the technological developments are causing shifts in media delivery systems. It is open because in America the economy is very good just now. It is open because lots of people are angry at the media's opportunism—the coverage of Princess Diana, of O.J Simpson, and of the Littleton high school shootings. There is almost a perceived crisis.

There is, in fact, a real crisis. The culture of this pluralistic, democratic nation is being stolen to satisfy the greed of big money.

It is not clear, however, that the public will seize this opportune timing and take action.

Perhaps the greatest obstacle to ending media gatekeeping is us—the public. Nicholas Johnson notes:

> Part of the problem when you're dealing with the media is that [we may be] like the character in George Orwell's *1984* who woke up in the morning and realized that he loved Big Brother. Look at all the kids who are voluntarily walking around wearing T-shirts advertising this product or that. Or they buy some designer shirt or jeans and there's the manufacturer's name splashed all over it. They don't think twice about advertising products. They don't think they're being ripped off. They don't see the incongruity. When I was a boy, people walking around with advertising billboards got paid for doing it. Nowadays you pay for the advertising billboard and you walk around in it. The point is that people get so caught up in this mediated life that they lead that they become less and less aware that that's what's happening to them. With the passage of time it gets more and more difficult to get people organized, even if you could get them out from in front of the television set and out of the house to attend a meeting. You hold a meeting and everybody's home watching TV. So you've got a real problem."[40]

I've made the point! Will you make the difference?

Notes

Chapter 1

1. Jane Alexander, movie actress and former chair of the National Endowment for the Arts, letter interview with author, April 18, 1999.

2. Nicholas Johnson, former FCC commissioner, telephone interview with author, August 21, 1999.

3. Ibid.

4. *U.S. Statistical Abstracts* (Washington, DC: U.S. Government Printing Office, 1997 numbers).

5. Jason Furlong, Emerson College media arts researcher, untitled paper, April 25, 1999.

6. Richard H. Fehlman, "Making Meanings Visible: Critically Reading TV," *English Journal* (Cedar Rapids, Iowa: University of Northern Iowa, November 1992).

7. Ibid.

8. Ibid.

9. D.A. Infante, A.S. Rancer, and D.F. Womack, *Building Communication Theory* (Prospect Heights, IL: Waveland Press, 1993).

10. Ian I. Mitroff and Warren Bennis, *The Unreality Industry* (New York: Oxford University Press, 1989) p.128.

11. George Hover, licensed psychologist and Jungian Institute participant, comment prepared in response to author's questions, May 1999.

12. Ibid.

13. Ibid.

14. *New Statesman*, August 7, 1998.

15. *Variety*, January 11, 1999.

16. Benjamin Svetkey, "In the Wake of Titanic," *Entertainment Weekly Online*, January 31, 1998, http://pathfinder.com/ew/.

17. Andrea Milford, Emerson College film and media arts researcher, untitled paper, spring 1999.

18. Ibid.

19. Denise Gorman, Emerson College media arts researcher of Nielsen ratings, untitled paper, 1999. *TV Guide* online, www.tvguide.com, 1998–early 1999.

20. A.J. Jacobs, "Heaven Can Rate," *Entertainment Weekly* online, February 5, 1999.

21. David B. Wolfe, "The Psychological Center of Gravity," *American Demographics* online, http://pathfinder.com/ew/, April 1998; Gorman, 1999.

22. Cheryl Russell, "The Ungraying of America," *American Demographics* online, July 1997.

23. Mircea Eliade, *The Myth of Eternal Return* (New York: Pantheon Books, 1954), p. 124.

24. Hover, ibid. interview, May 1999.

25. Chahn Chung, Emerson researcher, spring 1999.

26. James F. Iaccino, *Psychological Reflection on Cinematic Terror* (Westport, CT: Praeger, 1994).

27. Michael Wachter, Emerson College media arts researcher, untitled paper, spring 1999.

28. James Weathers, Emerson College media arts researcher, untitled paper, spring 1999.

29. Frank Newport, "One Fourth of Americans Still Smoke, but Most Want to Give Up the Habit," Gallup Organization, June 14, 1996. www.gallup.org

30. "Growing Epidemic," *Join Together* online, 1999, http://www.jointogether.org/gv/issues/epidemic.

31. Weathers, spring 1999.

32. Frank Newport, "Space Program Gets Positive Reviews from Public," Gallup Organization, December 5, 1998.

33. Chung, spring 1999.

34. Ibid.

35. Ibid.

36. Michael Strangelove, *Redefining the Limits to Thought Within Media Culture: Collective Memory, Cyberspace and the Subversion of Mass Media* (Ottawa: University of Ottawa Press, 1998); Wachter, spring 1999.

37. Hover interview, May 1999.

38. Clarissa Estes, *Women Who Run with the Wolves* (Cambridge: Ballantine, 1992).

39. Robert Bly, *Iron John* (Burlington, MA: Addison Wesley, 1990)

40. Hover interview, May 1999.

41. Malidoma Some, *Of Water and the Spirit: Ritual, Magic, and Initiation in the Life of an African Shaman*, (New York: Penguin, 1995).

42. Steven Foster and Meredith Little, *The Book of the Vision Quest* (New York: Simon and Schuster, 1992).

43. Hover interview, May 1999.

44. Sandy Flitterman-Lewis, "Psychoanalysis," in *Channels of Discourse, Reassembled*, 2d ed., ed. Robert C. Allen (Chapel Hill: University of North Carolina Press, 1992), p. 214; Joshua Goldman and John-Michael Trojan, Emerson College film researchers, untitled papers, spring 1999.

45. Robert L. Hilliard, "Ethics, Education, and the Necessity of Media Literacy," in *Media Ethics Update* (Boston: Emerson College, Fall 1998).

46. Susan Shaer, executive director, Women's Action for New Directions, 691 Massachusetts Ave., Arlington, MA 02476, interview with author in Arlington, June 1, 1999.

47. James Latham, *Vista*, Costa Rica: Radio for Peace International, January, April, and June 1998 issues.

48. Carla Brooks Johnston, "Radical Radio Redux," *Intelligence Report* (Montgomery, AL: Southern Poverty Law Center, Summer 1998) p. 17.

49. Robert L. Hilliard and Michael C. Keith, *Waves of Rancor* (Armonk, NY: M.E. Sharpe, 1999), p. 4.

50. Laura Flanders, "Far Right Militias and Anti-Abortion Violence: When will Media See the Connection?" *Extra*, Fairness and Accuracy in Reporting (FAIR), July/August 1995.

51. Paul Walker, Legacy program director, Global Green, U.S.A., Internet interview with author, July 21, 1999.

52. Carla Brooks Johnston, *Winning the Global TV News Game* (Boston: Butterworth Heinemann/Focal Press, 1995), p. 302.

53. "Reporting on the Gulf War," a Communications Forum Panel sponsored by the MIT Center for Technology, Policy and Industrial Development, Massachusetts Institute of Technology, Cambridge, October 17, 1991.

54. Johnston, *Winning*, p. 302.

55. Andreas Argyropoulos, Boston University mass communications researcher, paper, spring 1999.

56. Ed Asner, actor and former president Screen Actors' Guild, telephone interview with author, May 12, 1999.

57. Edward R. Murrow, article published by the Public Concern Foundation, Fairfax, VA. Vol. 12, no. 20 (November 1, 1986). Available from University Microfilms International, 300 N. Zeeb Rd., Ann Arbor, MI 48106.

Chapter 2

1. Michael Dukakis, former governor of Massachusetts and Democratic nominee for U.S. president, 1988, interview with author in Boston, May 3, 1999.

2. Definitions of culture are based on uncopyrighted material used in the University of Massachusetts College of Public and Community Services readings for teaching cultural awareness.

3. John Randolph, Tony Award winning actor and officer in Screen Actors' Guild, Actors Equity Association, and AFTRA (American Federation of Television and Radio Actors). Interview with author in New York City, April 10, 1999.

4. Andrea Milford, Emerson College Media arts researcher, paper, April 1999.

5. Mark Moi, "All Our Voices on Public TV Must Include Dissenting Ones," *Los Angeles Times*, February 1, 1993, p. F3. Adam Lippe, Emerson College film researcher, untitled paper, spring 1999.

6. Judith Michaelson, "PBS Finally to Air 'Building Bombs,'" *Los Angeles Times*, August 16, 1993, p. F12.

7. Robert Welkos, "Looking Beyond the 'Patriot Games' Incident at Variety," *Los Angeles Times*, August 4, 1972.

8. Michiru Onishi, Emerson College film researcher, untitled, March 29, 1999.

9. Ibid.

10. Denise Gorman, Emerson College media arts researcher, untitled paper, February 10, 1999.

11. Shaer interview, June 1, 1999.

12. Ibid.

13. Mark Potok, director of Public Affairs and Information, The Southern Poverty Law Center, 400 Washington Ave., Montgomery AL 36104, interview with author in Montgomery, May 12, 1998.

14. Arthur D'Lugoff, theatrical producer, interview with author in New York City, April 10, 1999.

15. Paul Starobin, "A Generation of Vipers: Journalists and the New Cynicism," *Columbia Journalism Review* (March/April 1995).

16. Dukakis interview, May 3, 1999.

17. D'Lugoff interview, April 10, 1999.

18. *U.S. Statistical Abstracts* (Washington, DC: U.S. Government Printing Office), www.access.gpo.gov/. Updated regularly. Table #747 has wealth data. Also see *Boston Globe*, February 16, 1997.

19. Herbert I. Schiller, *Information Inequality* (New York: Routledge, 1996), p. 143.

20. Interview of Jose Jorge Dias by Lauren Grossman, March 20, 1997.

21. Interview of Oscar Chacon by Lauren Grossman, March 1997.

22. Interview of Roosevelt Simil by Kheven Lee LaGrone, spring 1997.

23. Interview of Jean Marc Jean-Baptiste by Jeremy Thompson, March 20, 1997.

24. Michael Parenti, *Make Believe Media* (New York: St. Martin's Press, 1992), p. 70).

25. Asner interview, May 12, 1999.

26. Yegi Hong, Emerson College media arts researcher, untitled paper, October 1998.

27. Parenti, *Make Believe*, p. 100.

28. Ryan Lynch, Emerson College media arts researcher, "The Simpsons," paper, spring 1999.

29. Travis Searle, Emerson College Media Arts Researcher, untitled paper, April 22, 1999.

30. Jason Deparle, "Welfare to Work," *New York Times*, September 16, 1996, p. B4; Rachael Swarns, "The Nation: Behind the Tears," *New York Times*, April 5, 1997, p. D6.

31. Diane Dujon and Ann Withorn, *For Crying Out Loud* (Boston: South End Press, 1994).

32. Dirk Slater, The Welfare Law Center, 275 Seventh Ave., Suite 1205, New York, NY 1001–6708, www.welfarelaw.org.

33. Tom Bierbaum, "Index Brightens Peacock, NBC's Television Show 'Frasier' Doing Well in Ratings," *Variety*, December 14, 1998, p. 38. Jessica Aiches, Boston University mass communications reseacher, untitled paper February 17, 1999.

34. Quoted in Herbert I. Schiller, *Information Inequality* (New York: Routledge, 1996), p. 18.

35. "Uneven Progress," *Boston Globe*, September 20, 1998, p. F3.

36. Asner interview, May 12, 1999.

37. Don Aucoin, "TV Networks Under Fire for Diversity Gap," *Boston Globe*, July 15, 1999, p. 1.

38. Ibid.

39. Greg Braxton and Jan Breslauer, "Advocacy Groups Say Latinos Are Invisible on Network TV," *Boston Globe*, March 10, 1995.

40. Aucoin, "TV Networks Under Fire."

41. Lynn Elber, "BET Breaks Stereotypes with Black Romances and Mysteries," *Boston Globe*, July 8, 1999, p. C14.

42. Ibid.

43. Randolph interview, April 10, 1999.

44. www.latinolink.com.

45. Braxton and Breslauer, "Advocacy Groups."

46. Tori Rowe, College of Public and Community Service researcher on Latina Project, untitled paper, University of Massachusetts, Boston, April 24, 1999.

47. *Christian Science Monitor*, February 2, 1999, p. 7.

48. Amanda Escamilla, College of Public and Community Service researcher on Latina Project, untitled paper, University of Massachusetts, Boston, May 11, 1999.

49. Jenepher Gooding, College of Public and Community Service researcher on Latina Project, untitled paper, University of Massachusetts, Boston, spring 1999).

50. Juan Reynoso, College of Public and Community Service researcher on Latina Project, untitled paper, University of Massachusetts, Boston, spring 1999).

51. Hironobu Maeda, Emerson College Media Arts researcher, untitled paper, April 8, 1998.

52. Don Hazen and Julie Winokur, *We the Media* (New York: New Press, 1997), p. 110.

53. Sachiyo Yamamoto, Emerson College media arts researcher, untitled paper, fall 1998).

54. Evan Zehntner, Emerson College media arts researcher, untitled paper, fall 1998).

55. *60 Minutes*, CBS Television, June 27, 1999.

56. Jaci Ameer, Emerson College film researcher, untitled, fall 1998.

57. Randolph interview, April 10, 1999.

58. M. Butler and W. Paisley, *Women and the Mass Media: Sourcebook for Research and Action* (New York: Human Sciences Press, 1980).

59. Beth Sekul, Emerson College media arts researcher, untitled paper, October 6, 1998.

60. Janet Walker, *Couching Resistance: Women, Film, and Psychoanalytic Psychiatry* (Minneapolis: University of Minnesota Press, 1993), p. 93; Jessica Aichs, Boston University mass communications researcher, untitled paper, spring 1999.

61. Don Aucoin, "Kids TV Improves, but Violence Still a Worry," *Boston Globe*, June 28, 1999, p. C10.

62. Anthony Miller, Emerson College mass communications researcher, untitled paper, spring 1997.

63. *Television Digest*, January 2, 1995; Jeannine Aversa, "Public Broadcasters See Profits in Merchandising," *Marketing News*, March 27, 1995, p. 3.

64. Eric Schmuckler, "A Small World, After All: The Children's TV Business Is Now in the Hand of Only Four Companies," *Mediaweek*, January 27, 1997, p. 30.

65. *Television Digest*, May 1, 1995.

66. Jane Murphy and Karen Tucker, *Stay Tuned* (New York: Doubleday, 1996); Angela Olazabal, Emerson College media arts researcher, untitled paper, October 31, 1998.

67. http://tap.epn.org/cme/cta/tv-facts.html; also see Joan Anderson and Robin Wilkins, *Getting Unplugged* (New York: John Wiley and Sons, 1998); and Barrie Gunter and Jill McAleer, *Children and Television*, 2d ed. (New York: Routledge, 1997).

68. Gordon L. Berry and Joy Keiko Asamen, *Children and Television: Images in a Changing Sociocultural World* (Newbury Park, CA: Sage, 1993), p. 179.

69. Gunter and McAleer, *Children and Television*, p. 145.

70. Anne Norton, Emerson College media arts researcher, unpublished paper, fall 1998.

71. Altha Huston and John C. Wright, "Television and the Informational and Educational Needs of Children," *Annals of the American Academy of Political and Social Science* (May 1988): 9–24.

72. Lynette Rice, "Nets on Learning Curve with Kids," *Broadcasting and Cable*, October 13, 1997, pp. 10–11.

73. Ibid.

74. Amy Jordan and Emory H. Woodard IV, "Growing Pains: Children's Television in the New Regulatory Environment," *Annals of the American Academy of Political and Social Science* (May 1988): 83–96.

75. Asner interview, May 12, 1999.

Chapter 3

1. Asner interview, May 12, 1999.

2. Howard Kurtz, "Murder Rates Drop, but Coverage Soars," *Boston Globe*, August 13, 1997.

3. Laura Meckler, "Drop in Teen Crime Found," *Boston Globe*, July, 9, 1999, p. A3.

4. www.access.gpo.gov/su_docs/budget. This is where one examines what is included in the annual U.S. budget.

5. Robert Healy, "The GOP's Health Care Poster Boy," *Boston Globe*, October 26, 1995.

6. Anthony Pratkanis and Elliot Aronson, *Age of Propaganda* (New York: W.H. Freeman, 1991), p. 165.

7. Ibid., pp. 163–164.

8. Asner interview, May 12, 1999.

9. Times Mirror Center for People and the Press, a report on viewer opinions of American movies and TV programs, March 16, 1994.

10. "TV Violence: The Good News," *Harper's*, June 1996.

11. David Doi, "Media and Juvenile Violence: The Connecting Threads," *Nieman Reports* (winter 1998): 35–36; Gabrielle Chasis, Boston University mass communications researcher, untitled paper, May 1999.

12. Dennis Cauchon, "Coverage Is Closely Watched—by Media," *USA Today*, May 21, 1999.

13. Barrie Smith, Emerson College media arts researcher, untitled paper, April 26, 1999.

14. Benjamin Jacobson, Boston University mass communications researcher, untitled paper, November 17, 1998.

15. WBUR Radio, Boston, MA, June 17, 1999.

16. Don Aucoin, "Turning Down the Violence?" *Boston Globe*, August 8, 1999, p. N1.

17. Ibid.

18. Ibid.

19. Potok interview.

20. *SPLC Report* 29, no. 2 (June 1999): 1.

21. Potok interview, May 12, 1998.

22. Adam Goldberg, Emerson College media arts researcher, untitled paper, spring 1999.

23. Denise Gorman, Emerson media arts researcher, untitled paper, April 26, 1999.

24. Ibid.

25. Barrie Smith, April 26, 1999.

26. See http://www.drugfreeamerica.org/effective.html.

27. Goldberg, spring 1999.

28. See http://ej.kylz.com/songs/the.last.song.html. This is the Elton John site with lyrics.

29. Arnold Schulman, *And the Band Played On*, draft from script, March 12, 1992, Hollywood Scripts, Studio City, CA, p. 86; Aaron Hatin, Emerson College film researcher, untitled paper, April 28, 1999.

30. Christopher Sharrett, "The Urban Apocalypse," *USA Today*, January 1992, p. 61; Kishwanna M. Terry, Emerson College media arts researcher, untitled paper, February 24, 1997.

31. Paul Arthur, "Los Angeles as Scene of the Crime," *Film Comment* (July 1996): 20–27.

32. Karen Schwartz, "Good Marketing Lures Hollywood to Town," *Marketing News*, September 23, 1996, p. 22.

33. Neal Pierce, "Violent Filmmaking in Cities Impacts Public's Crime View," *Nation's Cities Weekly*, April 1994, p. 5.

34. Patricia Reed Scott, "Second Time Around," *Shoot*, June 1995, pp. 48–55

35. Karen Schwartz, "Good Marketing Lures Hollywood to Town," p. 25. Also see www.cityofchicago.org/SpecialEvents/FilmOffice/FilmOffice.html.

36. Stuart Miller, "Order," *Variety*, September 1995.

37. Carla Brooks Johnston, *Global News Access: Impact of the New Technologies* (Westport, CT: Praeger , 1998), pp. 110–116.

38. "NTSB Official Chastises Media," *Boston Globe*, August 25, 1999, p. F13.

39. W. James Potter, *Media Literacy* (Thousand Oaks, CA: Sage, 1998), p. 118.

40. Richard Zoglin, "The News Wars," *Time*, October 26, 1996, p. 58.

41. Alexander interview, April 18, 1999.

42. Rajesh Sawhney, chief manager-corporate, *The Times of India*, interview with au-

thor, February 23, 1999.

43. Minoru Sugaya, professor of media policy at Keio University, Japan, interview with author, March 1, 1999.

44. Joe Saltzman, "Celebrity Journalism, the Public and Princess Diana," *USA Today*, January, 1998, p. 65.

45. Richard Zoglin, *Time*, May 4, 1998; Michelle Ann Neves, Emerson College media arts researcher, untitled paper, March 22, 1999; Joliange Wright, Emerson College media arts researcher, untitled paper, February 17, 1999.

46. Don Hewitt, "Let's Not Compete with the Sitcom: What's Become of Broadcast Journalism," *Vital Speeches*, November 1, 1997, pp. 48–51.

47. Rebessa Heath, "Tuning in to Talk," *American Demographics* (February 1998): 48–54. Also Michelle Ann Neves, Emerson College media arts researcher and former worker in local TV reporting, untitled paper, spring 1999.

48. James Collins, "Talking Trash," *Time*, March 30, 1998, pp. 63–67.

49. Cynthia Littleton, "Charges of Fraud Don't Faze Springer Fans," *Variety*, May 11, 1998, p. 29.

50. Collins, "Talking Trash," p. 63.

51. Michael Blowen, "Witch Flick Scares Theater Owners," *Boston Globe*, August 8, 1999, p. N7.

52. Walter Lubars and John Wicklein, eds., *Investigative Reporting: The Lessons of Watergate* (Boston: BU School of Public Communication, 1975), p. 12; Adam Stoltz, Boston University mass communications researcher, untitled paper, fall 1998.

53. Zoglin, "The News Wars," p. 58; also Matthew Barone, Emerson College media arts researcher, untitled paper, fall 1998.

54. Alexander interview, April 18, 1999.

55. Michiru Onishi, Emerson College media arts researcher, untitled paper, April 28, 1999.

56. Claudia Eller, "Small 'Mussolini' Is MGM's Only Hit," *Boston Globe*, July, 5, 1999, p. B8.

57. Potok interview, May 12, 1998.

58. Lubars and Wicklein, *Investigative Reporting*, pp. 77–78.

59. "TV Show Liable in Death of Guest," *Boston Globe*, May 8, 1999.

60. Nat Segaloff, writer and producer, letter interview with author, July 1, 1999.

Chapter 4

1. Segaloff interview, July 1, 1999.

2. D'Lugoff interview, April 10. 1999.

3. Segaloff interview, July 1, 1999.

4. Chris Bastien, Emerson College media arts researcher, untitled paper, March 18, 1998.

5. Jack Newfield, "An Interview with Michael Moore," *Tikkun* (November–December 1998): 25–30.

6. Ibid.; Also Jessica Aichs, Emerson College media arts researcher, untitled paper, April 26, 1999.

7. Oliver Stone, untitled, address to the National Press Club, April 7, 1997.

8. Stacy Dubinsky, Emerson College media arts researcher, untitled paper, fall 1998.

9. Segaloff interview, July 1, 1999.

10. Dubinsky, fall 1998.

11. Dan Berkowitz, "Refining the Gatekeeping Metaphor for Local Television News," *Journal of Broadcasting and Electronic Media* 34 (1990): 55–63; Also Matthew Barone, Emerson College media arts researcher, untitled, October 24, 1998.

12. Michelle Ann Neves, Emerson College media arts researcher and former worker in local television TV reporting, untitled paper, spring 1999.

13. John Vivian, *The Media of Mass Communication* (Boston, n.p., 1995).

14. Potok interview, May 12, 1998.

15. Carla Brooks Johnston, "The Press and the Electoral Process," *Radcliffe Quarterly* (June 1992), p. 22.

16. Ibid., p. 24.

17. Dave Berkman, professor of mass communications, University of Wisconsin, Milwaukee, "A Dozen '98 Lows," *Media Musings*, work available through WHAD/90.7.FM. No date given.

18. Howard Kurtz, "Money Talks," *Washington Post Magazine*, January 21, 1996. *Hot Air: All Talk, All the Time* (New York: Times Books, 1995).

19. Project Censored, *Censored* (New York: Seven Stories Press), published annually.

20. Bastien, March 18, 1998.

21. Don Aucoin, "The News from Natalie," *Boston Globe*, March 31, 1998, p. C1; Dan McDuffie, Emerson College media arts researcher, untitled, spring 1999.

22. Ibid.

23. Susan Tyler Eastman, Sydney Head, and Klewis Klein, *Broadcast/Cable Programming*, 2d ed. (Belmont, CA: Wadsworth , 1985), p. 94.

24. Ken Tucker, "1998 the Best and Worst Television," *Entertainment Weekly*, December 25, 1998/January 1, 1999, pp. 124–126; Also Jessica Aichs, Boston University mass communications researcher, untitled paper, February 17, 1999.

25. ABC Capital Ratings, week of December 14–20, 1998.

26. Lynne Elber, "WB's Young Audience Is Where the Money Is, Network Chief Says," Associated Press, January 7, 1999.

27. "WB Lures Young Set vs. Prez," *New York Daily News*, January 21, 1999, p. 103.

28. Alexander Miltsch, Emerson College media arts researcher, untitled paper, March 25, 1998.

29. Jon LaFayette, "Critical ABC News Story on Disney Dies," *Electronic Media*, October 19, 1998, p. 1A; Also Matthew Barone, Emerson College media arts researcher, untitled paper, December 4, 1998.

30. Potok interview, May 12, 1998.

31. Bernard Mann, interview with the author in Greensboro, NC, May 9, 1998.

32. Dukakis interview, May 3, 1999.

33. Robert L. Hilliard, *The Federal Communications Commission (*Boston and London: Butterworth Heinemann/Focal Press, 1991).

34. Segaloff interview, July 1, 1999.

35. Johnson interview, August 21, 1999.

36. Mann interview, May 9, 1998.

37. W. James Potter, *Media Literacy* (Thousand Oaks, CA: Sage, 1998), p. 139.

38. Sut Jhally, "Moving Beyond the American Dream," in *We the Media*, ed. Don Hazen and Julie Winokur (New York: New Press, 1997), p. 40; Matthew Barone, fall 1998; Amanda C. Smith, Boston University mass communications researcher, untitled paper, November 17, 1998.

39. Vivian, *The Media of Mass Communication*, pp. 257–258.

40. Belinda Archer, "Should Advertisers Avoid Pandering to Prejudice?" *Campaign* (May 2, 1997): 16.

41. Michael McMenamin, "Tobacco Row: Controversy over TV Program's Interview of Former Tobacco Industry V.P. Who Accused Firm of Unethical Practices," *Reason* (February 1996); Also see Barone, fall 1998.

42. Tim Dickinson, "Updates: Tobacco-Friendly Media," *Mother Jones*, November/ December 1998, p. 18.

43. Steven Levingston, "Defender of the Civilized World," *Boston Globe*, July 13, 1999, p. F4.

44. Pamela Reynolds, "Bowing to Furor, Calvin Klein Pulls Ads," *Boston Globe*, August 29, 1995.

45. Chris Reidy, "Expression vs. Exploitation—Feds Disclose Investigation of Klein's Jeans Ads," *Boston Globe*, September 9, 1995.

46. Daniel Cohen, Boston University researcher, untitled paper, fall 1998.

47. Norman Klein and Stephen A. Greyser, "Benetton: The 'United Colors' Communication Campaign," *Harvard Business School* (1996); Jennifer N. Arkin, Boston University mass communications researcher, untitled paper, spring 1999.

48. Denise Gorman, Emerson College media arts researcher, untitled paper, spring 1999. Also do a Havista search for many articles on Bovine Growth Hormone.

49. Project Censored, *Censored*, Top 25 Stories, 1998.

50. http://www.specialk.com/ This site for Special K cereal describes their advertising. Bonnie Harary, Boston University mass communications researcher, untitled paper, November 17, 1998.

51. Elizabeth Claflin, Boston University mass communications researcher, untitled paper, November 17, 1998.

52. Erik Barnouw, media historian and author of *The Sponsor* (New York: Oxford University Press, 1961).

53. Elizabeth Jensen, quoted in *Brill's Content*, March 1999.

54. *1998 Report on Television* (New York: Nielsen Media Research, 1999), p. 14.

55. Ibid., p.20.

56. Bloomberg News, "Dutch Company to Buy Nielsen," *Boston Globe*, August 17, 1999.

57. Ibid.

58. *1998 Annual Report* (New York: Nielsen Media Research, 1999), p. 3.

59. Ibid., p. 2.

60. *1998 Report on Television*, p. 10.

61. Ibid., p. 31.

62. www.census.gov (the U.S. Census site). Also Gabriela Zelana, Emerson College media arts researcher, untitled paper, December 15, 1998.

63. *1998 Report on Television*, p. 33.

64. Don Aucoin, "Channel 7 Cancels Contract with Nielsen," *Boston Globe*, June 24, 1999, p. D20.

65. Lee Winblatt and Stephen A. Douglas, *A Presentation of the TV, Radio and Print Applications of the First Intermedia Personal Meter: A Review of Its Development, Strengths and Weaknesses* (Toronto, n.p., 1992), pp. 791–797.

66. Malcolm Belville, *Audience Ratings: Radio, Television, and Cable*, Lawrence Erlbaum Assoc., 1987, pp. 223–225, 294, 300, 307.

67. Maura Clancey, *How People Use Television* (Toronto: 1992), pp. 37–49.

68. Don Aucoin. "Local TV Stations Giving Nielson Low Ratings." *Boston Globe*, November 18, 1999, p. A4.

69. Nicholas P. Schiavone, Quality Methods, Quality Results! An Axiom. A Progress Report on the Work of CONTAM: Committee on Nationwide Television Audience Measurement (Toronto: n.p.), pp. 457–463. Also see Polykarpos Emilios Yiannoudes, Emerson College media arts researcher, untitled paper, May, 1998.

70. *Brill's Content*, March 1999, p. 89.

71. Segaloff interview, July 1, 1999.

72. Elisabeth Jensen, "Four Viewers Equal $50 million," *Brill's Content*, March 1999, p. 90.

73. Segaloff interview, July 1, 1999.

74. Robert Dole, "Giving Away the Airwaves," *New York Times*, March 27, 1997.

75. Chris Bastien, Emerson College media arts researcher, untitled paper, March 18, 1988.

76. Shaer, interview, June 1, 1999.

77. Bastien, March 18, 1998.

Chapter 5

1. Johnson interview with author, August 21, 1999.

2. Robert L. Hilliard, former chief of Public (Education) broadcasting, U.S. Federal Communications Commission, interview with author, August 16, 1999.

3. Ibid.

4. Johnson interview, August 21, 1999.

5. Ibid.

6. David Berkman, *Milwaukee Magazine*, November 1994.

7. Robert L. Hilliard and Michael C. Keith, *The Hidden Screen* (Armonk, NY: M.E. Sharpe, 1999), pp. 3, 34.

8. Mark Pinsky, "Low Power TV Gains Strength," *New York Times*, May 14, 1990, p. 8.

9. Hilliard and Keith, *The Hidden Screen*, p. 73.

10. Ron Sakolsky and Stephen Dunnifer, eds., *Seizing the Airwaves* (San Francisco: AK Press, 1998), p. 4.

11. Ibid., p. 26.

12. Stephen Labaton, "FCC to Approve Low-Power Radio, Seeking Diversity," *New York Times*, January 20, 2000, p. C27.

13. Ibid., p. 42.

14. Ibid., p. 173.

15. Jaime DeLong, Emerson College researcher, untitled paper, February 17, 1997.

16. Richard Tedesco, "Who'll Control the Video Streams? More and More Payers Are Muscling into Position to Dominate Video on the Web," *Broadcasting and Cable*, March 8, 1999, p. 20.

17. Carla Brooks Johnston, *Global News Access* (Westport, CT: Praeger, 1998), p. 86.

18. Nicholas Johnson, telephone interview with author, August 21, 1999.

19. Peter Phillips and Project Censored, *Censored: The News That Didn't Make the News and Why* (New York: Seven Stories Press, 1998).

20. Chris Bastien, Emerson College researcher, untitled paper, March 18, 1998.

21. Robert Hilliard, *Media, Education and America's Counter-Culture Revolution* (Stamford, CT: Ablex Books, 2000).

22. Ibid.

23. Don Hazen and Julie Winokur, eds. *We the Media* (New York: New Press, 1997), p. 57 (segment by Ronald Collins.)

24. D'Lugoff interview, April 10, 1999.

25. Johnson interview, August 21, 1999.

26. Ibid.

27. Nelson W. Polsby, *Political Innovation in America* (New Haven: Yale University Press, 1984).

28. Robert L. Hilliard, *The Federal Communications Commission* (Boston and London: Butterworth Heinemann/Focal Press, 1991), p. 71.

29. Johnson interview, August 21, 1999.

30. Mediascope, 12711 Ventura Boulevard, Studio City, CA 91604, Tel: 818–508–2080, Fax: 818–508–2088, www.mediascope.org.

31. Don Hazen and Julie Winokur, *We the Media*, p. 114; FAIR, 130 West 25th Street,

New York, NY, 10001, Tel: 212–633–6700, Fax: 212–727–7668, http://www.fair.org/fair).

32. Ibid., p. 34; Paper Tiger TV, 339 LaFayette St., New York, NY 10012, Tel: 212–420–9045, http://flicker.com/orgs/papertiger.

33. Union for Democratic Communication, University of San Francisco, 2130 Fulton St., San Francisco, CA 94118, www.udc.org.

34. Anne Norton, Emerson College researcher, untitled paper, fall 1998; see Carol Bodensteiner, "Are Media Tuned In or Worn Out on Your Issue?" *Public Relations Quarterly* (spring 1997: 30–33.

35. Linda P. Morton, "Gatekeepers as Public Targets," *Public Relations Quarterly* (summer 1995): 21–25.

36. Hilliard, *The Federal Communications*, p. 75.

37. Alexander interview, April 18, 1999.

38. Carla Brooks Johnston, *Reversing the Nuclear Arms Race* (Boston: Schenkman Books, 1986), p. 169.

39. Media Access Project, 1707 L St., NW, Suite 400, Washington, DC 20036, Fax: 202–466–7656).

40. Johnson interview, August 21, 1999.

Index

About the Author

Carla Brooks Johnston, author of seven books on the media and culture, has been awarded three advanced fellowships at Harvard and Radcliffe where she was a Bunting Fellow, a Loeb Fellow, and was awarded a research fellowship at the Kennedy School of Government. Her thirty-five years of professional work emphasize creating and sustaining policy innovation. Her current focus is on how the media affects public policy. Recent books include *Global News Access: Impact of New Communication Technologies* (1998), and *Winning the Global TV News Game* (1995). She is a retired university professor, the former head of state and local government agencies, and a former candidate for U.S. Congress. She lectures and consults internationally on policy innovation through her firm, New Century Polices.